The Business Cycle: Theories and Evidence

The Business Cycle: Theories and Evidence

Proceedings of the Sixteenth Annual Economic Policy Conference of the Federal Reserve Bank of St. Louis

edited by
Michael T. Belongia
Federal Reserve Bank of St. Louis

and

Michelle R. Garfinkel
University of California at Irvine

Kluwer Academic Publishers
Boston / Dordrecht / London

Distributors for North America:
Kluwer Academic Publishers
101 Philip Drive
Assinippi Park
Norwell, Massachusetts 02061 USA

Distributors for all other countries:
Kluwer Academic Publishers Group
Distribution Centre
Post Office Box 322
3300 AH Dordrecht, THE NETHERLANDS

Library of Congress Cataloging-in-Publication Data

Economic Policy Conference of the Federal Reserve Bank of St. Louis (16th: 1991: Federal Reserve Bank of St. Louis)
The business cycle: theories and evidence: proceedings of the Sixteenth Annual Economic Policy Conference of the Federal Reserve Bank of St. Louis / edited by Michael T. Belongia and Michelle R. Garfinkel.
p. cm.
Includes bibliographical references.
ISBN 0-7923-9239-6
1. Business cycles—United States—Congresses. I. Belongia, Michael T. II. Garfinkel, Michelle R., 1960- . III. Title.
HB3743.E24 1991
338.5′42′0973—dc20 92-11616
CIP

Printed on acid-free paper.

Set in 10/12pt Times Roman
by Graphicraft Typesetters Ltd., Hong Kong
Printed in the United States of America

Contents

Contributing Authors

Ben S. Bernanke
Princeton University
Robertson Hall
Princeton, NJ 08544–1013

Olivier Jean Blanchard
Department of Economics
E52–391
Massachusetts Institute of Technology
Cambridge, MA 02139

Alan S. Blinder
Department of Economics
Princeton University
Princeton, NJ 08544–1021

Michael R. Darby
Andersen School of Management
University of California
Los Angeles, CA 90024

Ray C. Fair
Yale University
Cowles Foundation
P.O. Box 2125 Yale Station
New Haven, CT 06520–2125

Benjamin M. Friedman
Harvard University
Littauer Center 127
Cambridge, MA 02138

Herschel I. Grossman
Brown University
Box B
Providence, RI 02912

David Laidler
Department of Economics
University of Western Ontario
Social Science Centre
London, Ontario N6A 5C2
Canada

Michael Parkin
Department of Economics
University of Western Ontario
Social Science Centre
London, Ontario N6A 5C2
Canada

James H. Stock
Harvard University
79 John F. Kennedy Street
Cambridge, MA 02138

Victor Zarnowitz
University of Chicago
Graduate School of Business
1101 East 58th Street
Chicago, IL 60637

Arnold Zellner
University of Chicago
Graduate School of Business
1101 East 58th Street
Chicago, IL 60637

President's Message

Asking what we know about business cycles seems, in one sense, a curious topic for a conference of professional economists. After all, it is not as though the cycle is a new phenomenon. From the less well documented ups and downs of the colonial economy through the various booms and busts of the 1800s, the turbulent decade of the 1920s, and the nine complete cycles of the postwar period, the U.S. economy has had ample experience with sustained economic expansion followed by periods of decline. The sum total of this experience, however, has produced few firm conclusions about the "whys" or "hows" of the business cycle.

To get a little perspective on the issue, I looked back to those days of the New Frontier when Walter Heller and Co. sat down "to the levers of control" as a *Time* magazine cover story described it. The first impression to catch my eye was the seeming harmony within the economics profession. *Time* asserted that "by broadening the areas of fact, the professionalization [of economics] has narrowed the areas of theory, of disagreement, and blurred old boundaries between liberals and conservatives." Indeed, the accepted wisdom of the day seemed to be that the cycle, though a bit of an annoyance, could be dealt with by the enlightened application of the appropriate mix of tax and budget policies. This state of affairs is in sharp contrast to the factional disputes that have dominated at least the last decade.

This confidence was based, again according to the *Time* story, not on the insights of Keynes's *General Theory* but on Wesley Clair Mitchell's *Business Cycles*. This book, labeled as "the most important of all U.S. contributions to economics," and Mitchell's call for "a body of statistical information on how the economy actually behaves under the impact of various policies" were cited as key to transforming economics from "the dismal science" to one of optimism. The new generation of economists was the first to use econometric models to evaluate the effects of pulling on different policy levers. They genuinely believed that it was possible to "tinker successfully" with the economy and "do a lot more good than harm in the process."

Kenneth Arrow summed up the prevailing view by claiming "you have to find a real crackpot to get an economist who doesn't accept the principle of government intervention in the business cycle." If this is what it means to be a crackpot, I know now why members of our staff here may have readily accepted the alternative designation, "maverick." They have argued, and I tend to agree, that the cycle is littered with all kinds of well-intentioned policies that have had all sorts of important, deleterious, and quite unanticipated effects.

The present time certainly is a different world from the confident optimism of the early 1960s. Moreover, the distinctions between liberal and conservative or activist and laissez faire economists, if they ever were blurred, now have widened to the point that splits among theories seem to preclude conversation between economists of different camps.

This is why we chose to devote our conference this year to a discussion of the cycle. I cannot envision the quality of policy making moving forward until there is agreement on a common language and until a path to resolving conflicts among competing theories is identified. Exactly *what* is this cycle we are trying to explain? Precisely *where* do our theories differ? And, *on what evidence* can we defend the idea that we are doing more good than harm by activist meddling with market forces?

Thirty years ago, in the same *Time* story I mentioned earlier, a panel of 17 economists were asked their views on the then-current recession and the prospects for recovery. Sixteen gave authoritative statements on when and why a recovery would begin. The seventeenth, John Kenneth Galbraith, said: "I do not believe anybody in this Administration makes the pretentious mistake of thinking he knows what is going to happen. One of the greatest pieces of economic wisdom is to know what you do not know." I hope that these proceedings offer some guidance both on what we know, and on what we don't know, about business cycles. The former will tell us how far we have come in the past 30 years; the latter will remind us how much further we have yet to go.

Thomas C. Melzer
President
Federal Reserve Bank of St. Louis

Preface

These proceedings, from a conference held at the Federal Reserve Bank of St. Louis on October 17–18, 1991, attempted to lay out what we currently know about aggregate economic fluctuations. Identifying what we know inevitably reveals what we do not know about such fluctuations as well. From the vantage point of where the conference's participants view our current understanding to be, these proceedings can be seen as suggesting an agenda for further research.

The conference was divided into five sections. It began with the formulation of an empirical definition of the "business cycle" and a recitation of the stylized facts that must be explained by any theory that purports to capture the business cycle's essence. After outlining the historical development and key features of the current "theories" of business cycles, the conference evaluated these theories on the basis of their ability to explain the facts. Included in this evaluation was a discussion of whether (and how) the competing theories could be distinguished empirically. The conference then examined the implications for policy of what is known and not known about business cycles. A panel discussion closed the conference, highlighting important unresolved theoretical and empirical issues that should be taken up in future business cycle research.

What Is a Business Cycle?

Before gaining a genuine understanding of business cycles, economists must agree and be clear about what they mean when they refer to the cycle. In the keynote chapter, "What Is a Business Cycle?" Victor Zarnowitz takes on the difficult task of defining a business cycle. Approaching this task from several perspectives, Zarnowitz argues that the business cycle is "pervasive." Although business cycles historically have differed in their duration and intensity, they are all generally characterized by a decline and contraction and a subsequent rise and expansion of aggregate economic activity, as measured by total employment, output, real income, and real expenditures. National in scope and typically lasting several years, business cycles manifest themselves in the co-movements of and interactions among many economic variables. Not all variables are perfectly synchronized, however. Some lead and others follow the cycle. In addition, while most economic variables are procyclical, they do not generally move with the cycle to the same degree; other variables are countercyclical.

Zarnowitz also finds that the characteristics of business cycles have changed over time and differ across nations. For example, Zarnowitz finds that, in the United States, postwar cycles have become milder: Business contractions have become shorter and less severe, and business expansions have become longer relative to the cycles experienced before the 1930s. As possible reasons for this observed change, Zarnowitz suggests "the shift of employment to production of services, automatic stabilizers, some financial reforms and avoidance of crises, greater weight and some successes of government actions and policies, and higher levels of public confidence." He also finds that the postwar recessions in France, Italy, West Germany, and Japan were even milder and attributes this difference to the relative strength of their economic growth.

Thus, in trying to explain cycles, we must be guided not only by the features common to all business cycles but also by their diversity and evolution. By limiting the focus to features shared by all cycles, economic analyses potentially fail to gain a comprehensive understanding of aggregate economic fluctutations. The processes by which shocks affect economic activity can depend on a nation's institutions and stage of economic development and thus could be changing also.

James Stock, in his comments on this chapter, commends Zarnowitz for his useful and thorough overview of the business cycle, including his analysis of international business cycles. In his discussion, Stock focuses on only two main points. First, by drawing on recent research, he argues that Zarnowitz's evidence of the shortening of postwar recessions and lengthening of postwar expansions might be "biased" by the National Bureau of Research's (NBER) dating chronology, which is based on different time series depending on the historical period: "The prewar dating relied on series with more cycles, longer contractions, and shorter expansions than the series used for the postwar dating." Stock notes that, alternatively, the differences in the series used might accurately capture fundamental changes in economic activity, so that the NBER's dating methodology does not create a bias. While there is evidence that weakens the credibility of this alternative interpretation, Stock argues that additional research is needed to resolve the issue satisfactorily.

Stock's second point builds on one of Zarnowitz's main themes—that historical business cycles are not identical but, rather, have evolved over time. Stock suggests that case study analyses of individual cycles are likely to yield new and significant insights into the sources of cycles and their propagation mechanisms as they have changed with the evolution of business cycles. The usefulness of this approach is illustrated by examining the 1990 recession and highlighting how it was unlike any other postwar recession. Stock's evidence indicates that "historical correlations between leading indicators and overall economic activity were not good guides to this episode." In contrast to other recent U.S. recessions, monetary indicators played a small role in the 1990 episode. Rather, the data suggest an important role for "unprecedented shifts in consumer expectations."

What Are the Sources of Business Cycles?

Despite the voluminous research on fluctuations in aggregate economic activity, there appears to be nothing resembling a consensus among economists and policy makers about the sources of such fluctuations. Although a consensus about macroeconomic fluctuations and their implications emerged in the 1950s, that consensus was short-lived. Differing opinions were sparked by theoretical and empirical advances in the late 1960s, culminating in a debate between the Keynesians and monetarists. Subsequent theoretical research attempting to establish the *microfoundations* of macroeconomic phenomena eventually shifted the focus of the debate to one between the new-Keynesians and the real business cycle theorists. The next two chapters trace the evolution of these debates and summarize their contributions to our understanding of why cycles occur.

In "The Cycle Before the New-Classical Economics," David Laidler describes the evolution of the debate between the Keynesians and monetarists. The consensus that remained intact in the 1950s and early 1960s downplayed the relevance of monetary factors in explaining macroeconomic fluctuations, emphasizing instead autonomous fluctuations in investment. Building on this general acceptance of Keynesian economics, business cycle research continued to make progress, incorporating the notion of the accelerator into the Keynesian framework to explain not only how fluctuations in investment affect aggregate demand but also how the economy's productive capacity affects investment and vice versa. As Laidler points out, the theories produced by this research interpret business cycles as *real* rather than monetary phenomena, in the spirit of Keynesian economics. Laidler argues that the eventual demise of this view of business cycles, which had integrated growth theory with business cycle theory, was driven by subsequent advances in the mainstream of macroeconomic research that undermined some of the theory's key assumptions.

Monetarism, which had gained popularity as a theory about cycles mainly because it filled the gap in macroeconomics opened by the demise of the multiplier–accelerator models of the business cycle, revitalized the empirical search for exogenous impulses of cycles. At the same time, Keynesians focused on developing and implementing large econometric models to identify the propagation mechanisms of cycles. The specific economic relationship that became the focal point of the debate was the Phillips curve, depicting a trade-off between nominal wage growth and unemployment—a relationship that was quickly absorbed into mainstream Keynesian economics. Monetarists, however, argued that the Phillips curve was inadequate as a long-run representation and that what matters in labor decisions is not the nominal wage but the real wage. This criticism was reinforced and extended by subsequent theoretical and empirical research, later referred to as "new-classical" economics, stressing the importance of microfoundations and internal consistency. Laidler argues that, while new-classical economics, in essence, drew attention away from the debate between the monetarists and Keynesians, the latter two views began to converge, with the remaining differences being quantitative, not qualitative.

In Laidler's view, this turn of events has proved to be unfortunate. Researchers adopted new modeling strategies that they considered theoretically appealing—that is, the application of general equilibrium theory to explain macroeconomic phenomena—without conforming to the facts (for example, price and wage stickiness), almost as though the beauty of the theory (derived from first principles) was sufficient to justify this approach. Laidler suggests, for future research, moving away from that strategy and toward an empirical challenge to the existing theories of business cycles.

In his discussion of this chapter, Ben Bernanke first focuses on Laidler's list of contributions by the monetarists. Agreeing with Laidler, he notes that one of the major contributions was to document the empirical relevance of money in economic fluctuations. Bernanke adds emphasis to the monetarist recognition of the now well-accepted notion that, in the long run, the unemployment rate equals the natural rate, and stresses the monetarist prescription for nonactivist policy or rules over activist policy or discretion. Second, Bernanke highlights the similarities and differences between the monetarists' and the real business cycle theorists' challenges to the Keynesian paradigm, as well as their respective contributions. To add a favorable note to the real business cycle approach, while admitting that it has not been overwhelmingly fruitful, Bernanke suggests that, in time, this general equilibrium approach could offer much insight to our understanding of the cycle. Thus, in contrast to Laidler, Bernanke reserves judgment until this methodology matures sufficiently to address macroeconomic issues.

In "For a Return to Pragmatism," Olivier Blanchard describes the progress made by macroeconomic researchers during the past two decades, taking the new-classical challenge to "macroeconomics, circa 1970" as a starting point.[1] According to Blanchard, the new-classical challenge, calling for theoretical reconstruction and thereby producing a "back-to-basics" mentality, was met in two phases. First, researchers incorporated the rational expectations hypothesis and the potential importance of supply shocks into their analyses. Second, starting roughly a decade ago, researchers began to analyze the structure of different markets more closely in an effort to provide the mainstream view of macroeconomics (circa 1970) with a stronger theoretical foundation. This effort was directed primarily to learning more about the processes of wage and price determination.

Blanchard questions whether the advances made here constitute important contributions to our understanding. Although Blanchard is impressed by the list of advances made, he is disillusioned by their lack of cohesiveness, by the general failure of researchers to extend their analyses to capture the increasing integration of national economies, and by the scarcity of attempts to test the theories empirically or extend them to explain the cyclical "facts." Like Laidler, Blanchard argues that the wave of research in the past two decades, in its narrow "back-to-basics" mode, has provided little insight into contemporary real-world issues and policy problems. His prescription for the profession is to "adopt a more flexible, more pragmatic approach to research."

Like Laidler, Blanchard argues that the wave of the new-Keynesian and real business cycle research has provided little insight into contemporary real-world policy problems. He also agrees with Laidler's prescription for the profession to get back to basics. In addition, he says, the wave has pushed econometrics in the wrong direction, away from the fundamental issues about characterizing the data structurally while handling simultaneity of the determination of economic variables. Blanchard encourages macroeconomists to adopt a common framework, one that sees demand shocks from home and abroad as dominant in explaining macroeconomic fluctuations, accounts for the changing nature of the shocks that generate the fluctuations, and explicitly allows for real if not nominal rigidities. Such a framework should permit an analysis of the interaction among technological change, recessions, and unemployment. Blanchard also draws attention to three areas of research that he believes should be addressed in this framework: the functioning of labor, goods, and credit markets.

How Might the Debate Be Resolved?

One of the overriding concerns among many conference participants was the movement away from empirical research in macroeconomics during the past two decades. In the absence of rigorous testing of the empirical validity of each of the competing theories, the debate concerning the sources and implications of business fluctuations appears to be vacuous. In "The Cowles Commission Approach, Real Business Cycle Theories, and New-Keynesian Economics," Ray Fair articulates this concern, using the Cowles Commission approach as a standard for judgment. This approach translates theoretical models into econometric ones that, in turn, enable estimation, testing, and prediction. He argues that the Lucas critique, which generated excitement about searching for the deep, structural parameters that are invariant to policy changes, might have led the profession astray, making it less able to deal with more difficult problems than those posed by the critique itself. While admitting that the critique is correct, Fair points out that its empirical significance remains to be seen. Testing of real business cycle models is difficult at best and thus will not fare well in competing with other models. Similarly, he criticizes the new-Keynesian approach for its failure to combine theories to produce a full model of the economy. This failure precludes the line of research from model estimation, testing, and prediction.

Given the lack of empirical content in both approaches, which have dominated macroeconomic research for nearly two decades, Fair is pessimistic that the debate will be resolved satisfactorily. He does, however, believe that empirical testing to distinguish the theories is possible. To do so would require more sophisticated and thorough testing and more econometric model building, by both the new-Keynesians and the real business cycle theorists, taking the approach of the Cowles Commission.

Arnold Zellner expresses general agreement with most of Fair's points. He is skeptical, however, about the fruitfulness of Fair's proposal to resolve the debate between the new-Keynesians and the real business cycle theorists empirically. Zellner points out, for example, that the actual structure of the economy is subject to much uncertainty. In addition, the estimated coefficients obtained from the Cowles Commission approach are not constant over time. Moreover, they are likely to change not only because of changes in policy, but also because of adaptive optimization by economic agents responding to large aggregate shocks. Zellner also expresses concern about the problems of aggregation, regime changes, measurement errors, and seasonal adjustments in the data.

He suggests, as an alternative to the Cowles Commission approach and fixed-parameter models, what he has dubbed the "structural econometric modeling, time series analysis" (SEMTSA) approach. With this approach, the researcher posits a *tentative* structural model based on theory and, from that model, derives "transfer" functions. In going back and forth between the structural formulation of the model and the transfer functions in estimation, the researcher ensures compatibility, thoroughly tests the structural model's components, and compiles them in a reasonable way to formulate a model. The result is a final model that can be tested further. Zellner believes that the SEMTSA approach might be quite successful in producing an empirical model that can explain the essential characteristics of business cycles and predict future outcomes with satisfactory precision.

What Are the Policy Implications?

Most economists would agree with the notion that understanding the causes and mechanisms of business cycles is necessary in making informed policy decisions. The issue receiving considerable attention in recent policy debates, however, is more fundamental—namely, whether macroeconomic policy could possibly enhance social welfare. Without sufficient empirical evidence to resolve the debate among competing camps of different normative (as well as positive) prior beliefs, one naturally wonders whether macroeconomics has anything to offer policy makers in the way of *useful* advice.

In "How Does It Matter?" Benjamin Friedman expresses his doubt that recent research on business cycles can be of much help to policy makers. His doubt is not driven by the lack of consensus among economists, however. Indeed, he argues that the principal distinction between new-Keynesian economics and real business cycle theories has less relevance for policy than is commonly thought. That is to say, whether the sources of business cycles originate on the demand side or the supply side of the economy might not matter in deciding whether a policy response would be welfare-improving. The reason is that exogenous shocks to the supply side typically generate shocks to the demand side, which often cannot be disentangled empirically or theoretically. Instead, Friedman argues, the distinction that is important for policy is whether the key assumptions of the real business cycle theories are consistent with the facts. Because the economy is better characterized by Walrasian rigidities and market imperfections rather than perfectly flexible prices and wages, frictionless markets, and nondistortionary taxes, Friedman argues, "there is room for macroeconomic policy to respond to even the purest of "supply shocks." Even then, Friedman argues, the existing theories have little to say about what policies should be implemented in response to exogenous shocks because they fail to incorporate heterogeneity of the population and thereby abstracts from the distributional questions that it raises.

Echoing both Laidler and Blanchard, Friedman also feels that research in business cycles has sacrificed relevance in its search for elegance. Specifically, the theories are incapable of addressing pragmatic policy issues about the differing effects on the welfare of various economic agents. Given that aggregate shocks generate "winners" and "losers," the notion of Pareto improvement "loses its practical relevance." Friedman argues that, to be able to provide reasonable guides for policy, theories of business cycles must account for heterogeneity in the population. In addition, Friedman suggests that economists should examine more closely the role of policy to influence expectations. In models exhibiting multiple equilibria, policy's influence on expectations could aid economic agents to coordinate on the *best* equilibrium.

While appreciating the strength of Friedman's arguments, Michael Darby challenges Friedman's view that monetary policy should pursue "contracyclical" or stabilization policies. In Darby's view, contracyclical policy promises a "cure that in actuality makes things worse." To be effective, such a policy requires a guide to determine the magnitude, direction, and timing of the policy response. Without such a guide and with institutional constraints that limit the role of fiscal policy, policies intended to stabilize aggregate income are likely to have destablilizing effects. Darby emphasizes that policy should avoid the temptation to stabilize income and aim for longer-term strategies and goals, such as price-level stability.

Where Do We Stand?

With so many unsettled issues in the study of business cycles, it might appear that the foundation on which future research should build is weak. That there is much room for further progress is hardly arguable. In the panel discussion closing this conference the participants offered their views on where we now stand and what areas of inquiry would likely prove most fruitful in future research.

Alan Blinder, in "Déjà Vu All Over Again," expresses much agreement with Laidler, Fair, and especially Blanchard in arguing that macroeconomic research since 1972 has made little progress in resolving the controversial issues about how the economy works. In addition, Blinder emphasizes, the "fact that such issues remain so controversial for so long is a condemnation of our profession." Although he is not inclined to condemn the new-Keynesians for the "nonempirical flavor" of their research, Blinder does question the real business cycle models for their lack of empirical basis. After reviewing the historical development of macroeconomic models, starting with the early Keynesians, he offers a "new, post-RBC consensus," which is hardly distinguishable from that reached in 1972 with the resolution of the positive issues of concern in the Keynesian–monetarist debate. The primary differences include the recognition of the importance of supply shocks and the general acceptance of rational expectations by macroeconomists. Blinder argues, in agreement with Fair and Laidler, that macroeconomists should return to empirical work, "the task that was so unfortunately abandoned in 1972."

In "Business Cycle Developments and the Agenda for Business Cycle Research," Herschel Grossman discusses how the evolution of research in this area was influenced by historical business cycle developments. These developments, in turn, suggest where it should go in the future. Before the mid-1970s, business cycle research centered on understanding the determination of nominal aggregate demand, its relation to real aggregate demand, and policies to stabilize nominal aggregate demand. The first development that influenced the direction of research, in Grossman's mind, was the oil price shock of 1973, which suggested that a possibly important source of economic fluctuations could be exogenous changes in resource endowments. He interprets the U.S. recessions of 1974–1975 and 1981–1982, as well as the recession of 1991, with their uneven regional and sectoral effects, as suggesting that research also should examine the determination of economic activity on regional and sectoral levels. In addition, experience in recent years suggests that the Federal Reserve System is able and willing to stabilize nominal aggregate demand without attempting to go beyond the nation's resource constraints. Grossman points out, nevertheless, that there is little to ensure that the Fed will continue to "give priority to this objective" indefinitely, for neither the preferences of our policy makers nor the institutions that constrain their choices have changed. Thus, he emphasizes, the events of the past two decades suggest that research efforts should be directed not only toward the implications of aggregate supply shocks and the cyclical aspects of economic activity from a regional and sectoral perspective, but also toward enhancing our "understanding of the political-economic structure underlying monetary and fiscal policy."

Michael Parkin, in "Where Do We Stand?" offers a characterization of the current debate quite different from that of Blanchard, suggesting that the current path of macroeconomic research might not be just a dead end. Parkin argues that the criticism against the new-classical research program—that it merely aims to "build beautiful models"—is not well founded. The research program currently being pursued by young macroeconomists aims to resolve economic puzzles by building models, with the ultimate goal of subjecting the models to empirical verification. In his view, the important distinctions between the new-Keynesians and the new-classical economists do not concern with methodology and ideology. Rather, they are "based on views about which abstractions might turn out to be useful and which might not." The new-classical economists emphasize intertemporal substitution to explain economic fluctuations. new-Keynesians, while accepting the importance of intertemporal substitution, emphasize problems of coordination and rigidities to explain economic fluctuations. But the new-classical economists do not deny the existence of these problems, and their modeling strategy does not preclude the incorporation of these features of the economy. Parkin suggests, in addition, that the empirical evidence offered by the new-classical economists should not be dismissed because of its lack of conformity with traditional empirical analyses, for that evidence is consistent with the view that "policy is a process, not an event." But, without a feasible commitment technology, this process is a discretionary one. Thus, Parkin believes that macroeconomists in the future should study alternative institutional arrangements to determine which would best stabilize the economy.

Over all, these proceedings offer many reasons for macroeconomists to feel humble about their work. At the same time, they contain a great deal of constructive criticism about which avenues of future research are most likely to produce useful results. Macroeconomists from all schools of thought should find plenty of stimulus in this volume for their own research agendas.

Note

1. It should be noted that Blanchard's chapter in this volume differs considerably from the paper he presented at the conference. This earlier paper, entitled "The New Classicals and the New Keynesians: The Long Pause" included comments on a variety of topics omitted in the published version. We regret that, due to time constraints, not all of conference participants were able to incorporate these changes in their own contributions to this volume.

Acknowledgments

The Bank's annual economic policy conference is organized by its Research and Public Information Department. Special thanks are due, however, to several people who did the lion's share of the work. Linda Moser coordinated all local arrangements, ranging from the mailing list to menus and hotel accommodations. Daniel Brennan helped edit the proceedings and worked closely with Zachary Rolnik and Judy Pereira of Kluwer Academic Publishers to produce this volume. Finally, Peggy Dooley typed, and kept organized, all of the conference correspondence in her usual conscientious and timely manner.

SESSION I

1 WHAT IS A BUSINESS CYCLE?

Victor Zarnowitz

Sober men, whose projects have been disproportioned to their capitals, are as likely to have neither wherewithal to buy money, nor credit to borrow it, as prodigals whose expence has been disproportioned to their revenue. Before their projects can be brought to bear, their stock is gone, and their credit with it. . . . When the profits of trade happen to be greater than ordinary, overtrading becomes a general error both among great and small dealers.

—Adam Smith (1776, p. 406)

When prices fall, production is arrested until the expences of production fall in equal degree; and whilst production is thus arrested, consumption *is also diminished . . . the inducements to employ labour . . . are diminished . . . and the prices of labour fall. The consumption of labour is thus diminished, and the prices of property again fall, and again act in depressing labour, and in crippling production. . . . It is the deficiency of money which has occasioned the depression of prices. . . .*

—Thomas Attwood (1817, pp. 99, 101)

We find [the state of trade] subject to various conditions which are periodically returning: it revolves apparently in an established cycle. First we find it in a state of quiescence,—next improvement,—growing confidence,—prosperity,—excitement,—overtrading,—convulsion,—pressure,—stagnation,—distress,—ending again in quiescence.

—Lord Overstone (1857, p. 44)

But though men have the power to purchase they may not choose to use it. For when confidence has been shaken by failures, capital cannot be got to start new companies or extend old ones. . . . In short there is little occupation in any of the trades which make Fixed capital. . . . Other trades, finding a poor market for their goods, produce less; they earn less, and therefore they buy less. . . . Thus commercial disorganization spreads. . . . The chief cause of the evil is a want of confidence.

—Alfred and Mary Marshall (1881, pp. 154–155)

1 The Emergence of Business Cycles in History and Economic Thought

1.1 Early Observations and Interpretations

Well before the concept of a business (or trade) cycle originated, serious episodes of commercial and financial instability were observed repeatedly by contemporaries. The preceding quotations, from Adam Smith (1776) to Alfred Marshall (1881), illustrate the reactions of some of the classical economists and politicians in England. Smith's brief mention of "overtrading" is the only one in *The Wealth of Nations*.[1] Attwood, a banker and politician, blamed reductions in the money supply under the gold standard for the resulting deflation and interacting declines in spending and incomes (see Link, 1958, pp. 6–35; Backhouse, 1988, pp. 134–34). The "famous words" of Lord Overstone, who may have been the first to write about a multistage "cycle of trade," were cited with approval by Marshall a quarter-century later. Marshall's stress of the confidence factor recalls not only Pigou of 1929 but also Keynes of 1936 (Marshall and Marshall, 1881). There is much in these and other early theories of crises and cycles that deserves to be rediscovered and reconsidered today.[2]

Because of the predominance of classical tradition, problems of long-term equilibrium constituted the principal concern of the prominent theorists in the nineteenth century, and short-term business cycle problems were at best a secondary interest. Yet throughout that century, from Sismondi and Malthus to Marx and Hobson, intense controversies prevailed about the validity of Say's law, that supply creates its own demand, and about the possibility of a "general glut" (Sowell, 1972). There can be little doubt that this controversy was so great because of the pressure of events: the need to account for the recurrent "crises," the related decreases in sales and profits, and the increases in unemployment.

A study of monetary statistics for France and England (since 1800) and the United States (since 1836) led Juglar (1889) to believe that crises are merely stages in recurrent business cycles. Although the title of his work refers to the "periodic return" of the crises, the durations of his cycles vary considerably.[3] According to Juglar, cycles are principally a feature of economies with highly developed commerce and industry, division of labor, external trade, and the use of credit. This idea was accepted and developed further by most of the leading scholars in the field.

The association of business cycles with modern capitalism is reflected in the National Bureau of Economic Research (NBER) reference chronologies, which begin (for annual dates of peaks and troughs) in 1792, 1834, 1840, 1866 for Great Britain, the United States, France, and Germany, respectively.[4] There is substantial agreement that wars, poor harvests, and other episodic disturbances played a greater relative role in the preindustrialization era than afterward, and the endogenous cyclical influences a smaller role. The main reason, presumably, is the pronounced cyclicality of investment in "fixed" capital—plant, machinery, and equipment. It was only after the great technological innovations of the latter part of the eighteenth century were adopted that the size of such investment, and its share in output, began to increase rapidly, in England, then in Western Europe and in the United States. In earlier times, processing of raw materials by labor must have represented a much larger part of total production. It is likely, therefore, that fluctuations of trade and inventory investment accounted for most of the overall economic instability prior to the Industrial Revolution. But these movements tend to be shorter in duration and more random in nature than the fluctuations related to investment in business plant and equipment.[5]

Differences of opinion still persist on when modern business cycles came into being. Schumpeter (1939, vol. 1, chap. 6B) argues that capitalism goes "as far back as the element of credit creation" and that "there must have been also prosperities and depressions of the cyclical type" in the seventeenth and eighteenth centuries.[6] Indeed, there is a modest amount of evidence on how harvests, grain prices, exports, imports, and sales and profits of a small sample of enterprises changed from year to year in Great Britain between 1720 and 1800. Four economic historians compiled chronologies of commercial crises for this period that show a fair amount of consensus. There may have been six or eight major contractions of credit and several more downturns of profit.[7] The problem is not with the existence of some substantial fluctuations but with their nature. How comparable are they with the later business cycles? Unfortunately, there is no conclusive answer because of severe limitations in the available data.

1.2 Popular Meaning

Unlike a theoretical concept such as that of equilibrium, a business cycle is principally an empirical phenomenon founded upon historical experience. People engaged in business and public affairs have long observed that economic conditions are generally satisfactory or good much of the time but weak or bad some of the time. An old term for the good times was *prosperity*, an old term for the bad times was *depression*. The transition from the former to the latter used to be called a *crisis* (and occasionally a *recession*, but this designation came to be reserved for a mildly depressed period and is so applied presently). The transition from depression to prosperity was called *revival* (today the term *recovery* is more common). It seems fair to say that these broad descriptions soon acquired a rather good intuitive meaning and wide acceptance in use.

The evidence comes from hundreds of official documents and contemporary reports in which such characterizations of the prevailing business situations are found over long sequences of years for market economies at various stages of development and industrialization. The terms denote phases of what later came to be called *business* (in England, *trade*) *cycles*, and their context was from the outset an economy with increasing population, labor force, productive capacity, and output. In the nineteenth century, long-term economic growth trends, like the fluctuations around them, became a widely recognized empirical phenomenon. Thus, prosperity soon acquired the connotation of an *expansion* and depression that of a *contraction*, although these terms came into use only later and were given a more explicit technical meaning by economists. Depressions were seen clearly as distressful interruptions of growth that was necessary to maintain prosperity. The dynamic nature of the perceived processes is well documented by the qualifiers frequently attached to the descriptions of the state of the economy. For example, a depression might be "mild" or "severe," a revival might be "slow" or "rapid," and so on.

Business annals based on a large collection of such materials were compiled by the NBER as one of its earliest projects (Thorp, 1926). They provide comprehensive qualitative records of general economic changes in a number of countries between 1790 and 1925.[8] The construction of the historical NBER business cycle chronologies for the United States, Great

Britain, France, and Germany was accomplished by a complementary use of the business annals and quantitative information drawn from a large collection of time series on aspects of general economic activity, price indexes, monetary and financial statistics, and the like (Burns and Mitchell, 1946). On the whole, a good agreement was found between the dates of the business cycle peaks and troughs suggested by the annals and the dates based on the statistical time series (for evidence, see Mitchell, 1927, pp. 20–31).

That many contemporaries were able to diagnose business conditions rather well in the face of great limitations of public data on the economy is a remarkable fact and a testimony to the persistence and pervasiveness of business cycles. It can take many months for downturns and declines to spread through the economy and for their effects to grow and recede. Such developments hurt the well-being of people in many occupations, industries, and regions and are therefore generally apprehended by them, although often with lengthy lags and great uncertainty. A similarly extended recognition process applies to economic upturns and rises. Business people track their sales and profits and learn when they are high or low, increasing or decreasing. Workers learn when jobs and wages are easy and when they are hard to get. Consumers know how much money they are able and willing to spend. One would expect sharp turning points and strong, sustained expansions or contractions to be recognized more promptly and reliably than gradual transitions and weak, erratic upward or downward movements.[9]

1.3 Economists' Definitions

It may be easy to recognize some manifestations of a business cycle, particularly the more extreme ones, but the history of events and ideas suggests that it is anything but easy to define what a business cycle actually *is*.[10] In recording sharp economic fluctuations, contemporaries and historians alike observe first the diverse disturbances, from bad weather to political upheavals and speculative manias and panics, that seem to account for crises and downturns. The concentration on isolated episodes and outside shocks precludes a definition of the entire fluctuation or cycle as an economic phenomenon and analytical target.

In contrast, economic theorists who accept the existence of general economic fluctuations are interested in the concept of "the" business cycle and its main cause or causes. In some cases the theory appears to rule the definition. For example, according to Cassel, "A period of boom is one of special increase in the production of fixed capital; a period of decline or a depression is one in which this production falls below the point it had previously reached. . . . This means that the alternation between periods of boom and slump is fundamentally a variation in the production of fixed capital, but has no direct connection with the rest of production" (see 1932, pp. 550, 552). Cassel, like Tugan-Baranovskii and Spiethoff before him, believed that changes in cost and value of capital goods are the main force driving the cyclical motion of the economy.

As another example, consider Hawtrey's statement that "the trade cycle is above all a periodical fluctuation in manufacturing activity and in the price level, the two fluctuating together" (1927, p. 471). Hawtrey's theory stressed the role of movements in bank credit, inventory investment, and prices in the relatively regular cycles of the pre–World War I gold standard era.

The search of literature for definitions of business cycles is on the whole frustrating. Most authors do not formulate such definitions by identifying empirically the principal "stylized facts" about what happens during expansions, downturns, contractions, and upturns. However, Mitchell proceeded along this way and arrived at a tentative working definition near the end of his 1927 volume (p. 468). With "some modifications suggested by experience in using it," that definition was restated by Burns and Mitchell (1946, p. 3):

> Business cycles are a type of fluctuation found in the aggregate economic activity of nations that organize their work mainly in business enterprises: a cycle consists of expansions occurring at about the same time in many economic activities, followed by similarly general recessions, contractions, and revivals which merge into the expansion phase of the next cycle; this sequence of changes is recurrent but not periodic; in duration business cycles vary from more than one year to ten or twelve years; they are not divisible into shorter cycles of similar character with amplitudes approximating their own.

The main point here is the co-movement of many economic variables or processes, which occurs with a rough synchronism (allowing for leads and lags of mostly moderate length) in the course of any business cycle. What matters is that many diverse activities tend to expand and contract together; also, it should be added, that they evolve over time and cannot be reduced to any single aggregate (Moore and Zarnowitz, 1986, p. 737). Hence, the question of what precisely constitutes "aggregate economic activity" is purposely and properly left open. The nature of business cycles depends on, and changes with, the major characteristics of the economy, society, and polity. The most common and salient feature of business cycles is their pervasiveness and persistence (the high cyclical conformity or coherence of numerous variables and their pronounced serial correlation). It is *not* the fluctuation of any single aggregate, however important.

In support of this argument, note that in the peacetime cycle before World War II, prices as well as quantities of industrial products tended to increase in expansions and decrease in contractions, which implies that nominal values of total output and income would have had larger amplitudes of procyclical movement than the real values. In contrast, in more recent times the overall level of prices continued to increase during contractions, albeit often at a slower pace (lower rates of inflation). Hence, real GNP is now a much more sensitive measure of cyclical changes in "aggregate economic activity" than nominal GNP is—whereas historically the opposite must have often been the case.

Of course, no statistics on GNP in either current or constant dollars were available before World War I, and none appeared on any regular basis in the interwar period. In fact, no single comprehensive measure of aggregate economic activity, with sufficient comparability of coverage and validity of estimation, exists for a long stretch of historical time. This applies to annual data and, still more so, to monthly and quarterly series that are much needed for the study of business cycles (as well as of short-term economic changes in general). It is therefore not only conceptually desirable but also statistically necessary to use a number of indicators rather than any single one. To be sure, they should include the most reliable and comprehensive time series data that can be had. In practice, for periods before 1914 or 1929, series representing various activities of production, consumption, investment, trade, and finance had to be collected and used as composite indexes of business activity, along with price indexes and other useful aggregates such as bank clearings and debits.[11]

The Burns–Mitchell definition refers to a broad range of durations (1–12 years), thereby accommodating both short and long cycles. It includes no strict amplitude criterion, but it rules out accepting movements smaller than usual as cyclical (this is roughly the intended effect of the last clause of the definition; see Burns and Mitchell, 1946, pp. 7–8). No distinction between major and minor cycles is made. The definition admits equally vigorous and weak expansions, severe and mild contractions.

1.4 Past Views on the Scope and Nature of Business Cycles

All descriptions and definitions of business cycles are guided in part by some theoretical ideas and in part by some observations and measures of what is going on in the economy. The data available to the early generations of students of the subject were meager indeed. Juglar, in the first large-scale work on the history of commercial crises and cycles (1862), assembled mainly monetary, banking, and price statistics. He showed that discounts and deposits were high in crisis (peak) years and low in liquidation (trough) years and that the reverse was true for bullion reserves. Prices rose before and fell after a crisis. Later, those economists who stressed the cyclical role of business investment in plant and equipment used various proxies, such as output of pig iron for production of capital goods and output of coal for total nonagricultural production (Tugan-Baranovskii, 1901; Cassel, 1932).

Note that the emphasis on some selected factors and data need not imply a view of business cycles as movements that are narrowly defined in spatial or temporal terms. On the scope and nature of the cycles, some economists have held widely different opinions. Referring to "cyclical fluctuations during the period 1870–1914," Cassel stated that they "have no absolute necessity, but are to a great extent caused by factors which represent passing phenomena of economic history, or which may be, if not eliminated, at least to a great extent controlled" (1932, p. 538). In contrast, according to Robertson (1937, p. 171), "In industrial fluctuation we are up against a problem very deep-seated in the nature of capitalist industry —perhaps of all modern industry—perhaps of man himself. I do not believe myself that we can solve it."

Overall, a perusal of the literature leaves a strong impression that most of the principal writers on business cycles recognized the large dimensions and importance of their problem and task. The interdependence of all parts of the economy, which essentially accounts for the wide diffusion of cyclical movements from any initial source, was well understood long before the advent of modern macroeconomic analysis. Indeed, the latter in some ways narrowed the approach to the study of business cycles, making it generally more aggregative and often also less dynamic. The pioneers in this field had a lively appreciation of the importance of endogenous cyclical processes and their connection with long-term economic growth and development. Many later contributions show less scope and vision in these respects. To be sure, the more recent work also displays the major benefits of using much more abundant, comprehensive, and accurate data as well as new techniques and insights of modern stochastic and econometric approaches.[12]

Those scholars who engaged in large-scale empirical research on the subject have been particularly insistent on seeing business cycles as complex phenomena of great importance: not only the main form of economic instability but also the uneven path of economic growth. Thus, to Burns and

Mitchell, "The problem of how business cycles come about is . . . inseparable from the problem of how a capitalist economy functions." They were "not content to focus analysis on the fluctuations of one or two great variables, such as production or employment" but "sought to interpret the system of business as a whole . . . to penetrate the facade of business aggregates and trace the detailed processes—psychological, institutional, and technological—by which they are fashioned and linked together."[13]

Similarly, Schumpeter's opening statement in his 1939 treatise that "analyzing business cycles means neither more nor less than analyzing the economic process of the capitalist era" conveys the sense of a most inclusive conception. Although "economic fluctuations properly so called [are] those economic changes which are inherent in the working of the economic organism itself," the effects of "external factors" or disturbances are also numerous and important; indeed in many instances they "entirely overshadow everything else" (1939, vol. 1, pp. 7, 12). But Schumpeter has no single definition of a business cycle. Rather, his "really relevant case" is that of interaction of "many simultaneous waves" (p. 212). The scheme involves 3–4, 7–10, and 48–60 year cycles (named after their investigators Kitchin, Juglar, and Kondratieff, respectively; see chap. 5). But there is little support from the data for periodicities in the occurrence of groups of major and minor cycles, although it is certainly true that individual cycles vary greatly in amplitude, duration, and diffusion (Burns and Mitchell, 1946, chap. 11; Zarnowitz and Moore, 1986, pp. 522–523).

1.5 New Developments and Ideas

Momentous developments bearing on thinking about business cycles occurred during the 1930s in the worlds of both real events and ideas. The Great Depression was not only an entirely unexpected calamity, it seemed to contradict the established ways and means of economic analysis. Seeking new explanations and remedies, Keynes claimed "to have shown . . . what determines the volume of employment at any time" and that therefore "our theory must be capable of explaining the phenomena of the Trade Cycle." Any particular cycle, he believed, "is highly complex and . . . every element in our analysis will be required for its complete explanation." But "the essential character of the Trade Cycle and, especially, the regularity of time-sequence and of duration which justifies us in calling it a *cycle*, is mainly due to the way in which the marginal efficiency of capital fluctuates" (1936, p. 313). Investment depends on the MEC as compared with the rate of interest, which recalls Wicksell's (1936) account of the relation between the value and the cost of capital goods, and Fisher's (1907) concept of the "rate of return over cost." But Keynes adds the *ex ante* discrepancies between investment and saving, the multiplier, and the cycle-induced changes in the liquidity preference and the propensity to consume. He stresses the instability of investment due to sharp fluctuations in business confidence under uncertainty about long-run returns.

Keynes' leading role in the development of the macroeconomics of income determination is beyond doubt, but his analysis of business cycles was quite fragmentary and his influence on the subsequent work in this area proved rather limited.[14] Formal models of dynamic disequilibrium based mainly on an interaction of the investment accelerator and the consumption multiplier enjoyed considerable popularity between the late 1930s and the early 1950s (Samuelson, 1939; Metzler, 1941; Hicks, 1950).[15] But it soon became apparent that these models are limited to a mechanical treatment of relations between a few aggregates and neglect potentially important factors of prices, money, finance, and expectations. A more lasting impact is attributable to the general idea that random shocks and changes in exogenous factors provide impulses that are propagated into cyclical movements by the dynamics of the interdependent market economy. This conception had some earlier origins but was first formalized by Frisch (1933).

Starting in the 1930s, econometric models came into use as vehicles for testing business cycle theories (Tinbergen, 1939). Their early postwar versions were heavily influenced by the Frisch impulse-propagation model and the Keynesian *I-S* model of Hicks (1937). The development of macroeconometric models depended critically on the growth of modern statistics, and particularly the system of national income accounts.

Hansen (1964, p. 4) defines the business cycle as "a fluctuation in (1) employment, (2) output, and (3) prices." Although he refers to Mitchell's 1927 definition, he is content to use only the aggregative measures of output and employment, plus the indexes of consumer and wholesale prices. More recent studies tend to restrict the criteria further to measures of real income and output, dropping the comprehensive price indexes because of their continued rise during the business contraction of the past 30 to 40 years. Other measures, such as those of the diffusion of cyclical movements, attract little attention. However, the dates of business cycle peaks and troughs as identified by the NBER continue to be generally accepted.

Views on the nature and scope of business cycles remain disparate. The once prevalent theories of endogenous or self-sustaining cycles have been in retreat for some time, though surviving in various nonlinear macrodynamic models and lately experiencing some resurgence. The predominant type is theories of cyclical response to various exogenous disturbances. The main controversies concern the source of the originating shocks: Are they real or monetary? To aggregate demand or aggregate supply? Monetarists stress the instability of growth in money supply due to errors in monetary policy. Keynesians stress the instability of private spending on capital goods and consumer durables. Both groups see the main shocks as arising on the demand side, but some new equilibrium theorists give more attention to supply shocks that impact the relative prices of oil and other major inputs, technology, and productivity.

This is no place to discuss in any detail the recent evolution and present state of business cycle theories (for a treatment of this subject, see Zarnowitz, 1985, 1991). Only a few remarks are in order here, but more will be made later in the context of a descriptive analysis of past and recent business cycles.

The range of contemporary views is indeed remarkably wide. Some theories predict the recurrence of serious financial crises and business depressions (Minsky, 1982). Others see the "cycles" as phenomena of moving equilibrium, no more than adjustments to random shocks (to technology, for example,) and of low social cost (Plosser, 1989). Most of the writings can be located somewhere between these extremes.

The debate increasingly concerns the underlying institutional and market conditions. Increases in the weight of the public sector and the role of government actions first resulted in rising beliefs that business cycles can be not only reduced but even entirely eliminated by proper stabilization policies. The focus of such expectations shifted over time from fiscal to monetary policies, and from purely discretionary to more rules-oriented policies. But in the process the high hopes of banning all boom-and-bust sequences were repeatedly disappointed. The celebrated inflation–unemployment tradeoff had seemed to vanish altogether in the 1970s, but this was a temporary eclipse reflecting the worsening inflation (actual and expected) and the novel supply shocks (huge oil price jumps). What became clear is that the tradeoff is neither stable nor predictably exploitable for purposes of stabilization policy but is itself dependent on the varying sources and characteristics of business cycles.

A related issue is the cyclical sensitivity of prices and wages. The new classical economists believe that prices in general are flexible, reacting promptly to clear the markets. The new-Keynesian economists believe that industrial prices and wages are sticky, reacting only slowly. In this view, both nominal and real (or relative) rigidities exist, and they are presumed to have good reasons, that is, to be consistent with considerations of self-interest of individuals and more or less organized groups. These reasons, however, are not yet well understood, so the causes of price and wage stickiness are in urgent need of much further research.

1.6 Some Basic Reflections and Further Steps

The preceding sections have shown that the documented history of business cycles goes back at least two hundred years. The popular awareness of recurrent crises and alternations of prosperous and depressed times is reflected in similarly long records. Serious thought about the nature and causes of major economic fluctuations accompanied serious thought about the nature and causes of industrial development and economic growth since the early writings on political economy.

If this is so, should it then not be clear by now what a business cycle is? Why the need to raise this question time and again? The reason is that business cycles are changing as well as complex. A process that repeats itself with substantial regularity over long periods of time will not withhold its secrets from inquiring minds over many decades of intensive study, even if it were quite complicated. But business cycles involve many interacting processes (economic, political, and broadly social) whose roles vary and evolve. They are most probably caused in part by uncontrollable outside disturbances and in part by errors of public policy and private decision makers that may be avoidable, but they are also, just as plausibly, to a large extent self-sustained and self-evolving. They are certainly not the same at all times and in all developed market economies, although they show a great deal of international interdependence.

To improve our understanding of business cycles, it is necessary to learn from their past as well as present and to study both their common features and diversity, continuity and change. In what follows, I shall consider the main lessons from the chronologies of business cycles in the United States and abroad and from research on the indicators and measures of cyclical and related processes. The discussion will include examples of stable and changing behavior and of some international similarities and differences.

2 The Changing Dimensions of Business Cycles

2.1 The Historical Reference Cycle Chronologies of the NBER

Annual chronologies of "reference cycles," that is, business cycle peaks and troughs, as estimated by Burns and Mitchell (1946) from time series studies and Thorp's annals, are available for the United States and Great Britain between 1790 and 1858. Monthly (as well as quarterly and annual) reference chronologies from the same source cover the United States and Britain for 1854–1938, France for 1865–1938, and Germany for 1879–1932. Table 1–1 sums up the record of durations of business expansions, contractions, and full cycles as derived from these dates. Part A lists the means and standard deviations for the overall periods covered and consecutive segments of 3–6 (mostly 4 and 5) cycles each. Part B lists the shortest (S) and the longest (L) durations over the same periods and somewhat fewer successive subperiods.

It is clear that the durations have varied greatly, as shown by the huge S–L ranges in part B. For example, the U.S. expansions ranged from 10 to 72 months, contractions from 8 to 72 months, and full cycles from 24 to 108 months (trough-to-trough) or 17 to 101 months (peak-to-peak). The results for the other countries are very similar: slightly larger S–L differences still for the British cycles, slightly smaller for the shorter histories of the French and German cycles.

These are comparisons between outliers, however, that can greatly overstate the more common differences between the duration measures. Indeed, U.S. business expansions in peacetime averaged 22–26 months in each of the four segments of 1854–1938 and 25 months in the period as a whole.[16] Remarkably, the corresponding contractions were not much shorter, averaging 19–20 months in three segments, 27 months in one, and 21 months over the total 1854–1938 period. Expansions varied relatively much less than contractions, as shown by the standard deviations attached to these averages. For full cycles, most of the mean durations are close to four years, with overall standard deviations of 18–20 months. These statistics disclose no systematic changes in phase and cycle durations. They surely justify the phrase "recurrent but not periodic" in the NBER definition. Still, the central tendency of the duration figures suggests a modest degree of regularity. Thus, 15 of the 19 peacetime expansions of 1854–1938 (79%) fall into the range of 1½ to 2½ years, and the same proportion applies to contractions in the range of 1 to 2 years.

The cycles in the other countries show more variability in durations both across and within subperiods. The U.S. cycles tended to be more numerous and shorter.[17] They numbered 21 in 1854–1938, averaging 4 years, while the British cycles numbered 16 and averaged 5⅓ years. For the longest common period, 1879–1938, the comparison is shown in the following table. Figure 1–1 compares the timing of business cycle peaks and troughs in the four countries by means of a schematic diagram. It suggests a fairly high degree of correspondence between the chronologies. Of the total of

Table 1–1. Durations of Business Expansions and Contractions in Four Countries, Selected Periods Between 1790 and 1938

A. *Phase and Cycle Durations, in Months: Means and Standard Deviations (S.D.)*

Line	*Period (No. of Business Cycles)*[a] *T to T* (1)	*P to P* (2)	*Expansion*[b] *Mean* (3)	*S.D.* (4)	*Contraction*[c] *Mean* (5)	*S.D.* (6)	*Full Cycle (T to T)* *Mean* (7)	*S.D.* (8)	*Full Cycle (P to P)* *Mean* (9)	*S.D.* (10)
					United States					
	Excluding Civil War & WWI									
1	1854–1879 (4)	1857–1882 (4)	26	7	27	26	53	31	61	27
2	1879–1897 (5)	1882–1899 (5)	25	7	19	11	44	17	41	11
3	1897–1915 (5)	1899–1913 (4)	22	8	20	5	42	4	40	11
4	1919–1938 (5)	1918–1937 (5)	26	15	20	13	46	16	45	29
5	1854–1938 (19)	1857–1937 (18)	25	9	21	14	46	18	46	21
	All cycles[d]									
6	1854–1938 (21)	1857–1937 (20)	26	11	22	14	48	18	48	20
7	1790–1938 (35)	1790–1938 (33)	28	14	23	16	50	24	50	20
					Great Britain					
	Excluding WWI									
8	1854–1879 (5)	1857–1882 (5)	40	9	36	28	76	37	79	32
9	1879–1914 (5)	1882–1912 (5)	43	17	25	16	68	26	67	36
10	1919–1938 (5)	1918–1937 (5)	26	24	20	10	47	21	45	33
11	1854–1938 (15)	1857–1937 (15)	36	18	27	19	63	29	64	34
	All cycles[d]									
12	1854–1938 (16)	1857–1937 (15)	37	18	26	19	63	29	64	33
13	1790–1938 (29)	1796–1937 (28)	39	18	22	16	60	24	62	28

					France					
	Excluding WWI									
14	1865–1887 (5)	1867–1881 (5)	22	3	30	23	52	25	56	31
15	1887–1914 (5)	1881–1913 (4)	39	21	26	14	65	28	67	32
16	1919–1938 (6)	1920–1937 (6)	24	11	15	8	39	14	38	10
17	1865–1938 (16)	1867–1937 (15)	28	15	23	17	51	24	52	26
	All cycles									
18	1865–1938 (17)	1867–1937 (16)	29	15	22	16	51	23	52	25
					Germany					
	Excluding WWI									
19	1879–1914 (6)	1882–1913 (5)	39	16	32	21	71	26	75	34
20	1919–1932 (3)	1918–1929 (3)	29	12	23	15	53	25	43	8
21	1879–1932 (9)	1882–1929 (8)	36	15	29	18	65	26	63	31
	All cycles									
22	1879–1932 (10)	1882–1929 (9)	37	14	27	18	64	24	63	29

Table 1–1. (Continued)

B. *Shortest (S) and Longest (L) Durations, in Months*

		No. of Business Cycles		*Expansion*[b]		*Contraction*[c]		*Full Cycle (T to T)*		*Full Cycle (P to P)*	
Line	*Period*[e] (1)	*T to T* (2)	*P to P* (3)	*S* (4)	*L* (5)	*S* (6)	*L* (7)	*S* (8)	*L* (9)	*S* (10)	*L* (11)
				United States							
23	1790–1855	14	13	12	72	12	72	24	108	24	84
24	1854–1899	10	10	18	46[f]	8	65	30	99	30	101
25	1899–1938	11	10	10	50	7[f]	43	28	64	17	93
				Great Britain							
26	1792–1858	14	14	24	72	12	36	36	84	36	108
27	1854–1900	6	6	30	64	6	81	39	135	36	123
28	1900–1938	10	9	8	61	6[f]	37	26	79	17	98

				France							
29	1865–1895	6	5	19	41	11	68	34	95	33	109
30	1900–1938	11	11	8	52	8	30	24	92	24	110
				Germany							
31	1879–1904	4	3	17	61	18	61	35	102	41	122
32	1904–1932	6	6	16	52	12	40	28	77	34	69

Source: National Bureau of Economic Research. For details, see Moore and Zarnowitz (1986, tables A.2 and A.3).

[a] The years are those of the initial and terminal business cycle troughs (T) in column 1, and those of the initial and terminal business cycle peaks (P) in column 2, according to the NBER monthly chronology. The numbers in parentheses refer to complete T to T or P to P cycles in the given period. The entries in columns 7 and 8 correspond to the dates in column 1; the entries in columns 9 and 10 correspond to the dates in column 2. The wartime cycles consist of expansions during the Civil War (for the United States) and World War I (WWI) for all four countries, and of the immediately following contractions (for the T to T cycles) or the immediately preceding contractions (for the P to P cycles).

[b] Measured from troughs (T) to peaks (P).

[c] Measured from peaks (P) to troughs (T).

[d] The reference cycle chronologies contain annual segments for the United States, 1790–1855, and Great Britain, 1792–1858. In Part A, lines 7 and 13, observations based on these dates but converted from annual to monthly durations are combined with the observations based on the monthly reference chronologies that begin in 1854 for both the United States and Great Britain.

[e] Years refer to the earliest and latest reference dates in each segment. Entries in lines 23 and 26, columns 4–10, are converted from annual to monthly durations (see note d).

[f] Refers to a wartime cycle.

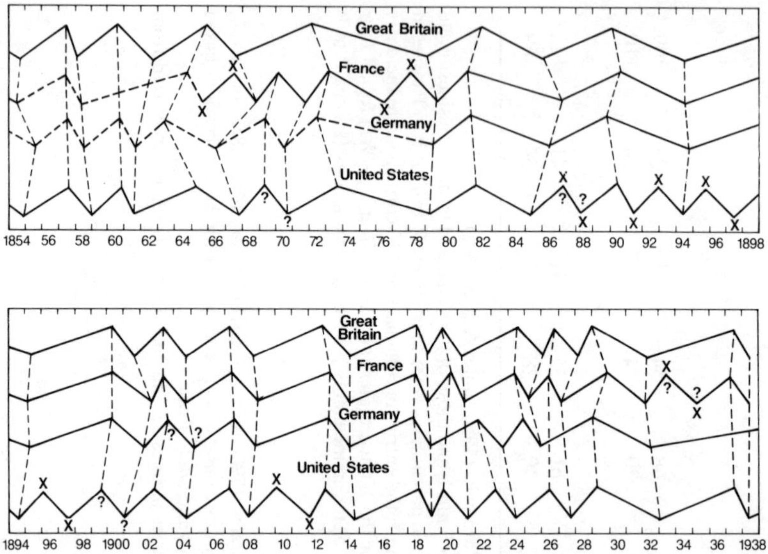

Figure 1–1. Timing of reference cycles for four countries and matched turning points, 1854–1938

Note: For each country, the lines connect the dates of business cycle peaks (upper turning points) and troughs (lower turning points). Thus, the upward-sloping segments of each country line represent expansions, the downward-sloping segments, contractions. The dashed links between the country lines connect the matched peaks or troughs for two or more countries. The sign × denotes an unmatched turn. For France before 1865 and for Germany before 1879, the reference dates are annual. They are plotted at the midpoint of the given calendar year and connected with dashed and dotted lines. All other reference dates are monthly and are connected with solid lines. Question mark (?) denotes a dubious turning point (see text).

Sources: German annual turning points 1855–1963 estimated from Hoffman by Rostow (1980, pp. 38–39). All other dates are from Burns and Mitchell (1946, pp. 78–79).

146 turning points shown, 92 (63%) match for all four countries and another 36 (25%) for three countries. Four turning points can be matched for two countries, and only 14 (10%) are unmatched. Practically the same proportions apply to peaks and troughs taken separately.

	United States	*Great Britain*	*France*	*Germany*
Number of cycles (T to T)	17	13	14	10
Mean duration (months)	48	65	53	64
Standard deviation (months)	18	31	25	24

When examined more closely, figure 1–1 shows that during the first quarter-century covered, French and German cycles diverged considerably, probably in part because of annual dating. The U.S. cycles conformed better to the British and German than to the French cycles. In the period 1879–1914—the heyday of the pre–World War I gold standard—the conformity between the business cycles in the European countries was particularly close, but the U.S. economy followed a different pattern of shorter and more frequent fluctuations. The timing of the wartime expansions (1914–1918) and contractions (1918–1919) was very similar in all four countries. In the 1920s and 1930s the European economies were much less in phase with each other than in the preceding 40 years, but the degree of conformity between their cycles and those in the United States increased (see Morgenstern, 1959, chap. 2).[18]

2.2 A Cautionary Note

The limitations of data, particularly for the early times, might have produced various errors in the identification of the reference cycles. A particularly likely type of error is that of mistaking a serious slowdown (phase of a low, that is, below-trend but still mainly positive, growth) for a contraction (phase of an absolute decline in overall economic activity). One reason to suspect an error is that the reference contractions are so much longer and more frequent in the pre–World War II era than for the more recent times about which there is much better and more complete statistical information (see section 2.3). Another reason is that business annals and indexes representing deviations from "normal" business conditions (where the "normal" levels or trends themselves are not quantified) were extensively used in determining the U.S. reference dates for the period before 1873, and these sources may be especially susceptible to the suspected bias (Zarnowitz, 1981, pp. 494–499).

A reassessment of the evidence must consider that the historical contractions may represent declines in real or nominal aggregates or both, depending on the strength and persistence of the concurrent movements in the general price level. Deflations greatly aggravated some past depressions, and wholesale price indexes are among the oldest important cyclical indicators. Both real and nominal representative time series must therefore be considered carefully, and when this is done the NBER chronology is found to be in good overall agreement with dating by other economic historians and generally well supported by the available evidence (Burns and Mitchell, 1946, pp. 107–113; Zarnowitz, 1981, pp. 494–505; Moore and Zarnowitz, 1986, pp. 755–764).

This does not mean, however, that all the identified cycles (let alone their precise dates) are equally well confirmed. A few episodes are doubtful. They include four NBER contractions: 1845–1846, 1869–1870, 1887–1888, and 1899–1900, of which the first one is most uncertain. (The peaks and troughs of the last three are denoted by a question mark (?) in figure 1–1.) The information on hand seems to me insufficient to make a conclusive determination of whether these were periods of actual declines or retardations below average growth. There are some problems with a few other minor contractions as well, but they are easier to resolve (Zarnowitz, 1981).

If these episodes were treated as slowdowns instead of contractions, the average durations of expansion ($\bar{E}$) would be considerably increased, both absolutely and relative to those of contractions ($\bar{C}$). The following tabulations shows this for the two periods principally affected.[19]

	1834–1855		*1854–1919*	
Number of cycles (T to T)	5	4	16	13
Expansion, months ($\bar{E}$)	26	36	27	37
Contraction, months ($\bar{C}$)	24	27	22	23
Ratio ($\bar{E}/\bar{C}$)	1.1	1.3	1.2	1.6

Some of the reference dates for the other countries may also be questioned. Burns and Mitchell (1946, p. 113) mention explicitly the German 1903–1905 contraction[20] and France "after 1932." Consequently, in figure 1–1, question marks denote these French and German contractions (as well as the three pairs of U.S. turning points already noted). In addition, the authors of the NBER dating methodology warn that "the chronology for France in the 1860s and 1870s requires careful consideration." It is therefore possible that some of the several discrepancies between the French and the other turning-point dates in this period are spurious (but, for lack of more specific information, these dates are left unquestioned in the diagram).

Figure 1–1 indicates that elimination of such dubious phases as U.S. 1887–1888 and France 1933–1935 would clearly improve the intercountry correlation of cyclical movements. But in other cases the opposite effects are suggested: Note U.S. 1899–1900[21] and Germany 1903–1905. Treating the U.S. 1869–1870 period as a slowdown rather than a contraction would improve the conformity with Great Britain but worsen the conformities with Germany and France (the dates for which, however, are themselves uncertain).

2.3 The Last Half-Century: Long Expansions, Short Contractions

The NBER chronology identifies 15 business cycles measured from peak to peak in 1857–1918, that is, on average one every four years. In 1918–1945 there were six cycles with a mean duration of about 4½ years. Between 1945 and 1990, nine cycles occurred, averaging approximately five years. Consequently, according to these estimates (see table 1–2, lines 7–9), the length of U.S. business cycles increased and their frequency diminished gradually. However, these differences are small and could be due largely to errors in a few early reference dates.[22] The predominant feature of the average full-cycle durations, when compared across such long eras, is their relatively high degree of stability.

What table 1–2 definitely demonstrates is that business expansions tended to be much longer, and contractions much shorter, after World War II than before. In the 1854–1919 period, expansions averaged 27 months and contractions 22 months; for 1919–1945 the mean durations of the respective phases are 35 and 18 months; and for 1945–1990 they are 50 and 11 months. Excluding wartime episodes would make the averages slightly smaller for expansions and slightly larger for contractions, but it would not alter significantly the changes between the periods.

Even allowing for the largest plausible errors in the early dating would still leave a large contrast between the pre-1945 and post-1945 cycles with respect to their relative divisions by phase. Thus the $\bar{E}/\bar{C}$ ratio for 1854–1919 can be estimated at 1.2–1.6 (see tabulation on page 22). The $\bar{E}/\bar{C}$ ratio for 1919–1938 is 1.9; that for 1945–1990 is 4.5 (based on the entries in lines 8 and 9). In other words, in the last 50 years the economy has been in expansion phases about 80% of the time; before then, perhaps only 55% to 60% of the time.

Business expansions have become not only longer but also more variable, hence less predictable with regard to their durations. The standard deviations of the latter, in months, increased from 10 before 1918 to 26 in 1919–1945 and 31 in 1945–1990. The range of peacetime expansions was 10 to 50 months before 1945 and 12 to 92 months thereafter (the longest wartime expansions lasted 80 months in 1938–1945 and 106 months in 1961–1969; see lines 7–14, columns 3 and 4).

In contrast, business contractions have become not only shorter but also more uniform in length, hence in this sense more predictable. Their standard deviations, in months, dropped from 13 and 14 in 1857–1919 and 1920–1945, respectively, to 4 in 1945–1982. The range of peacetime contractions was 8 to 65 months before 1945 and 6 to 16 months thereafter (see lines 7–14, columns 5 and 6).

Table 1–2. Durations of Business Expansions and Contractions in the United States, Selected Periods between 1938 and 1990 and between 1854 and 1990

	Period (No. of Business Cycles)[a]		*Expansion*[b]		*Contraction*[c]		*Full Cycle (T to T)*		*Full Cycle (P to P)*	
Line	*T to T (1)*	*P to P (2)*	*Mean (3)*	*S.D. (4)*	*Mean (5)*	*S.D. (6)*	*Mean (7)*	*S.D. (8)*	*Mean (9)*	*S.D. (10)*
	1938–1990, excl. wartime cycles									
1	1938–1961 (3)	1945–1990 (3)	33	8	10	2	43	8	42	9
2	1961–1982 (3)	1960–1990 (4)	50	34	13	6	48	18	62	38
3	1938–1982 (6)	1945–1990 (7)	43	26	11	4	46	13	53	30
	1938–1990, all cycles									
4	1938–1961 (5)	1945–1960 (5)	45	21	9	1	54	20	55	23
5	1961–1982 (4)	1960–1990 (5)	61	39	12	5	65	38	73	41
6	1938–1982 (9)	1945–1990 (10)	53	31	11	3	59	28	64	33
	1854–1990, all cycles									
7	1854–1919 (16)	1857–1918 (15)	27	10	22	14	48	19	49	18
8	1919–1945 (6)	1918–1945 (6)	35	26	18	13	53	22	53	32
9	1945–1982 (8)	1945–1990 (9)	50	31	11	4	56	27	61	33
10	1854–1982 (30)	1857–1990 (30)	35	23	18	12	51	22	53	26

			Shortest (S) and Longest (L) Durations, in Months							
			S	L	S	L	S	L	S	L
	Excluding wartime cycles									
11	1938–1982 (6)	1945–1990 (7)	12	92	6	16	28	64	18	108
12	1854–1938 (19)	1857–1945 (19)	10	50	8	65	30	99	17	101
	All cycles									
13	1938–1982 (9)	1945–1990 (9)	12	106[d]	6	16	28	117[d]	18	116[d]
14	1854–1938 (21)	1857–1945 (21)	10	80[d]	7[d]	65	28	99	17	101

[a] T denotes initial and terminal troughs, P denotes initial and terminal peaks. Entries in columns 7 and 8 correspond to the dates in column 1; the entries in columns 9 and 10 correspond to the dates in column 2. The wartime cycles consist of expansions during the Civil War, World Wars I and II, the Korean War, and the Vietnam War, and of the immediately following contractions (for the T to T cycles) or the immediately preceding contractions (for the P to P cycles).

[b] Measured from troughs (T) to peaks (P).

[c] Measured from peaks (P) to troughs (T).

[d] Refers to a wartime cycle.

Both expansions and contractions, and hence full cycles, increased in length and variability between the early part of the recent era (the 1940s and 1950s) and the later part (the 1960s, 1970s, and 1980s). This is true for both peacetime and all cycles, as shown in some detail in table 1–2, lines 1–6.

2.4 Phase Durations in Eras of Inflationary and Deflationary Trends

Through the great contraction of the early 1930s, prices in the United States and Europe followed alternating upward and downward trends (table 1–3). This is best seen in the wholesale or producer price indexes, which also have the longest records, but even the less flexible consumer price indexes show alternating periods of inflation and deflation. The complete upswings in wholesale prices lasted generally between 20 and 30 years; the downswings varied more, from 9 to 32 years. Over long stretches of time the deflations nearly offset the inflations, even when the war periods are included, so that the level of wholesale prices at the bottom of the depression in 1932 was not much higher than in the early times of the Republic, more than 140 years earlier. However, no significant deflationary trends appeared in the nearly 60 years since, only brief price declines in the recessions of 1937–1938 and 1948–1949. Ours is the age of the most persistent and pervasive inflation on record.

The long-period averages in table 1–3, column 2, are instructive, even though they conceal much variability over shorter time intervals. Before 1950 comprehensive price indexes had generally, in addition to the longer trends, clear procyclical movements, up in expansions and down in contractions. Thereafter, disinflation replaced deflation as a frequent concomitant of business recessions and some major slowdowns. Inflation became a grave and stubborn problem primarily because the deflationary slumps have disappeared, not because the booms have grown more inflationary. This is a very important but relatively neglected point.

Periods of rising trends in prices witnessed relatively long business expansions and relatively short contractions, whereas periods of declining trends in prices witnessed the opposite. This was observed as early as 1926 by Mitchell (in his introductory chapter to Thorp, 1926, pp. 65–66) and confirmed by Burns and Mitchell in 1946 (pp. 437–438, 538). Table 1–3 provides a summary of their findings and of the generally consistent later results (see also Moore, 1983, chap. 15; Zarnowitz and Moore, 1986, pp. 525–531). In times of rising prices, the expansion–contraction duration ratios $\bar{E}/\bar{C}$ averaged 2.1–2.5; in times of falling prices, $\bar{E}/\bar{C}$ averaged 0.8–1.0. These are large and systematic differences based on U.S. data for 1789–1990 and on European data for periods beginning 1854–1895 and ending in the 1930s. The documented relationship is robust: It does not depend on the inclusion of the highly inflationary wartime expansions, for example, or on our use of average rather than total phase durations.[23]

The longest and most severe contractions in the history of U.S. business cycles were associated with major deflations, including 1873–1879, 1882–1885, 1895–1897, 1920–1921, and 1929–1933. This last world depression was ascribed by Irving Fisher (1932, 1933) mainly to "debt-deflation," that is, an overexpansion of debts in the preceding expansion followed directly by sharp downturns in prices and profits.[24] Similar ideas on the role of overindebtedness, credit restrictions, and liquidation reappear in some recent theories that also stress, along the lines of Keynes, the instability of real investment and are adapted to the present environment of large government and persistent inflation (as in Minsky, 1982). But one does not need to accept all these ideas to agree that the avoidance of major deflations greatly helped the postwar economies to avoid major depressions as well. Many monetarists and Keynesians alike would probably accept this statement.

Let it be made immediately clear that to argue against deflation does not mean at all to argue for inflation. Recent experiences with high inflation in developing countries and with stagflation in North America and Europe leave no doubt that any long and sizable inflation is harmful to both real growth and economic stability. Once allowed to develop, inflation, like deflation, is difficult to control and can be self-accelerating by generating perfectly reasonable expectations about its own future. But it is also true that a small rate of inflation really amounts to the desired state of stability in the general price level, given the inevitable technical limitations of price-index measurement. Further, expansions favor price raises, while contractions favor cost and price cuts.[25]

2.5 *Some Other Analytical Uses of the Duration Data*

Are business expansions, contractions, and full cycles more likely to end or less likely to end as they grow older; that is, do they exhibit a positive or a negative duration dependence? Diebold and Rudebusch (1990, 1991) attempt to answer this question by fitting hazard functions to the NBER duration data.[26] Using an exponential-quadratic hazard model, which is relatively flexible yet parsimonious, they find evidence of a positive

Table 1–3. Trends in Wholesale Prices and the Business Cycle Phase Durations, United States 1789–1990 and Three European Countries between 1854 and 1935

Line	Trend in Wholesale Prices: Direction and Dates in Years[a] (1)	First to Last Year Change (percent p.a.)[b] (2)	Business Expansions[c]: Number (3)	Average Duration ($\bar{E}$) in Months (4)	Business Contractions[c]: Number (5)	Average Duration ($\bar{C}$) in Months (6)	Ratio of Average Durations, $\bar{E}/\bar{C}$ (7)
	United States						
	Rising						
1	1789–1814	3.1	5	42	4	22	1.9
2	1843–1864	4.7	6 (5)	32 (30)	5	15	2.1 (2.0)
3	1896–1920	5.1	7 (6)	23 (20)	6	18	1.3 (1.1)
4	1932–1990[d]	4.1	11 (8)	53 (44)	10	11	4.6 (3.8)
5	Total or Average[d]	4.2	29 (24)	40 (34)	25	16	2.5 (2.1)
	Falling						
6	1814–1843	–3.1	6	27	7	27	1.0
7	1864–1896	–3.2	7	25	8	26	1.0
8	1920–1932	–6.9	3	23	4	22	1.0
9	Total or average	–3.9	16	25	19	25	1.0

			Great Britain				
	Rising						
10	1854–1873, 1896–1920	3.6	10	30	8	17	2.2
	Falling						
11	1873–1896, 1920–1933	–2.3	5	30	7	38	0.8
			France				
	Rising						
12	1865–1873, 1896–1926	6.4	11	31	9	15	2.1
	Falling						
13	1873–1896, 1926–1935	–2.6	4	30	6	34	0.9
			Germany				
	Rising						
14	1895–1923	2.3	6	40	6	18	2.2
	Falling						
15	1922–1933	–4.2	4	32	4	42	0.8

[a] Through 1932 based on Burns and Mitchell (1946, p. 432). For 1932–1982, see Moore (1983, p. 240).

[b] For the United States 1789–1982, see Zarnowitz and Moore (1986, p. 527). For other countries, see the sources listed in Burns and Mitchell (1946, p. 432). Author's calculations are based on the data for the initial and terminal years; the averages are weighted by the durations in years of the periods covered.

[c] The NBER monthly business cycle chronologies are used. See Zarnowitz and Moore (1986, pp. 528–529). Entries in parentheses exclude wartime expansions (Civil War, World Wars I and II, Korean War, and Vietnam War).

[d] Updated by author's calculations.

duration dependence for pre–World War II business expansions in the United States, Great Britain, France, and Germany. Thus, the longer these expansions lasted beyond their minimum durations, the more likely they were to end. On the other hand, the pre-1940 business contractions show no duration dependence at all in any of these four countries. For full cycles (both T-to-T and P-to-P) there is evidence of some positive duration dependence but less than for expansions.

The U.S. business cycles of the post–World War II era present just the opposite situation, according to the estimates by Diebold and Rudebusch. Here the expansions show no duration dependence, and neither do the full cycles whose length reflects largely that of the expansions. In contrast, the contractions display a strong positive duration dependence.

These results are definitely associated with the findings reported earlier in section 2.2 of this chapter: Prewar expansions and postwar contractions have both stable average durations and positive duration dependence; prewar contractions and postwar expansions have neither. These tendencies are of great interest but difficult to explain. They are not consistent with models of purely random "Monte Carlo" fluctuations that would show no systematic duration dependence for either upward or downward movements. They are also not consistent with models that would produce positive duration dependencies in both expansions and contractions.

It is important to note that a strong periodicity of expansions implies that business cycle peaks, in large measure, should be predictable. But they are not: Even the best reputed professionals seldom make good forecasts of an approaching downturn, and the public often recognizes a recession tardily, with a surprise. Moreover, if the timing of economic downturns were predictable, strong efforts would probably be made to prevent them, or at least to diminish them greatly, so as to avoid the large individual losses and social distress they cause. If such efforts fully succeeded, business cycles as they are known now would no longer be with us. If they were repeatedly frustrated, we would try to learn why. In any event, the experiment remains only a mental one; were it actually performed, the working of the economy itself could well be significantly altered. The upshot of the argument is simply that strong periodicities of expansion are not to be expected. This is quite consistent with indications of a significant positive duration dependence in pre-World War II expansions.

For contractions, stable durations have different implications and are not so difficult to imagine. That contractions have become much shorter in the postwar age can be explained in part by changes in the structure of the economy and in part by the direct and indirect effects of much increased efforts of government policy makers to combat recessions and unemployment. The experience of more persistent growth helped to generate expectations that a recession, once known to be under way, will prove to be over soon. A business recovery in the near future is always a highly welcome event (worries about an inflationary boom can wait), and forecasts of a recurrence of such an event are always popular and apt to spread.

2.6 *On Theories and Evidence Relating to Periodic Business Fluctuations*

The duration data based on the reference cycle chronologies give no encouragement to any theories that imply strong phase and cycle periodicities, but they do not exclude the possibility of some weak and latent periodicities.[27] The class of strongly periodic theories includes the early deterministic versions of multiplier–accelerator interaction and nonlinear limit cycles (Samuelson, 1939; Kaldor, 1940; Metzler, 1947; Hicks, 1950; Goodwin, 1951). Adding shocks can relax the periodicities of the cycles generated by these models. Adding relations involving money, finance, and expectations can enrich and diversify the models. None of these refinements, however, is likely to produce any systematic asymmetries and shifts in phase durations.

Nor is it probable that the answer lies in any single impulse or propagation mechanism. The models of "forced oscillations" driven by factors that are themselves periodic are the simplest and also the easiest to dismiss. The oldest example here is that of weather and harvest cycles that used to be attributed to variations in sunspots or other extraterrestrial influences (Jevons, 1884; Moore, 1914). There is no doubt that changes in weather can and do cause major and recurrent fluctuations of production, prices, wealth, and welfare in poor agricultural countries. Some of these may be strongly or weakly periodic and occasionally are very large.[28] But today the weather and other "seasonal" hypotheses have hardly any plausibility as *the* explanation of business cycles in modern industrialized countries (including their farm sectors).

A more timely and currently much debated hypothesis is that of a "political business cycle" linked to the electoral cycle in democratic countries. Here, too, there are elements of forced oscillations, though not ordained by nature but due to events with a calendar rhythm imposed by a nation's laws and institutions. That economics and politics interact in various ways is important and widely acknowledged. But the notion of a regular political business cycle encounters serious theoretical problems, being based on assumptions that would enable the government to pursue a purely self-interested and myopic but highly effective fine-tuning policy. Not surprisingly, good evidence in support of this hypothesis is hard to find.[29]

Cycles with a positive duration dependence, and indeed a substantial degree of periodicity, can be produced by damped linear models with small and dense white-noise shocks and the required structural properties. This hypothesis, in the form developed by Frisch (1933), has strongly influenced the theory and, particularly, the econometric modeling of business cycles. It belongs to a class of models of "free oscillations," which explain the cycles by the way the economic system responds to the forces that impinge upon it, not by the cyclicality of these forces. This is a useful approach when given a sufficiently broad interpretation. But the empirical validity of models with purely random shocks was never adequately demonstrated. Indeed, the conclusion from simulation studies that used macro-econometric models driven only by such shocks is that the so generated movements lack the dimensions and properties observed in the actual data on business cycles (Hickman, 1972).

One of the needed extensions is to large shocks, which contribute to macroeconomic instability, along with the small ones (Blanchard and Watson, 1986). Large shocks presumptively occur at irregular intervals but are often serially correlated: Think of wars, shifts in policy, embargoes, price-level disturbances, speculative waves, financial crises, major bankruptcies, and strikes. In general such events and their direct and indirect effects are likely to increase the diversification and irregularity of business cycles over time.

2.7 The Moderation of U.S. Business Cycles

Business contractions in the United States have become not only much shorter but also much milder in the post–World War II era compared with earlier times. Severe depressions like those of the 1870s, 1880s, and 1930s appear to have disappeared for good. Table 1–4 compares measures of depth and diffusion for the five contractions of 1920–1938 and the eight contractions of 1948–1982. The former set includes two major depressions (1920–1921 and 1937–1938), one disastrous depression (1929–1933), one mild recession (1926–1927), and one more severe recession (1923–1924). The latter set includes three mild recessions (1960–1961, 1969–1970, and 1980) and five more severe recessions (1948–1949, 1953–1954, 1957–1958, 1973–1975, and 1981–1982). The presently available, incomplete data indicate that the U.S. recession of 1990–1991 (not covered here) will qualify as another mild one.

Table 1–4 leaves no doubt about the relative shallowness of even the most severe of the recent recessions (1973–1975 and 1981–1982), which contrasts sharply with the depth of either of the two interwar depressions, let alone that of the 1929–1933 collapse. Despite the upward trend in joblessness during the recent period, the maximum unemployment rate in the early 1980s was still less than half those reached in the 1930s (column 5). Consistent evidence is also provided by diffusion measures, although here the differences are less striking, with the proportions of industries with declining employment ranging from 71% to 100% (column 7).

For the pre–World War I period, comprehensive estimates of economic activity are scarce and their quality leaves much to be desired. Quarterly data used in table 1–5, lines 1–3, suggest that output was 1½ times more volatile in 1919–1945 than in 1875–1918 and twice as volatile in 1919–1945 as in 1946–1983 (column 3).[30] Although the pre-1919 figure may be an overestimate (Romer, 1986), there is little doubt about the ranking of the three periods in terms of both quarter-to-quarter and cyclical variability. In percentage terms and on average, the trough-to-peak increases were the largest in 1919–1945 and somewhat larger after 1945 than before 1919 (column 6). The peak-to-trough decreases were very large in 1919–1945, much smaller in 1875–1918, and the smallest by far in 1946–1983 (column 9).

Before 1945 wholesale prices tended to rise in expansions and fall in contractions, as shown clearly in table 1–5 (see lines 4–6, columns 6 and 9). The trend in prices was just moderately up in 1875–1918 and mildly down in 1919–1945, despite the big inflations of World Wars I and II, but it was strongly up in 1946–1983 (column 2).

Even though economic growth decreased and cyclical instability increased in the latter part of the postwar era (since the early 1970s), business cycles remained moderate in comparison to the pre–World War I and, *a fortiori*, the interwar periods. In other major countries with higher growth rates, business contractions became much less frequent and much milder still (see section 3). Several not mutually exclusive hyptheses may explain the observed reduction of the business cycles in the United States. I can only list them briefly here (Zarnowitz, 1991, offers an extended discussion).

1. Employment in service-producing industries and government, which is only weakly procyclical or acyclical, increased greatly relative to employment in goods-producing industries, which is strongly procyclical.

Table 1–4. Depth and Diffusion of Business Contractions in the United States, 1920–1982

		Percentage Change[b] in			Unemployment Rate		Nonfarm Employment, % of Industries Contracting[d]
Line	Business Cycle Contraction[a] (1)	Real GNP (2)	Industrial Production (3)	Nonfarm Employment (4)	Maximum[c] (5)	Percentage Increase[c] (6)	(7)
			A. Selected Business Contractions				
1	1/1920–7/1921 (D)	n.a.	−32.4	n.a.	11.9	10.3	97
2	10/1926–11/1927 (M)	−2.0	−7.0	n.a.	4.4	2.4	71
3	8/1929–3/1933 (GD)	−32.6	−53.4	−31.6	24.9	21.7	100
4	5/1937–6/1938 (D)	−13.2	−32.4	−10.8	20.0	9.0	97
5	11/1948–10/1949 (S)	−1.5	−10.1	−5.2	7.8	4.5	90
6	8/1957–4/1958 (S)	−3.3	−13.5	−4.3	7.3	3.7	88
7	10/1969–11/1970 (M)	−1.0	−6.8	−1.5	5.9	2.6	80
8	11/1973–3/1975 (S)	−4.9	−15.3	−2.9	8.8	4.3	88
9	1/1980–7/1980 (M)	−2.3	−8.5	−1.4	7.7	2.2	77
10	7/1981–11/1982 (S)	−3.0	−12.3	−3.1	10.7	3.6	79

			B. Averages by Degree of Severity				
11	Two major depressions[e]	−13.4	−32.4	−10.6	16.0	9.6	97
12	Six severe recessions[f]	−3.3	−13.1	−3.8	7.7	3.8	88
13	Four mild recessions[g]	−1.7	−3.8	−1.7	6.2	2.3	77

Source: Moore and Zarnowitz (1986, Table A.7).

n.a. = not available.

[a] Symbols in parentheses classify the contractions as follows: GD, Great Depression of 1929–1933; D, depression; S, severe recession; M, mild recession.

[b] Measured from peak to trough in quarterly data for real GNP and monthly data for industrial production and nonfarm employment.

[c] Entries for 1920–1933 (lines 1–3) are annual averages (monthly data not available).

[d] Before 1948 based on cyclical changes in employment in 41 industries. Since 1948 based on changes in employment over six-month spans in 30 industries (1948–1959); 172 industries (1960–1971); and 186 industries (1972–1982).

[e] 1920–1921 and 1937–1938 (as marked D above).

[f] Includes the recessions of 5/1923–7/1924 and 7/1953–5/1954 in addition to the four marked S above.

[g] Includes the recession of 4/1960–2/1961 in addition to the three recessions marked M above.

Table 1–5. Variabilities of Relative Change and Amplitudes of Cyclical Movement, Real GNP and Prices, 1875–1918, 1919–1945, and 1946–1983

		Log Differences		*Expansions*[b]			*Contractions*[b]		
Line	*Period*[a] *(1)*	*Mean (2)*	*S.D. (3)*	*Number (4)*	*Mean Duration (quarters) (5)*	*Mean Amplitude (percent) (6)*	*Number (7)*	*Mean Duration (quarters) (8)*	*Mean Amplitude (percent) (9)*
				Real Gross National Product					
1	1875–1918	1.0	2.4	12	8.9	17.3	12	3.2	–5.1
2	1919–1945	0.8	3.6	4	11.0	30.1	5	6.0	–14.1
3	1946–1983	0.8	1.2	7	16.3	20.9	8	2.6	–2.5
				Wholesale (Producer) Price Index					
4	1875–1918	0.3	3.3	11	6.6	12.1	10	6.9	–11.8
5	1919–1945	–0.2	4.1	4	8.2	15.4	5	8.6	–21.6
6	1946–1983	1.1	2.3	4	12.0	8.7	5	5.0	–4.8

Source: Calculated from data in Balke and Gordon (1986, pp. 788–810) (see note 30).

[a] Number of quarterly observations per series: 1875–1918, 175; 1919–1945, 107; 1946–1983, 151. The annual dates refer to the first and last turning points of the series during each period.

[b] Identified by specific cycle peaks and troughs in the series. Expansions are measured from peaks to troughs, contractions from troughs to peaks. Only complete upward and downward movements are counted.

2. Fiscal automatic stabilizers relating to procyclical income taxes and countercyclical transfer payments became quite effective, particularly before the rise in inflation and its distortionary tax effects.
3. Federal deposit insurance prevented general banking panics, although lately at high cost to the taxpayers.
4. The rates of change in money supply were more volatile in 1875–1917 and, particularly, 1919–1939 than after 1946.
5. The record of discretionary fiscal and monetary policies, although quite mixed over time, was on balance sufficiently positive to help avert depressions and persistence of high unemployment.
6. The gradual recognition that business contractions have become shorter and milder strengthened the confidence of business people, workers, and consumers and made them adopt behavior that promoted growth (but this was partially offset in more recent times by the expectational effects of rises in inflation and unemployment).

3 Some International Comparisons of Cyclical Movements and Growth Trends

3.1 The Major Market Economies After World War II

World War II devasted the economies of Continental Europe and the Far East. The physical wealth and capital of once rich nations—cities, factories, machinery—lay in ruins and in dire need of reconstruction. But human capital was much better preserved; that is, people retained their high productive potential—education, skills—and the backlog of effective demand was huge. Monetary, fiscal, and political reforms enabled both the defeated nations and the nations liberated by the Allies to make a relatively smooth transition from closed-war to open-market economies, and from totalitarian and oppressive to democratic and free social systems. Further, foreign aid, mainly from the United States, was made available to friend and former foe alike.

The result of this historically rare, perhaps unique, combination of circumstances was that France, Italy, West Germany, and Japan (as well as a number of smaller countries) soon came to enjoy extraordinarily high rates of real economic growth. Of course, the initial activity levels were very low, which helps explain the long persistence of very high and only gradually declining growth rates, but nevertheless the progress achieved in the 1950s and 1960s was spectacular, particularly in the case of West Germany and Japan.

As long as the steep upward trends in employment and output (much of it exported) continued, real growth in Continental Europe and the Far East was interrupted infrequently and mostly by slowdowns rather than absolute declines in overall economic activity. Thus, the benefits of high growth were augmented by those of high cyclical stability.

Figure 1–2 presents the evidence. The data, collected and processed by the Center for International Business Cycle Research (CIBCR) at Columbia University Business School, are composite indexes of coincident indicators that combine monthly and quarterly measures of aggregate activity (total output, industrial production, employment, real sales, inverted unemployment) and have trends made equal to those of the corresponding series for real GNP or GDP. Note that West Germany had its first postwar recession in 3/1966–5/1967, Japan (for which the index begins in 1954) in 11/1973–2/1975 (see figure 1–2A). For France (since 1955) the first postwar contraction shown is in 4/1958–4/1959, for Italy it is in 10/1963–3/1965 (figure 1–2B). Meanwhile, Canada and the United Kingdom (figure 1–2C) and the United States and Australia (figure 1–2D), all countries that suffered much smaller direct wartime damages, had less need of domestic reconstruction, slower growth rates, and earlier and more frequent recessions.

Economic growth slowed markedly everywhere during the 1970s and 1980s, and recessions became both more common and more severe. They spread worldwide in 1974–1975 after the oil embargo and the huge increases in the OPEC cartel oil prices, and again in 1980–1982 after new price shocks and strong counterinflationary policy moves in the United States. However, the index for Japan shows only a brief decline in late 1980; its growth after the mid-1970s was much slower than before but also remarkably steady. The index for France shows frequent but only short and shallow declines throughout, except in 1958–1959 and 1974–1975 (its sharp decline in the spring of 1968 largely reflects the concurrent political unrest).

3.2 Estimated Dimensions of Business Cycles in Eight Countries

There is no NBER-type international reference chronology of business cycle peaks and troughs for the post–World War II period. Perhaps the main reason is the belief that recessions have been generally replaced by mere retardations of growth in most countries. But this is a vague view or expectation, not a well-established fact. What is certainly true is that contractions of total output and employment have been short and few and far between in developed and developing countries that achieved high average rates of real growth.

The laborious and data-intensive task of identifying and dating business cycles in different economies cannot be attempted here. However, much can be learned from the rich data bank of CIBCR, and particularly the coincident indexes, covered in figure 1–2.

The black dots in figure 1–2 mark peaks and troughs of specific cycles in the indexes. The so-identified declines last several months (as a rule, six or more) and have amplitudes of several or more percentage points (as a rule, at least 1%). They presumably reflect business contractions. The open dots mark shorter and/or smaller declines that do not qualify as recessions but may be associated with significant retardations in general economic activity. However, substantial business slowdowns can occur without any noticeable decreases in the levels of the index series, particularly in places and times of very high overall growth (see, for example, West Germany, 1956–1957, and Japan, 1957 and 1964).

The charts show some important similarities between the country indexes, notably the concentration of long expansions in the 1960s and 1980s, of mild recessions or slowdowns in the mid- or later 1960s, and of more severe contractions in the mid-1970s and early 1980s. But the differences are even more pronounced, and it is clear that they are primarily related to the longer growth trends. The main point here is that high growth helps to reduce the frequency and depth of business contractions.

Thus periods of rapid and recession-free growth are observed for West Germany and Italy before 1962, for France in most of the 1960s and again after 1985, for Japan before 1973, for Canada between 1961 and 1981, and for Australia between 1961 and 1973. The economies of the United States and United Kingdom had relatively low rates of real growth and most cyclical variability. In sharp contrast, Japan had both the fastest growth and least cyclicality; indeed, one can say that business cycles as we know them were essentially absent there.[31]

Figure 1–2 suggests that the postwar business cycles were shorter and more numerous in the United States than in any other of the seven countries. In 1955–1990, the longest common period covered, the numbers of complete peak-to-peak cycles in the indexes were as follows: United States, 6; United Kingdom and Italy, 5 each; France and Australia, 4 each; Canada and West Germany, 3 each; and Japan, 2. Comparisons between fewer countries over longer periods yield generally consistent results. Further, inspection of the charts suggests that the greater frequency of U.S. cycles was mainly due to the shorter durations of U.S. expansions. On the whole, it was the expansions that differed greatly across the countries in

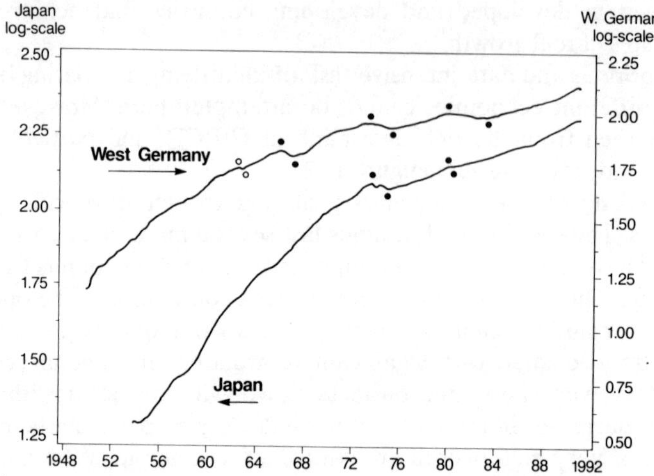
Japan
log-scale
W. Germany
log-scale
West Germany
Japan
2.50
2.25
2.00
1.75
1.50
1.25
2.25
2.00
1.75
1.50
1.25
1.00
0.75
0.50
1948
52
56
60
64
68
72
76
80
84
88
1992

A

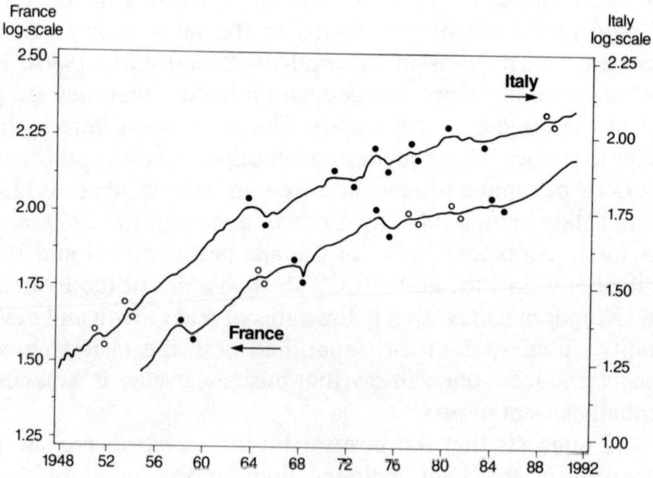
France
log-scale
Italy
log-scale
Italy
France
2.50
2.25
2.00
1.75
1.50
1.25
2.25
2.00
1.75
1.50
1.25
1.00
1948
52
56
60
64
68
72
76
80
84
88
1992

B

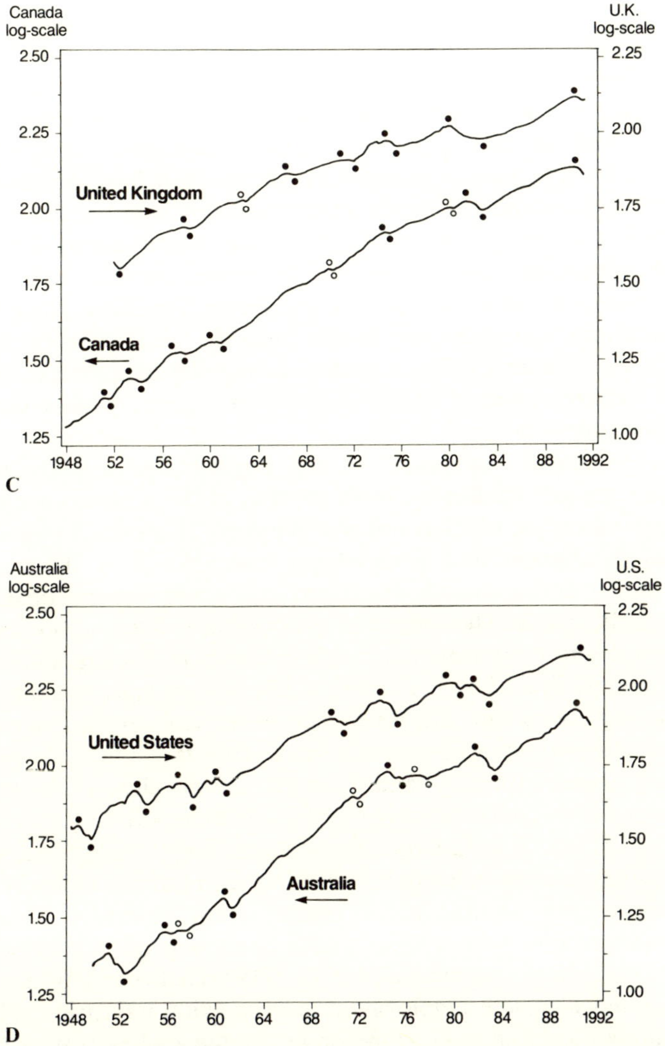

Figure 1–2. Coincident indexes (adjusted). *A*: Japan and West Germany; *B*: France and Italy; *C*: Canada and United Kingdom; *D*: Australia and United States

both length and amplitude, whereas the contractions varied much less in both dimensions.

Table 1–6 presents a summary based on the data plotted and the specific-cycle turning points identified in figure 1–2. It demonstrates that the cyclical rises in the U.S. index were on average much shorter than the rises in the foreign indexes (column 6), and also much smaller in percentage terms than the indexes for the other countries, with the sole exception of the United Kingdom (column 7). As for the cyclical declines in the U.S. index, they were on average considerably deeper than the declines in the other indexes, but not particularly long (columns 9 and 10). The entries on mean durations and mean amplitudes quantify the impression from the charts that expansions differed greatly across the countries (even apart from the extreme cases of West Germany and Japan), while contractions differed only moderately.[32]

A comprehensive assessment of how business cycles in the different countries compare would require an analysis of the performance of many individual indicators, which is not possible here. However, I examined the industrial production and employment components of the coincident indexes under consideration and found that a few general observations deserve to be made. The industrial production indexes cover sectors of high cyclical sensitivity (manufacturing everywhere, mining and/or public utilities in most countries).[33] Therefore they have at least as many specific cycles as the coincident indexes (which cover less sensitive sectors and processes as well), often significantly more. Thus the industrial production series for Japan (mining and manufacturing) clearly shows seven expansions and six contractions in the 1953–1990 period.

In the United States, although nonfarm employment has a much broader coverage than industrial production, the cyclical profiles of the two indicators are quite similar. This is definitely not the case in some of the other countries, however. In Japan total employment of "regular workers" had only one cyclical contraction (4/1975–5/1976) between 1954 and 1990.[34] In the United Kingdom employment in production industries followed a gradual *downward* trend since 1966, and the same applies to West German employment in manufacturing and mining from 1971 until mid-1984 as well as to French nonfarm employment between mid-1974 and mid-1985. In contrast, in the United States an upward trend in employment prevailed throughout. It is well known that, after having stayed very low in the earlier postwar years, unemployment in Western Europe increased rapidly (quadrupled) between 1970 and 1985, from well below to well above the U.S. levels. Yet, despite the downtrends in employment and clear cyclical movements around them, business cycles apparently remained milder in

Table 1–6. Average Durations and Amplitudes of Expansions and Contractions in Composite Indexes of Coincident Indicators, Eight Countries, 1948–1991

			Dates of Turning Points		Expansions			Contractions		
Line	Country (1)	Period Covered (2)	First[a] (P or T) (3)	Last[b] (P or T) (4)	Number (5)	Mean Duration (months) (6)	Mean Amplitude (percent) (7)	Number (8)	Mean Duration (months) (9)	Mean Amplitude (percent) (10)
1	U.S.	1948–1991	48(P)	90(P)	8	49	30.4	8	13	–9.1
2	Canada	1948–1991	51(P)	90(P)	5	82	57.8	5	12	–3.4
3	U.K.	1952–1991	52(T)	90(P)	6	63	29.2	5	15	–4.1
4	France	1955–1991	58(P)	91(P)	4	88	47.6	4	11	–5.8
5	Italy	1948–1991	48(T)	91(P)	6	77	60.2	5	18	–4.9
6	W. Germany	1950–1991	50(T)	91(P)	4	101	110.8	3	26	–6.5
7	Japan	1954–1991	54(T)	91(P)	3	140	430.7	2	10	–4.6
8	Australia	1950–1991	51(P)	90(P)	5	81	65.1	5	12	–7.5

Source: Center for International Business Cycle Research, Graduate School of Business, Columbia University.

[a] The following initial or early low values are assumed to represent trough dates: Italy, 1/1948; West Germany, 1/1950; Japan, 6/1954 (see figures 1–2A and 1–2B).

[b] The following late or terminal values are assumed to represent peak dates: France, 1/1991; Italy, 1/1991; West Germany, 4/1991; Japan, 2/1991 (see figures 1–2A and 1–2B).

Europe than here. This suggests that the persistent rise in European unemployment was largely noncyclical in nature, which is consistent with most recent hypotheses.[35]

3.3 Possible Reasons for the Observed Differences

There are no tested hypotheses, let alone accepted knowledge, on why the United States may be subject to more frequent and deeper recessions than Japan, West Germany, or France. However, there is much debate about the sources of differences in longer-term growth rates between the major industrial and trading countries. Insights from this literature bear on the present problem insofar as higher growth is in fact conducive to greater cyclical stability.

The central argument here is simple. Investment in human and physical capital produces advances in knowledge, technological progress, and increased rates of growth in factor productivity, output, and real income. What is desired, therefore, is higher maintained rates (and shares in total output) of saving-cum-investment in real terms.[36] There is no need here to cite the voluminous theoretical and empirical work on sources of economic growth, which generally supports this basic position. As a practical outcome, there is considerable consensus that the most successful economies are those that have the highest average long-term rates of capital investment. For some time, the United States has had relatively low shares of private saving and total productive investment; hence it is widely and variously urged to perform better in this respect, as its main competitors in Europe and the Far East do.

On the other hand, fluctuations in business and consumer capital outlays have long been recognized to be a major source of cyclical instability in aggregate demand. The preceding argument seems to ignore or assume away the problem. Since investment is much more cyclical than consumption, is it not necessarily true that a larger share of investment will increase the fluctuations of the economy, along with its growth?

The short answer is no. Investment can be both high and stable, provided it is a part of, and a response to, growth in aggregate demand that is sufficient to keep the economy near full employment. As the classical long-run version of the accelerator theory has it, net investment is in the end only justified by growth in the demand for the product of the new capital (which ought to be given the broadest interpretation). But, as noted before, it is equally true that growth itself depends positively on prior rates of investment. Increases in real capital, physical and human, generate improvements in productivity that can reduce costs and prices. This fact is particularly important in the competitive world of open economies.

In sum, higher rates of saving, investment, and growth can coexist with, and indeed may favor, greater cyclical stability. The problem is how to maintain them. But several heavily export-oriented countries in Europe and Asia did very well on this score, and their experiences may hold useful lessons.

The other side of the argument that more growth promotes more stability is that economic fluctuations can have costly long-term consequences in the form of suboptimal investment and growth. In a recent model, firms must make technology commitments in advance, and unanticipated volatility causes errors in these decisions (for example, on the scale of a new plant or size of the work force) that have substantial negative output effects (Ramey and Ramey, 1991).[37]

To be sure, there are other factors to be considered. Business cycles have historically been more frequent and shorter in the United States than in Europe, as shown in section 2.1 and table 2–1. This difference points in the same direction as that observed in recent times, but it is much weaker and there are no large and systematic disparities in country growth trends to account for it. To my knowledge, it was never explained. Possible reasons include a larger role of short inventory fluctuations in the United States and more frequent financial disturbances.

3.4 Growth Cycles

In countries where growth persisted at high rates and business contractions occurred rarely and remained mild for a considerable time, even mere slowdowns cause much public concern and indeed are often treated as actual recessions are treated elsewhere. The reason is that the slowdowns are themselves of significant duration, result in some rise in unemployment and weak business conditions generally, and are usually associated with absolute declines in some more cyclically sensitive activities and sectors. In the 1960s, when confidence about the long-lasting era of high growth and rising prosperity reached its peak, business cycles seemed increasingly "obsolete" and interest shifted to "growth cycles," that is, fluctuations around the upward trend in a nation's economic activity expressed in real terms (Bronfenbrenner, 1969; Mintz, 1969, 1974).

The concept of growth cycles is an old one, as illustrated by the fact that early indexes of general business conditions and trade were more often than not available only in the form of percentage deviations from estimated trend or "normal" curves (see Zarnowitz, 1981, for a brief history of this approach and references). Implicitly, the idea of growth cycles has also long been popular with textbook authors, who refer vaguely to business cycles being "fluctuations around the trend" and stress the transitory nature of departures of the actual from the potential (full employment) output. But it is very important to distinguish clearly between business cycles and growth cycles because the two differ qualitatively and not just in degree. A slow expansion is still an expansion; the problems posed by a contraction are quite distinct. Moreover, trends interact with cycles, vary over time, and are difficult to isolate and measure.

In spite of these difficulties, much interesting work has been done in the last 20 years on the postwar growth cycles in many countries, particularly by Mintz at the NBER and by Moore and his associates at the CIBCR.[38] When cautiously interpreted, the results can yield lessons on when and how expansions speed and slow and retardations do or do not develop into contractions.

The chronology of growth cycles is derived from the observed consensus of the corresponding turning points in series of *deviations from trend*, just as the chronology of business cycles is derived from the consensus of turning points in series of *levels*. In both cases, the same basic set of data is used, namely, a country's principal coincident indicators—the main comprehensive measures of GNP or GDP, personal income, sales, employment, and industrial production (all deflated or in physical units). In both cases, too, peaks and troughs mark specific cycles in the indicators used (whether they relate to the original levels or those in the trend-adjusted series). The trends should be flexible and as free of any cyclical components as possible (in the CIBCR studies they are determined by interpolation between segments of the series determined with the help of selected long-term moving averages).

This chapter is mainly concerned with business cycles, not growth cycles, but a brief review of how the two units of observation are related is in order. Figure 1–3 presents in schematic form the timing of growth cycle peaks and troughs in six countries. The initial and terminal dates of slowdowns that ended in renewed expansions are marked by ordinary dots, the dates of slowdowns that ended in contractions are marked by heavier black dots. The following table indicates that slowdowns without recession prevailed strongly in Japan, less so in West Germany and Canada, while slowdowns with recession were more common in the other three countries, most notably the United States.[39] Growth cycles include both types of slowdown; hence they are much more numerous than business cycles that are defined by the presence of absolute decreases in aggregate activity

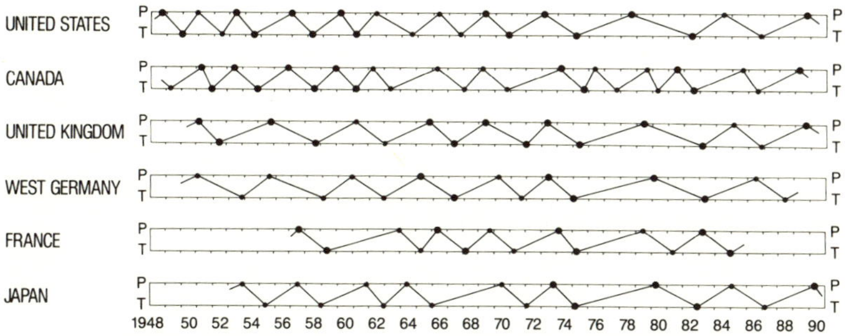

Figure 1–3. Timing of growth cycles in six countries, 1948–1980

Note: In each schematic diagram, the drawn-out lines connect the dates of the consecutive peaks (P) and troughs (T) in growth cycles for the given country. Heavy black dots identify slowdowns that became recessions.

Sources: For the U.S. business cycle chronologies—National Bureau of Economic Research, Inc. For the growth cycle chronologies of Canada, United Kingdom, West Germany, France, and Japan—Center for International Business Cycle Research, Graduate School of Business, Columbia University.

(recessions). In the trend-adjusted indicator series, all major retardations are reflected in specific-cycle declines that make up growth cycle contractions; some of these movements descend into the negative region, others stop short of it.

	U.S.	*Canada*	*U.K.*	*West Germany*	*France*	*Japan*
Slowdown without recession	4	7	3	5	3	6
Slowdown with recession	7	5	5	3	4	2

Slowdowns occur either in the late stages of business expansions (some time before peaks) or they interrupt long expansions. As a result, expansions are shorter and contractions longer in growth cycles than in business cycles. Growth cycles are more nearly symmetrical and less variable than business cycles with respect to both durations and amplitudes of their phases. Growth cycle peaks tend to occur before the corresponding business cycle peaks, while the troughs of the matching growth cycles and business cycles tend to be roughly coincident.

Figure 1–3 suggests a high degree of international correspondence in the timing of growth cycles. Thus much (though not all) of the time the diagrams for the United States and Canada, and those for the United Kingdom and West Germany, display nearly synchronous movements. Indeed, these chronologies are considerably more similar than those of business cycles that can be inferred from figure 1–2. This presumably reflects the effects of the elimination or reduction of the divergencies in the national trends.

4 The Observed Tendencies, Disturbances, and Regularities

4.1 Endogenous Cyclical Variables

As we have seen, business cycles vary greatly in duration and intensity, less in diffusion. They are not only diverse but also evolving. What they have in common is not their overall dimensions but the makeup, features, and interaction of their many constituent processes.

Thus in each cycle—whether long or short, large or small—production, employment, real incomes, and real sales tend to expand and contract together in many industries and regions, though at uneven rates. Other variables—for example, hours worked per week, real new orders for manufactured goods, and changes in prices of industrial raw materials—rise and fall correspondingly but earlier, with variable leads. Still others—for example, inventory-sales ratios, real business loans outstanding, and changes in unit labor cost—also rise in business expansions and fall in contractions but somewhat later, with variable lags. These sequential movements usually recur in each successive cycle. They all are significantly persistent and pervasive.

Systematic differences exist not only in the timing of cyclical movements in different variables but also in their relative size and conformity or coherence (that is, correlation with business cycles). Among the earliest and most important observations in this area is that activities relating to durable (producer and consumer) goods have particularly large and well-conforming cyclical fluctuations. Other variables long and rightly viewed as highly cyclical are business profits; investment in plant, equipment, and inventories; and cost and volume of bank credit used to finance such investments.

More than any other sector of the modern economy, manufacturing has historically been central to both economic growth and fluctuations. Mining, construction, transportation, communication, and public utilities have varying but significant degrees of cyclical sensitivity. Other nonfarm sectors, which produce largely services rather than goods, tend to be much less responsive to business cycles. Employment in broadly defined service industries (including government) followed a strong and smooth upward trend. Agriculture, which underwent a long and strong downward trend in employment and a huge secular rise in productivity, is but weakly cyclical, except for prices. In sum, business cycles, which developed in the age of industrialization, still affect most strongly industries producing goods, especially durables (Zarnowitz and Moore, 1986, pp. 536–539).

Given the weight of these "stylized facts," it is not surprising that the predominantly endogenous theories of business cycles, old and new, stress the role of those variables that have clear patterns of regular participation in the motion of the economy at large. These variables, which may be called "cyclical," and the corresponding theories, follow;[40]

- Business fixed investment (overinvestment, vertical maladjustments, accelerator).
- Inventory investment (multiplier–accelerator models with feedback effects).
- Business profits (cost–price imbalances, profit margins and expectations).
- Credit and interest rates (unstable supply of bank credit; discrepancies between, and changes in, the money, real, and natural rates of interest).

The cyclical variables are endogenous—generated by the system of relationships within which they interact. For these variables to be primarily responsible for business cycles, the system must have the required dynamics in the form of some essential nonlinearities, or leads and lags, or both. Such elements are undoubtedly important, but we are still far from really understanding how they work and hence how far the endogenous models can go in explaining business cycles.

4.2 Exogenous Variables and the Role of Money

Recent theories view economic fluctuations as resulting mainly from changes in observable exogenous factors (variables) or unobservable random shocks (errors). Here the cyclical variables, although still important as propagators of business cycles, are no longer seen as the central part of a system that can produce self-sustaining cycles.

Important policy variables such as the monetary base, tax rates, and federal government spending have been traditionally treated as exogenous, although this cannot be strictly true since they are clearly influenced by the economy as well as influencing it. Money supply variables are of even more mixed nature in this regard. The extent to which a central bank controls the stock of money or (which is more relevant) its rate of growth depends on factors that vary across countries and over time. They include the national and international monetary systems; the powers, objectives, and performance of the bank; and the definition and composition of the supply of money.

In the United States, narrowly and broadly defined monetary aggregates normally trend upward in both expansions and contractions, though often at reduced rates before downturns. Long absolute declines in M1 or M2 are rare and as a rule associated with business depressions or stagnations. Monetary growth rates tend to lead at business cycle peaks and troughs but by intervals that are highly variable and on average long (Friedman and Schwartz, 1963*a*, 1963*b*). Cyclical changes in the deposit-reserve ratio and particularly the deposit-currency ratio, which reflect the chain of influence that runs from business activity to money, contribute on average strongly to the patterns of movement in money growth during business cycles (Cagan, 1965; Plosser, 1991). Money shows a systematic tendency to grow faster in business expansions than in contractions, and so does the domestic nonfinancial credit, but the stability of monetary relationships in the cyclical context is subject to much doubt and debate (Friedman, 1986; Meltzer, 1986). Certainly, there is more regularity in the long-term relation between money growth and changes in the price level, and in the procyclical behavior of interest rates and the income velocity of money (allowing for its long trends).

For all of this, there is no denying that business cycles have important monetary and financial aspects. A six-variable, four-lag quarterly vector autoregressive (VAR) model applied to postwar and earlier U.S. data by Zarnowitz and Braun (1990) shows that the rate of change in real GNP was significantly affected by lagged rates of change in the monetary aggregates (base, M1, and particularly M2) but much more strongly yet by lagged values of short-term interest rates. However, the influence of changes in the planned volume of fixed and inventory investment and purchases of durable goods (represented by series of new orders and contracts) proved to be strong as well.[41]

4.3 Monetary, Real, and Expectational Shocks

In the original monetarist theory, the money supply was treated as the main exogenous factor driving the business cycle. In the more recent equilibrium version with rational expectations, anticipated money growth can influence only prices, not output; that is, only unanticipated money shocks have real effects. Tests of this hypothesis have produced evidence that is mixed but mostly unfavorable in the sense of not confirming the importance of the distinction between the effects of the anticipated and unanticipated components of monetary change.[42]

Full exogeneity of money is one extreme and unrealistic assumption; full endogeneity of money is another, at the opposite end of the spectrum. The latter view posits that changes in inside money accommodate the money stock to the level of economic activity; it is accepted both in some Keynesian disequilibrium models and the real business cycle (RBC) models in which fluctuations are strictly equilibrium phenomena.[43]

In the RBC model, stochastic oscillations in the economy's real growth path result from a mixture of transitory and permanent shocks to productivity (Kydland and Prescott, 1982). There is a long gestation lag in the production of capital goods, which imparts some persistence to output movements. As productivity gains fluctuate, so do real wages (or, more accurately, real returns on the work effort) to which labor supply responds very elastically.

But the cyclical sensitivity of real wages is low, and tests of the hypothesis of high intertemporal substitution of leisure are mostly negative (see, for example, Altonji, 1982). To explain booms and busts, sufficiently large and frequent shocks to productivity would be necessary, yet the evidence for them is hard to find (or nonexistent: Has there been any technological *regress* of a large-scale or recurrent nature?). When interpreted as productivity shocks, the procyclical movement of the Solow residual supports the RBC hypothesis, but it overlooks the high probability that much of this movement reflects the effects of labor hoarding and measurement errors (as noted in several critiques; see, for example, Eichenbaum, 1990). Indeed, a recent study, whose authors include two RBC theorists, finds that productivity disturbances account for no more than 35% to 44% of total output fluctuations in a cointegrated VAR model with both real and nominal variables (King et al., 1991).

Much of the recent work that seems to be concerned with explaining business cycles is actually preoccupied with such perennial theoretical issues as the rationality of economic expectations and behavior and the neutrality of money. The predominant view is that stable growth at full employment would prevail in the absence of outside shocks; moreover, the shocks tend to be reduced to one or two broad categories per model. Thus, as already noted, the equilibrium theorists concentrate either on unanticipated changes in money and prices or on shifts in technology. Some attention is given to shifts in preferences and desired consumption (Hall, 1986). One study singles out sectoral demand shifts (Lilien, 1982), another oil price shocks (Hamilton, 1983). The role of shocks to, and imperfections of, credit markets is stressed by some authors (Wojnilower, 1980; Greenwald, Stiglitz, and Weiss, 1984), while the direct effects of independent shifts in monetary policy are central to others (Romer and Romer, 1989).

However, there is also considerable and perhaps increasing recognition that macroeconomic fluctuations may have many important sources. Blanchard and Watson (1986) distinguish four major categories of shocks—to aggregate demand, aggregate supply, fiscal policy, and money supply—and conclude that each made a roughly equal contribution to U.S. postwar cycles. Occasional large disturbances are at work along with frequent small shocks, so that business cycles are quite differentiated. Recent papers by Blanchard and others generally assume that the effects of supply shocks are more persistent than those of demand shocks.

That a variety of factors can and do serve as proximate causes of business cycles is an old idea embodied in the synthetic theories of several early writers, such as Aftalion, Mitchell, Schumpeter, and very explicitly Pigou (1927). Evidence from recent macroeconometric models supports this concept. Unlike the early Keynesian models dominated by demand factors and fiscal policy, the present models give considerable attention to supply factors as well and actually have monetary policy matter more than fiscal. In large multisector models the distinction between demand and supply shocks is rather blurred anyway.

Since the incisive and detailed analysis of the monetary history of the United States by Friedman and Schwartz (1963*a*), the monetarist interpretation of business cycle developments gained and still retains a wide acceptance, despite critical countercurrents within the profession. It is simply very difficult to deny that strong restrictive monetary measures designed to combat inflation have contributed to subsequent economic downturns at least in some well-known episodes (notably the Federal Reserve increases of the discount rate in 1920 and of reserve requirements in 1936–1937). Similarly, the shift to a policy of lower money growth and sharply higher interest rates, first signaled in October 1979, was followed by the "Volcker disinflation" and the recessions of 1980 and 1981–1982. In each case, however, these monetary shocks were accompanied by changes in factors unrelated to monetary policy that must have also contributed to the recessions that followed (fiscal stringencies in 1920 and 1936–1937, an oil shock and financial deregulation in the late 1970s, a fall in money velocity in the early 1980s). So monetary and real disturbances (or unusual developments) coincided, and their effects are difficult to disentangle.

Nor are these the only types of disturbances to be considered, since there are also the "psychological" factors emphasized early by Pigou, that is, the shifts in expectations that may at times spread widely enough to become self-fulfilling. In contemporary models of financial crises or speculative price bubbles, multiple equilibria exist, many of them involving expectations that appear arbitrary *ex post* yet are rational *ex ante*: Many act on them because they believe that others will (see Woodford, 1987, for a brief review).

The controversy about real versus monetary theories of business cycles is now very old; although it has been instructive, prolonging it further is apt to produce more heat than light. It is time to recognize that short-term variations in economic activity are influenced by forces of each of the three types—real, monetary, and expectational. Their mix varies, and the really important question is how they interact and why.

The 1990–1991 recession presents an interesting example, although more time and data will be needed to assess it. It was preceded by a long slowdown starting early in 1989 following a sharp decrease in monetary growth and increase in interest rates. Both monetary policy and credit conditions tightened. Efforts to counteract the persistently large government deficits made fiscal policy quite tight, too. Real disposable income and real domestic final sales flattened and then turned down early. So both monetary and real factors worked to depress enconomic activity. They were finally joined by a sharp drop in consumer expectations and business confidence, which occurred after Iraq's invasion of Kuwait raised oil prices, the threat of war, and the general level of uncertainty about inflation and unemployment. Thus the last blow was delivered to the old and by then seriously weakened expansion.

4.4 Leads and Lags

Presumably, one important reason for the differentiation of business cycles is that they are affected by large disturbances of all kinds, including shifts in policies. Also, changes in the economy's structure contribute to an evolution of cyclical behavior that is more predictable, though not without some important exceptions.[44] Still, business cycles are like individuals of a species: diverse yet also alike in many essential respects (think of other events of which the same can be said, wars, for example). The main common element, as we already know, consists of the properties of co-movements in cyclical variables.

Table 1–7 covers 32 U.S. monthly indicators for which there are available both the traditional measures of cyclical timing and variability

Table 1–7. Selected Measures of Average Cyclical Timing, Variability, and Correlation with an Index of Coincident Indicators, 32 Monthly Series, 1948–1980 and 1959–1989

		Median Timing (months)[b]			*Average Change (%)*[c]		*Correlation w/New ICI*[d]		
Line	*Series Title (BCD Number)*[a] (1)	*Peaks* (2)	*Troughs* (3)	*All Turns* (4)	*Series (s.a.)* (5)	*Cyclical Component* (6)	*Transformation* (7)	*Lag (k) (months)* (8)	*r(k)* (9)
1	Average workweek, mfg (*1)	−11	−1	−4.5	.5	.2	N	−1	.79
2	Unempl. insur. claims, inv. (*5)	−12	0	−5.5	5.4	2.4	DLN	−2	−.87
3	Help wanted index (46)	−7	+2	−2.5	2.9	2.2	DLN	−1	.95
4	Capacity utilization, mfg (82)	−11	+1	−1.5	1.6[x]	1.4[x]	D	−1	.96
5	New orders, dur. goods, c$ (7)	−8	−1	−3	3.4	1.4	DLN	−1	.90
6	N.O., cons, goods & mtls, c$ (*8)	−12	−1	−4.5	2.8	1.3	DLN	−2	.89
7	Vendor performance (*32)	−6	−4	−6	3.8[x]	2.4[x]	N	−2	.67
8	Contr. & orders, plant & equip (*20)	−8	−1	−3.5	6.2	1.6	DLN	−1	.76
9	New bldg permits, priv. housing (*29)	−13	−3	−9.5	5.1	2.4	N	−6	.59
10	New bus. incorporations, no. (13)	−10	−1.5	−5	2.5	1.0	DLN	−3	.55
11	Change in mfg & trade invent. (31)	−6	−2	−3.5	7.1[x]	1.4[x]	DLN	6	.79
12	Stock price index, S&P 500 (*19)	−9.5	−4	−5.5	2.7	1.6	DLN	−6	.55
13	Change in sensitive mtls prices (*99)	−9.5	−3.5	−5.5	.3[x]	.2[x]	DLN	0	.55

14	Change in money stock, M1 (85)	−15	−3	−14	.3^x	.03^x	DLN	−3	.25
15	Money supply M2, c$ (*106)	−16	−3	−10	.42	.37	DLN	−6	.68
16	Change in bus. & cons. credit (*111)	−11	−2	−7	2.9^x	.8^x	N	−2	.67
17	Liab. of bus. failures, inv. (14)	−14	−2	−10	27.8	2.5	DLN	−3	−.40
18	Employees on nonag. payrolls (*41)	0	0	0	.32	.28	DLN	1	.92
19	Pers. income – transfer pmts, c$ (*51)	0	−0.5	0	.5	.4	DLN	0	.87
20	Mfg & trade sales, c$ (*57)	−3	−1	−1.5	1.0	.6	DLN	−1	.94
21	Index of industrial production (*47)	−2	0	0	.9	.7	DLN	0	.99
22	Indus. prod., dur. mfg (73)	−3	0	0	1.4	1.0	DLN	0	.98
23	Indus. prod., nondur. mfg (74)	−1	−1	−1	.7	.6	DLN	−1	.92
24	Retail sales, c$ (59)	−4	−2	−2.5	1.1	.5	DLN	−2	.69
25	Unempl., aver. duration, inv. (*91)	0	+8	+3.5	3.6	1.6	N	6	−.88
26	Invent./sales, mfg & trade, c$ (*77)	+8	+13	+10	.02^x	.01^x	N	−2	−.79
27	Unit labor cost, mfg, detrend. (*62)	+5	+13	+10	.6^x	.3^x	DLN	−2	−.69
28	Comm. & indus. loans outst., c$ (*101)	+4	+6	+4.5	.9	.7	DLN	10	.63
29	Cons. instal. credit/pers. inc., % (*95)	+4	+7	+6	.07^x	.05^x	DLN	6	.57
30	Treasury bill rate. 3 mo. (114)	+1.5	+3.5	+2	.28^x	.17^x	D	1	.52
31	Federal funds rate (119)	+2	+5	+2.5	.38^x	.26^x	D	1	.59
32	Yield, high grade corp. bonds (116)	+1	+2	+1.5	.18^x	.09^x	D	−12	−.45

Table 1–7. (Continued)

Sources: U.S. Department of Commerce (1984, Tables 8 and 9A, pp. 167–68, 172–68, 172–75 [for columns 1–6]); Stock and Watson (1990, table 1 [for columns 7–9]).

[a] Series titles are abbreviated. The BCD numbers in parentheses are series numbers used by the U.S. Department of Commerce in its monthly publications *Business Conditions Digest* (*BCD*, through March 1990) and *Survey of Current Business* (*SCB*, current). * identifies a series included in the composite index of leading or coincident or lagging indicators (referring to the indexes of the Bureau of Economic Analysis in the Commerce Department as of 1984).

[b] The measures cover the seven pairs of business cycle peaks and troughs between 1948 and 1980. The median is the middle value in an odd-numbered array and the average of the two middle values in an even-numbered array. Minus (–) signs are leads at business cycle turning points; plus (+) signs are lags.

[c] Entries in column 5 are average changes, without regard to sign, between consecutive values in a seasonally adjusted (s.a.) series. Entries in column 6 are average changes, without regard to sign, between consecutive values in the cyclical component, which is a smooth, flexible moving average of the seasonally adjusted series. Entries marked [x] are average actual changes in the series, in its original units of measurement; all other entries are average percentage changes.

[d] The transformation codes (column 7) are N = no transformation; D = first differences of the series; DLN = first differences of the natural logs of the series (i.e., growth rates). The transformations are generally from the original levels of the (s.a.) series. Entries in column 8 (k) are leads (–) or lags (+), in months, which are associated with the maximum correlations $r(k)$, as listed in column 9. These statistics are based on the cross-correlogram between filtered log ICI and the filtered series, using the 24-month moving average filter $a_{24}(L)$. ICI is the new experimental index of coincident indicators by Stock and Watson; it covers the period January 1959 to May 1989.

Abbreviations: mfg = manufacturing; dur. = durable; insur. = insurance; mtls = materials; invent. = inventories; contr. = contracts; comm. = commercial; cons. = consumer; instal. = installment; pers. = personal; inc. = income; outst. = outstanding; pmts. = payments; nonag. = nonagricultural; / = ratio (inventory/sales in Line 26; credit/income in Line 29); c$ = in constant dollars; inv. = inverted (peaks in the series are matched with business cycle troughs, troughs in the series are matched with business cycles peaks); detrend. = adjusted for (deviations from) trend.

(columns 2–6) and new measures of filtered cross correlation with an index designed to approximate aggregate economic activity in real terms. The first set of statistics, from the Bureau of Economic Analysis (Commerce Department), refers to the 1948–1980 period; the second, from an NBER study by Stock and Watson (1990), refers to the 1959–1989 period. The two are entirely independent and based on very different methods, yet they are generally consistent and complementary.

The first 17 series listed in table 1–7 are classified as leading at both peaks and troughs of business cycles and include ten components of the BEA index of leading indicators as of 1984 (marked with an asterisk, "*"). They reflect marginal employment adjustments, which under uncertainty are made ahead of decisions that result in changes of employment and unemployment (lines 1–3); adjustments of delivery periods and activities marking the early stages of investment processes, which tend to lead production, shipments, construction, and installation of equipment (lines 4–10); changes in inventories and sensitive prices (lines 11–13); and changes in money and credit conditions (lines 14–17).

Such series have a long history of leading at business cycle peaks and troughs. They are heavily represented in a group of 75 series whose median timing at 15 peaks and 16 troughs of the 1885–1937 period was –6 (5) and –5 (3), respectively (that is, leads of six and five months, with standard deviations of five and three months; for sources and detail, see Zarnowitz and Moore, 1986, pp. 565–571). In 1948–1980 the means (s.d.), in months, of the median leads were –11 (3) at peaks and –2 (2) at troughs (as calculated from the entries in table 1–7, lines 1–17, columns 2 and 3). Thus, the relative timing of these indicators remained remarkably consistent over the past century, although the leads at peaks have become longer and the leads at troughs shorter since 1948.[45]

Leads maximize correlations with an index of coincident indicators in 1959–1989 for all but two of the series used in table 1–7, lines 1–17, columns 7–9.[46] This is a strong confirmation of the tendency of these series to move ahead of aggregate economic activity (output, employment, real income, and real sales). But because these leads (column 8) average – 2 (3) months, they are considerably shorter than the corresponding "all turns" leads (column 4), which average -6(3) months.

This would be expected for the following reasons. The differences in timing are likely to be larger and more systematic for the major cyclical movements than for the many small and short variations that may often be caused by random influences affecting many variables more or less simultaneously. The cyclical measures in table 1–7, columns 1–3, refer mostly to the indicator levels (except where the title specifies change), but the correlation measures in columns 7–9 refer mostly to smoothed rates of change, including those in the coincident index itself (note the prevalence of DLN = Δ ln in column 7).[47] Thus the former relate directly to business cycle turning points, whereas the latter relate directly to all observations for growth cycles. The series that lead at business cycle turns also tend to lead at growth cycle turns, in the United States and elsewhere (Klein and Moore, 1985). But the leads at business cycle peaks are particularly long, reflecting high levels of demand and capacity utilization, large backlogs of unfilled orders, and extended delivery periods. Growth cycle peaks typically occur several months before business cycle peaks and have shorter leads and signals (Zarnowitz and Moore, 1982).

It should be noted that table 1–7 covers monthly indicators only. Hence the table omits one particularly important class of leaders available in quarterly form only, namely, corporate profits (totals, rates, and margins, before and after taxes, in current and constant dollars; also net corporate cash flows). Profits decline in late stages of expansion well before sales do because costs start rising faster than selling prices, depressing profit margins in many businesses. Labor markets get tight and wages rise even as productivity slackens; interest rates and the cost of holding inventories rise; but product prices tend to increase less, being held back by prior commitments and domestic and international competition for market shares. (Mitchell hypothesized such developments as a major cause of business cycles in his earliest treatise of 1913). Stock price indexes tend to have strong cyclical leads (line 12) because they anticipate or reflect the early movements in profits and also in inverted interest rates, as well as probably other changes such as those in money and credit (lines 15 and 16).

Roughly coincident indicators of employment, production, real personal income, and real sales are listed in lines 18–24 of table 1–7 (the four marked with an asterisk are components of the BEA coincident index). Here coincidences (0) or very short leads (−1) dominate both the all-turns and maximum-correlation timing (columns 4 and 8), but in a few cases longer leads appear, mainly at peaks, for industrial production and sales. All of these series have pronounced growth trends and are used in log differences for the correlation measures.

The indicators listed in lines 25–32 of table 1–7 are classified as lagging in the historical NBER studies and BEA reviews of cyclical indicators (the five marked with an asterisk are components of the BEA lagging index). The common feature of these series is their association with the cost of doing business. Increases in the duration of unemployment increase the private and social burdens of joblessness and insurance against it. Labor cost per unit of output is the largest component of average costs on an economywide scale. Interest rates measure the costs of credit and financing investments of various types. The larger the inventories are relative to sales, and the larger the volume of credit is relative to income, the heavier are the costs of finance, given the level of interest rates. Accordingly, the lagging increase in these cost factors around the business cycle peak works to discourage economic activity, and their lagging decrease around the trough works to encourage it. Indeed, when inverted (divided into one), the lagging index shows the earliest cyclical signals that anticipate even the turning points in the leading index (Moore, 1983, chap. 23).

The eight series in the last section of table 1–7 have sizable median lags, averaging in months about +3(3) at peaks, +7(4) at troughs, and +5(3) at all turns (columns 2–4). It is broadly consistent with the lagging nature of these indicators that five of them also show the best correlations for lags (which are long, except for the two series of first differences in short-term interest rates; see columns 7–9). For three series that tend to lag at business cycle turns (inventory–sales ratio, unit labor cost, and corporate bond yields), the correlations with the coincident index refer to leads, but they are negative. This is consistent with the old and well-established finding that the inverted lagging indicators lead.[48]

4.5 Co-movements and Amplitudes

The typical leads and lags of the major economic variables constitute important and relatively enduring features of cyclical behavior. Another class of such characteristics relates to how close the co-movements of the variables tend to be in the course of business expansions and contractions. Still another consists of relative amplitudes of cyclical change in the different processes.

The correlations in the last column of table 1–7 provide estimates of the co-movements of the selected indicators with an index that approximates well aggregate economic activity on a monthly basis. The Stock–Watson index of coincident indicators (denoted ICI for simplicity) resembles the BEA coincident index rather closely but has a formal probabilistic interpretation. Of the leading series (lines 1–17), capacity utilization, the help-wanted index, and the two aggregates of new orders show the highest positive $r(k)$ of .89–.96, while unemployment insurance claims has –.87 (lines 2–6). Average workweek, contracts and orders for plant and equipment, and inventory change show $r(k)$ correlations of .76–.79; seven other indicators, including in descending order real money supply, change in credit, vendor performance, housing permits, and stock prices, have an $r(k)$ of .55–.68; and for two series these measures are very low indeed (–.40 for failure liabilities and .25 for M1 growth).

Not surprisingly, the correlations of the individual coincident indicators with the ICI are high (lines 18–24). They range from .92 to .99 for five of the series, are .87 for real personal income less transfer payments, but are only .69 for real retail sales. Industrial production indexes for total and durable manufacturing show the highest $r(k)$ coefficients.

The co-movements of the lagging indicators with the ICI are not very close. The highest correlations here are the negative ones for unemployment duration, inventory-sales ratio, and unit labor cost (lines 25–27). Two series on credit and two on short-term interest rates have an $r(k)$ of .52–.63, and the bond yield has one of only –.45 (lines 28–32).

The conventional method of analyzing time series for the study of business cycles is to estimate and then eliminate their seasonal components. Working with seasonally adjusted series (just as working with trend-adjusted or heavily smoothed series) is often covenient but not without risks.[49] Even after seasonal adjustment, the month-to-month change in most series contains a large component of short, random variations; the cyclical component represents a much longer and smoother movement that is often much smaller than the total change on a per-month basis (compare the paired entries in columns 5 and 6).[50] Some leading indicators show great volatility of monthly change, which obscures the relatively small trend- cycle movement (inventory investment and business failures provide extreme examples; see lines 11 and 16). In contrast, some other early-moving series are remarkably smooth to begin with and are dominated by cyclical fluctuations (for example, the help-wanted index, capacity utilization, and vendor performance, lines 3, 4, and 7) or by the trend-cycle (for example, real money supply, line 15). Most of the leading indicators fall somewhere in the broad intermediate range; that is, they display great overall sensitivity and have both clear, specific cycles and many smaller random oscillations.

The coincident indicators have generally much smaller, and also more uniform, amplitudes of monthly total and cyclical change than the leading indicators. The following tabulation, which uses only percentage entries from columns 5 and 6, brings out the contrast between the two groups. Behind it are important particulars. Thus consider manufacturing of durable goods, where much of the production is to order. Here new orders move in large swings that are followed with variable but significant lags and much smaller fluctuations in output and shipments. The resulting changes in backlogs of unfilled orders and average delivery lags are also large, leading, and procyclical. Production of nondurable goods is both less cyclical and less volatile than that of durable goods (lines 22 and 23), and production of services (not shown) is least, again on both counts.

	Total Change	*Trend-Cycle Change*
Leading (11 series)	5.4 (7.6)	1.5 (0.8)
Coincident (7 series)	0.8 (0.4)	0.6 (0.2)

Other related or similar examples may be mentioned.[51] New housing permits (and starts) lead residential investment, which is somewhat smoother. New orders and contracts for plant and equipment lead business capital outlays, which fluctuate much less and lag behind considerably, particularly at troughs. Other commitments and activities marking the early stages of investment processes are new capital appropriations, new business formations and incorporations, and new bond and equity issues (all strongly procyclical and leading), whereas other late-stage processes are completions of industrial and commercial construction projects, shipments, and installations of machinery.

Interest rates tend to lag at business cycle turns, especially troughs, but they are both strongly influenced by, and themselves strongly influence, general business conditions. All vary procyclically, but the short-term rates have larger cyclical movements than do long-term rates (lines 30–32). Their changes are measured in their own units, as is also the case for some other series in this group (lines 25–26), so no amplitude comparisons can be made here with measures expressed in terms of percent changes. But let us note that several important lagging indicators have strongly predominant trend-cycle components and are very smooth (notably so for commercial and industrial loans outstanding and the ratio of consumer installment credit to personal income; see lines 28 and 29).

5 General Conclusions

In this chapter I have considered the short but not-so-easy question, "What is a business cycle?" from several angles. Section 1 looked at economic history and at the development of thinking about business cycles. Section 2 reviewed the chronologies of business expansions and contractions, the lessons from the duration data, the concepts of periodicity of cycles and phases, and the evidence and reasons for the apparent moderation of macroeconomic fluctuations in the post–World War II era. Section 3 compared the postwar business cycles and growth cycles in several major industrialized, market-oriented countries. Section 4 discussed the behavior of endogenous and exogenous variables; the role of monetary, real, and expectational shocks; the systematic timing sequences (tendencies to lead or lag); and the regularities of cyclical co-movements and amplitudes. Understanding business cycles can be aided by each of these modes of analysis.

Some sections of this study interpret history, others literature; some discuss old, others new, findings and ideas. Many of the results refer to particular aspects of theory and evidence, and there is no need to restate any of them. Hence only a few general conclusions are collected here.

1. A business cycle includes a downturn and contraction followed by an upturn and expansion in aggregate economic activity, which ideally should be represented by comprehensive and reliable measures of total employment, output, real income, and real expenditures. (But nominal income aggregates and price indexes can serve as good criteria, provided that the fluctuations extend to a broad class of sufficiently flexible prices, as was the case in the now rather distant past.)

2. A business cycle is pervasive in the sense that it consists of co-movements and interactions of many variables. The regularity, magnitude, and timing of the fluctuations vary across the variables, and these differences are in part systematic. Thus most activities are procyclical, mildly or strongly, but some are countercyclical. Some variables tend to have approximately coincident timing, others tend to lead, and still others tend to lag. These patterns might or might not be symmetrical; for example, timing might be systematically different at peaks and troughs.

3. A business cycle is at least national in scope, that is, it involves most industries and regions of a country, though again with variations in intensity and timing. It can attain much larger dimensions when transmitted across countries through channels of international trade and finance.

4. As a rule, a business cycle lasts several years and so is sufficiently persistent for serially correlated as well as intercorrelated movements in many variables to develop sequentially in the downward as well as upward direction. The movements tend to cumulate before reversing themselves.

5. In most but not all business cycles, prices in general move procyclically, at least apart from their long trends (in the last half-century, upward). This indicates a long and large role for the fluctuations of, and disturbances to, aggregate demand. These can be of real, monetary, or expectational origin and can well involve interactions between any or all such factors. But supply shifts are also part and parcel of business cycles, and they can be dominant in some. (The two major oil price shocks in the 1970s have been associated with inflationary recessions.) The cyclical

instability of profits, investment, and credit has a long history and is well-documented.

6. Business cycles have varied greatly over the past 200 years in length, spread, and size. They included vigorous and weak expansions, long and short; mild and severe contractions, again some long, some short; and many moderate fluctuations of close-to-average duration (about three to five years). But since the 1930s the United States suffered no major depression. Business expansions have become longer, recessions shorter and milder. The probable reasons include the shift of employment to production of services, automatic stabilizers, some financial reforms and avoidance of crises, greater weight and some successes of governmental actions and policies, and higher levels of public confidence.

7. The postwar recessions are much fewer and generally milder still in France, Italy, and particularly West Germany and Japan. These countries also had much higher average rates of real economic growth than the United States, especially in the early reconstruction phase of the post-1945 era. In the 1970s and 1980s growth decreased everywhere and the recessions became more frequent and serious. All this suggests that countries and periods with stronger growth trends are less vulnerable to cyclical instability. This is a potentially important proposition in need of explanation and testing (with possible extensions to regions, industries, and the like).

8. In sum, business cycles make up a class of varied, complex, and evolving phenomena of both history and economic dynamics. Theories or models that try to reduce them to a single causal mechanism or shock seem to me altogether unlikely to succeed.

Notes

1. In a letter of June 27, 1772, David Hume informed Smith that "We are here in a very melancholy situation: Continual bankruptcies, universal loss of credit.... Do these events any-wise effect your theory?" Smith's answer is unknown (see Mirowski, 1985, pp. 15–18).

2. See Haberler (1964), Zarnowitz (1985), Moore and Zarnowitz (1986), Backhouse (1988), and Sherman (1991).

3. Thus, for England he listed 14 crises in 1803–1882 at intervals averaging 6.1 years, with a standard deviation of 2.6 and a range of 1–10 years (see also Burns and Mitchell, 1946, p. 442).

4. See Burns and Mitchell (1946, table 16, pp. 78–79).

5. For arguments and some evidence consistent with the previous discussion, see Backhouse (1988, chs. 2 and 5).

6. Schumpeter refers to Mitchell and Spiethoff as disagreeing with him on this point.

7. See Mirowski (1985, pp. 201–213). The other sources of the crisis chronologies in question are Bouniatian (1908), Ashton (1959), and Deane (1967). All authors agreed on two dates, three agreed on six, and two agreed on ten (out of the 13 dates proposed by Ashton). For 1700–1802, Ashton suggested a sequence of 16 "cycles," with durations averaging about five years and concentrated mainly in the three-to-six-year range (Moore and Zarnowitz, 1986, pp. 741–743).

8. The coverage of the annals is United States and England, 1790–1925; France, 1840–1925; Germany, 1853–1925; Austria, 1867–1925; and 12 other countries on four continents (various periods between 1890 and 1925).

9. This is certainly consistent with the recent evidence on the performance of business outlook analysts, policy makers, and forecasters (see Fels and Hinshaw, 1968; Zarnowitz, 1967, 1974).

10. Of course, many seemingly familiar facts or events are complex or controversial enough to elude a tight formulation of meaning, say, in a definitional or legal sense. One is reminded, for example, of Justice Potter Stewart's writing, in the 1964 case of *Jacobellis* vs. *Ohio*, that obscenity was indeed difficult to define, but "I know it when I see it."

11. For some detail on the historical statistics applied in the construction of the business cycle chronology for the United States, see Zarnowitz (1981) and Moore and Zarnowitz (1986), and references therein.

12. For a further analysis along these lines, see Zarnowitz (1985, 1992).

13. From the introduction by Burns to the posthumous book by Mitchell (1951, pp. VII–VIII).

14. Something similar could be said as well about some earlier important influences, notably that of Marx.

15. Early accelerator models made investment a function of changes in output (Aftalion, 1913; Clark, 1917). The more general and satisfactory formulation equates investment to some fraction of the gap between the desired and actual capital stock.

16. This excludes the expansions during the Civil War and World War I periods, which were longer than the average and different in some respects. Business contractions that followed these expansions had shorter than average durations. But these distinctions are blurred by the fact that some peacetime expansions were even longer and some peacetime contractions were shorter. Compare lines 5 and 6 in table 1–1.

17. The rest of this section draws on material in Moore and Zarnowitz (1986, pp. 754–758).

18. During the short but sharp and widespread 1920–1921 decline, Germany was insulated by hyperinflation and the associated floating exchange rate (Friedman and Schwartz, 1963*a*, p. 362). During the similarly diffuse and painful 1937–1938 contraction, Germany was no longer a free market economy but a controlled economy under the Nazi dictatorship and heavily engaged in arming for the war, annexing Austria, invading Czechoslovakia, and threatening other neighboring countries.

19. The first of these is covered mainly by annual data (the duration measures are expressed in monthly terms for comparability). Combining the two periods would add little to the story.

20. This contraction is omitted from the chronology of Spiethoff (1955, vol. I., p. 147).

21. However, Friedman and Schwartz do not recognize the 1901 trough and the 1903 peak included in the NBER chronology for Britain (1982, p. 74).

22. Thus, assuming that 1869–1870, 1887–1888, and 1899–1900 represented major slowdowns rather than marginal recessions, the 1857–1918 period would contain 12 (not 15) business cycles with an average length of 5 (not 4) years.

23. Indeed, using the latter would only strengthen the case, since the relative frequency of expansions has been somewhat greater in the long upswings of prices, that of contractions in the long downswings (Zarnowitz and Moore, 1986, p. 530).

24. The results of this combination include a sharp increase in real debt burdens; distress selling of assets to pay off the debts; contraction of deposits; declines in production, trade, and employment; depressed confidence; and lower nominal but higher real interest rates. When the liquidation process and the debts and costs are reduced sufficiently in real terms, however, confidence will gradually return, hoarding will give way to new buying and lending, and reflation will pave the way to another recovery.

25. For more on the association between the price trends and the relative duration of business cycle phases, see Zarnowitz and Moore (1986, pp. 530–531).

26. A hazard function shows the dependence of the termination or "failure" probability on the duration of the process; in this case, the probability of a peak (trough) as a function of the length-to-date of the preceding expansion (contraction). Let $F(t) = Pr(T < t)$ be the probability that the duration random variable T is less than some value t; $f(t) = dF(t)/dt$ be the corresponding density function; and $S(t) = 1 - F(t)$ be the corresponding "survivor function." Then the general form of the hazard function is $\lambda(t) = f(t)/S(t)$ (see Kiefer, 1988).

27. The following discussion draws in part on material from Zarnowitz (1985, 1987).

28. Consider the consequences of such natural disasters as cyclones and storm surges in the Bay of Bengal (for India and Bangladesh) and hurricanes and shifts in ocean currents (for fishing off the coast of Peru).

29. See Alt and Chrystal (1983). For some more positive appraisals and recent contributions, see Willett (1988).

30. The measures are based on estimates by Balke and Gordon (1986, pp. 788–810) that use the historical annual series by Gallman and Kuznets and more recent series of the Department of Commerce. Persons' index of industrial production and trade (1875–1918) and the Federal Reserve System index of industrial production (1919–46) were used as quarterly interpolators.

31. Similarly, the index for Taiwan available since 1961 shows only one serious decline, of 9.1%, in 12/73–2/75 (a minor decline of 1.3% occurred in 1/90–8/90). Unlike Taiwan and Japan, the economy of South Korea escaped a recession in 1973–1975 but had one in 1979–1980. The Korean index declined by 10.3% in 3/79–11/80, its only lapse from growth since its beginning in 1963.

32. Taking into account the divergences between the periods covered by the indexes does not alter this conclusion.

33. For a description of the international indicators, see Moore and Moore (1985).

34. The Japanese series refers to the number of employees on payrolls in all nonagricultural establishments (private and government-owned). The series for the United States, Canada, France, and Italy cover nonfarm employment; for the United Kingdom, manufacturing, mining, construction, and public utilities; and for West Germany, mining and manufacturing.

35. The theories of hysteresis explain the persistence of high unemployment by making long-run equilibrium depend on history. Adverse shocks reduce demand for physical or human capital or both as well as the demand for labor. Or "insider" workers keep real wages high and "outsider" workers out of jobs (Blanchard and Summers, 1986).

36. This assumes that investment is predominantly productive in nature, well allocated by market forces, and supported rather than hindered by government policies.

37. In this model, volatility is associated with productivity shocks, but I suspect that the analysis of the Rameys has broader applicability.

38. See Klein and Moore (1985), Klein (1990), and Lahiri and Moore (1991).

39. This count does not include the 1990–1991 recessions in the United States, Canada, and the United Kingdom or the concurrent slowdowns or possibly recessions in any of the other three countries. Although the initial dates (peaks) of some of these movements have been established, at least tentatively (see figure 1–3), their severity and duration cannot as yet be known.

40. The listing uses broad labels and offers only selected types of theory. The theories are in general not mutually exclusive and are often used in combinations, with varying emphases. See Haberler ([1937] 1964) and Zarnowitz (1985) for surveys of the literature.

41. Still other, weaker effects accounted for in this model are those of changes in a fiscal policy variable and in the price level. One should remember that a VAR model shows the lead–lag interactions among all the selected variables, allowing also for the effects of their own lagged values (for the serial correlations that are high in many important economic aggregates).

42. On the monetary policy ineffectiveness in the new classical macroeconomics, see Lucas (1972, 1973) and Sargent and Wallace (1975); on tests, see Barro (1978), Boschen and Grossman (1982), and Mishkin (1983).

43. That is, prices clear markets, expectations are rational and adjust promptly, and all opportunities for mutually beneficial transactions are used up.

44. Thus, the shift from production of goods to production of services made employment much less cyclical, as already noted in section 2.7 (see also Zarnowitz and Moore, 1986, pp. 536–538). But the 1990–1991 recession, although relatively mild, was unusually harsh in causing a shrinkage of jobs in many service-producing industries. It is much too early to tell, however, whether this constitutes a reversal of the trend previously observed, and if so to what extent.

45. It can also be shown that the opposite change occurred for the lagging indicators, where the lags have become shorter at peaks and longer at troughs (see Zarnowitz and Moore, 1986, pp. 567–71). These changes are explained by the shift toward longer business expansions and shorter recessions in the postwar era.

46. The two exceptions are the change in sensitive materials prices (line 14), where the indicated k_{max} timing is 0 (coincident), and the change in inventories (line 11), where it is a lag of six months. This last result seems puzzling, since inventories tend to lag in levels but lead in changes.

47. Only the average workweek, the diffusion index of slower deliveries (vendor performance), housing permits, and change in business and consumer credit—all series with little trend—are used in level form *(N)* for the entries in columns 7–9.

48. The leads are particularly long in the case of inverted bond yields (line 32) or, which amounts to much the same, indexes of corporate bond prices (Zarnowitz, 1990). Note also that the average duration of unemployment, like other series on unemployment, is naturally taken in inverted form to match like turns in business activity. This indicator has a roughly coincident timing at peaks but substantial and regular lags at troughs (line 25).

49. The big difference between seasonal and business cycles is that seasonal movements are much more periodic (more truly "cyclical") and much more capable of being anticipated. Over short spans within the year, seasonal fluctuations dominate the changes in many variables, but over longer spans of several years it is the movements associated with business cycles (the "specific cycles") that are predominant. The risk is that seasonal and cyclical movements may interact so that their workable separation is impeded.

50. The cyclical (actually, trend-cycle) component is estimated as a weighted moving average (Henderson curve) chosen on the basis of the relative amplitude of the irregular and

cyclical movements. Most series are smoothed with a 13-month device, but a nine-month formula is used for relatively smooth and a 23-month formula for very volatile series. See Zarnowitz and Boschan ([1975] 1977, p. 173).

51. Any documentation would require more data, mainly in quarterly form.

References

Aftalion, A. 1913. *Les Crises Périodiques de Surproduction*. Paris: Rivière.

Alt, J.E., and K.A. Chrystal. 1983. *Political Economics*. Berkeley: University of California Press.

Altonji, J.G. 1982. "The Intertemporal Substitution Model of Labour Market Fluctuations: An Empirical Analysis." *Review of Economic Studies* 49: 783–824.

Ashton, T.S. 1959. *Economic Fluctuations in England, 1700–1800*. Oxford: Clarendon Press.

Attwood, T. 1817. "A Letter to Nicholas Vansittart, on the Creation of Money, and on Its Action upon National Prosperity." Birmingham: R. Wrightson.

Backhouse, R. 1988. *Economists and the Economy: The Evolution of Economic Ideas 1600 to the Present Day*. Oxford: Basil Blackwell.

Balke, N.S., and R.J. Gordon. 1986. "Historical Data." In *The American Business Cycle Today*, pp. 781–850. In Gordon (1986).

Barro, R.J. 1978. "Unanticipated Money, Output, and the Price Level in the United States." *Journal of Political Economy*. 86: 549–580.

Blanchard, O.J., and L.H. Summers. 1986. "Hysteresis and European Unemployment Problem." In S. Fischer, ed. *NBER Macroeconomics Annual 1986*. Cambridge, MA: MIT Press.

Blanchard, O.J., and M.W. Watson. 1986. "Are Business Cycles All Alike?" In *The American Business Cycle Today*, pp. 123–156 and 178–179. See Gordon (1986).

Boschen, J.F., and H.I. Grossman. 1982. "Tests of Equilibrium Macroeconomics Using Contemporaneous Monetary Data." *Journal of Monetary Economics*. 10: 309–33.

Bouniatian, M. 1908. *Geschichte der Handelskrisen in England, 1640–1840*. Munich: Ernst Reinnhardt.

Bronfenbrennner, M., ed. 1969. *Is the Business Cycle Obsolete*? New York: Wiley-Interscience.

Burns, A.F., and W.C. Mitchell, 1946. *Measuring Business Cycles*. New York: National Bureau of Economic Research.

Butler, W.F., R.A. Kavesh, and R.B. Platt, eds. 1974. *Methods and Techniques of Business Forecasting*. Englewood Cliffs, N.J.: Prentice-Hall.

Cagan, P. 1965. *Determinants and Effects of Changes in the Stock of Money, 1875–1960*. New York: Columbia University Press for NBER.

Cassel, G. [1923] 1932. *Theory of Social Economy*. Harcourt, Brace and Company.

Clark, J.M. 1917. "Business Acceleration and the Law of Demand: A Technical Factor in Economic Cycles." *Journal of Political Economy*. 25: 217–235.

Deane, P. 1967. *The First Industrial Revolution*. Cambridge: Cambridge University Press.

Diebold, F.X., and G.P. Rudebusch. 1990. "A Nonparametric Investigation of Duration Dependence in the American Business Cycles." *Journal of Political Economy* 98(3): 596–616.

———. 1991. "Turning Point Predictions with the Composite Leading Index: An *Ex ante* Analysis." Chapter 14 in K. Lahiri and G.H. Moore, eds., *Leading Indicators: New Approaches and Forecasting Records*. Cambridge: Cambridge University Press.

Eichenbaum, M. 1990. "Real Business Cycle Theory: Wisdom or Whimsy?" NBER Working Paper no. 3432, (September) Cambridge, MA.

Fels, R., and C.E. Hinshaw. 1968. *Forecasting and Recognizing Business Cycle Turning Points*. New York: NBER.

Fisher, I. 1907. *The Rate of Interest*. New York: Macmillan Co.

———. 1932. *Booms and Depressions: Some First Principles*. New York: Adelphi Co.

———. 1933. "The Debt-Deflation Theory of Great Depressions." *Econometrica* 1: 337–357.

Friedman, B.M. 1986. "Money, Credit, and Interest Rates in the Business Cycle." In Gordon (1986, pp. 395–438, 456–458).

Friedman, M., and A.J. Schwartz. 1963*a*. *A Monetary History of the United States, 1867–1960*. Princeton, N.J.: Princeton University Press for NBER.

———. 1963*b*. "Money and Business Cycles." *Review of Economics and Statistics* (Supplement) 45: 32–64.

———. 1982. *Monetary Trends in the United States and the United Kingdom: Their Relation to Income, Prices; and Interest Rates; 1867–1975*. Chicago: University of Chicago Press for NBER.

Frisch, R. 1933. "Propagation Problems and Impulse Problems in Dynamic Economics." *Economic Essays in Honor of Gustav Cassel*. London: George Allen & Unwin.

Goodwin, R.M. 1951. "The Non-linear Accelerator and the Persistence of Business Cycles." *Econometrica* 19: 1–17.

Gordon, R.J. 1986. *The American Business Cycle Today: Continuity and Change*. Chicago: University of Chicago Press for NBER.

Greenwald, B.C., J.E. Stiglitz, and A. Weiss. 1984. "Informational Imperfections in the Capital Market and Macroeconomic Fluctuations." *American Economic Review* 74: 194–199.

Haberler, G. [1937] 1964. *Prosperity and Depression*. League of Nations. Reprinted Cambridge, MA: Harvard University Press.

Hall, R.E. 1986. "The Role of Consumption in Economic Fluctuations." In R.J. Gordon (1986, pp. 237–266).

Hamilton, J.D. 1983. "Oil and the Macroeconomy Since World War II." *Journal of Political Economy* 91: 228–248.

Hansen, A.H. [1951] 1964. *Business Cycles and National Income* (expanded edition). New York: W.W. Norton (first edition 1951).

Hansen, A.H., and R.V. Clemence. 1953. *Readings in Business Cycles and National Income*. New York: W.W. Norton & Co.

Hawtrey. R.G. 1927. "The Monetary Theory of the Trade Cycle and Its Statistical Test." *Quarterly Journal of Economics*. 671–686. Reprinted in Hansen and Clemence (1953, pp. 139–149).

Hickman, B.G., ed. 1972. *Econometric Models of Cyclical Behavior* (2 vols.). *Studies in Income and Wealth*, no. 36. New York: Columbia University Press for NBER.

Hicks, J.R. 1937. "Mr. Keynes and the 'Classics': A Suggested Interpretation." *Econometrica* 5: 147–159.

———. 1950. *A Contribution to the Theory of the Trade Cycle*. Oxford: Clarendon Press.

Hoffman, W. 1965. *Das Wachstum der deutschen Wirtschaft seit der Mitte des 19. Jahrhunderts*. Berlin: Springer-Verlag.

Jevons, W.S. 1884. *Investigations in Currency and Finance*. London: Macmillan & Co.

Juglar, C. [1862] 1889. *Des Crises Commerciales et leur Retour Periodique, en France, en Angleterre et aux Etats-Unis*. Paris: Guillaumin.

Kaldor, N. 1940. "A Model of the Trade cycle." *Economic Journal* 50: 78–92.

Keynes, J.M. 1936. *The General Theory of Employment, Interest and Money*. London: Macmillan.

Kiefer, N. 1988. "Economic Duration Data and Hazard Functions." *Journal of Economic Literature* 26: 646–679.

King, R.G., C.I. Plosser, J.H. Stock, and M.W. Watson. 1991. "Stochastic Trends and Economic Fluctuations." *American Economic Review* 81: 819–840.

Klein, P.A., ed. 1990. *Analyzing Modern Business Cycles: Essays Honoring Geoffrey H. Moore*. Armonk, N.Y.: M.E. Sharpc.

Klein, P.A., and G.H. Moore. 1985. *Monitoring Growth Cycles in Market-Oriented Countries: Developing and Using International Economic Indicators*. Cambridge, Mass.: Ballinger Publishing Company for NBER.

Kydland, F., and E.C. Prescott. 1982. "Time to Build and Aggregate Fluctuations." *Econometrica* 50: 1345–1370.

Lahiri, K., and G.H. Moore, (Eds.). 1991. *Leading Economic Indicators: New Approaches and Forecasting Records*. Cambridge, MA: Cambridge University Press.

Lilien, D.M. 1982. "Sectoral Shifts and Cyclical Unemployment." *Journal of Political Economy* 90: 777–793.

Link, R.G. 1959. *English Theories of Economic Fluctuations, 1815–1848*. New York: Columbia University Press.

Lucas, R.E., Jr. 1972. "Expectations and the Neutrality of Money." *Journal of Economic Theory* 4: 103–124.

———. 1973. "Some International Evidence on Output-Inflation Tradeoffs." *American Economic Review* 63: 326–334.

Marshall, A., and M. Marshall. 1881. *The Economics of Industry*. (2nd ed.) London: Macmillan.

Meltzer, A.H. 1986. "Comment (on B.M. Friedman, 1986)." In Gordon (1986, pp. 441–450).

Metzler, L.A. 1941. "The Nature and Stability of Inventory Cycles." *Review of Economic Statistics*. 23: 113–129.

———. 1947. "Factors Governing the Length of Inventory Cycles." *Review of Economic Statistics* 29: 1–15.

Minsky, H.P. 1982. *Can 'It' Happen Again? Essays on Instability and Finance*. New York: M.E. Sharpe.

Mintz, I. 1969. *Dating Postwar Business Cycles: Methods and Their Application to Western Germany, 1950–67*. New York: NBER.

———. 1974. "Dating United States Growth Cycles." *Explorations in Economic Research* 1(1): 1–113.

Mirowski, P. 1985. *The Birth of the Business Cycle*. New York & London: Garland.

Mishkin, F.S. 1983. *A Rational Expectations Approach to Macroeconometrics: Testing Policy Ineffectiveness and Efficient-Markets Models*. Chicago: University of Chicago Press for NBER.

Mitchell, W.C. 1913. *Business Cycles*. Berkeley: University of California Press.

———. 1927. *Business Cycles: The Problem and Its Setting*. New York: NBER.

———. 1951. *What Happens During Business Cycles: A Progress Report*. New York: NBER.

Moore, G.H. 1983. *Business Cycles, Inflation, and Forecasting* (2nd ed.; 1st ed., 1980). Cambridge, Mass.: Ballinger for NBER.

Moore, G.H., and M.H. Moore. 1985. *International Economic Indicators: A Sourcebook*. Westport, Conn.: Greenwood Press.

Moore, G.H., and V. Zarnowitz, 1986. "The Development and Role of the National Bureau's Business Cycle Chronologies." In Gordon (1986).

Moore, H.L. 1914. *Economic Cycles: Their Law and Cause*. New York: Macmillan Co.

Morgenstern, O. 1959. *International Financial Transactions and Business Cycles*. Princeton: Princeton University Press for NBER.

Overstone, S.J.L. 1837. "Reflections Suggested by a Perusal of Mr. J. Horsley Palmers' Pamphlet on the Causes and Consequences of the Pressure on the Money Market."

Pigou, A.C. 1927. *Industrial Fluctuations*. London: Macmillan.

Plosser, C.I. 1989. "Understanding Real Business Cycles." *Journal of Economic Perspectives* 3: 51–77.

———. 1991. "Money and Business Cycles: A Real Business Cycle Interpretation." In M.T. Belongia, ed., *Monetary Policy on the 75th Anniversary of the Federal Reserve System*. Boston: Kluwer Academic Publishers.

Ramey, G., and V.A. Ramey. 1991. "Technology Commitment and the Cost of Economic Fluctuations." NBER Working Paper no. 3755.

Robertson, D.H. 1937. "The Trade Cycle: An Academic View." *Lloyds Bank Review* (September): 504–510. Reprinted in Hansen and Clemence (1953, pp. 166–174).

Romer, C.D. 1986. "The Prewar Business Cycle Reconsidered: New Estimates of Gross National Product, 1869–1918." NBER Working Paper no. 1969.

Romer, C.D., and D.H. Romer, 1989. "Does Monetary Policy Matter? A New Test in the Spirit of Friedman and Schwartz." In O.J. Blanchard and S. Fischer, eds., *Macroeconomics Annual 1989*. Cambrige, Mass.: MIT Press, pp. 121–170.

Rostow, W.W. 1980. "Cycles in the Fifth Kondratieff Upswing." In *The Business Cycle and Public Policy, 1929–80*. A Compendium of Papers Submitted to the Joint Economic Committee, Congress of the United States, Washington, D.C.: Government Printing Office.

Samuelson, P.A. 1939. "Interactions Between the Multiplier Analysis and the Principle of Acceleration." *Review of Economic Statistics* 21: 75–78.

Sargent, T. J., and N. Wallace. 1975. "Rational Expectations, the Optimal Monetary Instrument, and the Optimal Monetary Rule." *Journal of Political Economy* 83(2): 241–254.

Schumpeter, J.A. 1939. *Business Cycles: A Theoretical, Historical, and Statistical Analysis of the Capitalist Process*. New York: McGraw-Hill.

Sherman, H.J. 1991. *The Business Cycle: Growth and Crises Under Capitalism*. Princeton, N.J.: Princeton University Press.

Smith, A. 1776. *The Wealth of Nations*. Cannon ed., Modern Library, 1937.

Sowell, T. 1972. *Say's Law: An Historical Analysis*. Princeton, N.J.: Princeton University Press.

Spiethoff, A. 1955. *Die wirtschaftlichen Wechsellagen* (2 vols.). Tübingen: Mohr.

Stock, J.H., and M.W. Watson. 1990. "Appendixes to Business Cycle Properties of Selected U.S. Economic Time Series, 1959–1988." NBER Working Paper no. 3376.

Thorp, W.L. 1926. *Business Annals*. New York: NBER.

Tinbergen, J. 1939. *Statistical Testing of Business-Cycle Theories* (2 vols.). Geneva: League of Nations, Economic Intelligence Service.

Tugan-Baranovskii, M.I. [1894, 1901] 1913. *Les Crises Industrielles en Angleterre* (2nd ed.). Paris: Giard & Brière. (Published first in Russian, then in German)

U.S. Department of Commerce. Bureau of Economic Analysis. 1984. *Handbook of Cyclical Indicators: A Supplement to the Business Conditions Digest*. Washington D.C.: U.S. Government Printing Office.

Wicksell, K. [1896] 1936. *Interest and Prices: A Study of the Causes Regulating the Value of Money*. London: Macmillan.

Willett, T.D. 1988. *Political Business Cycles: The Political Economy of Money, Inflation, and Unemployment*. Duke University Press.

Wojnilower, A.M. 1980. "The Central Role of Credit Crunches as Recent Financial History." *Brookings Papers on Economic Activity* 2: 277–339.

Woodford, M. 1987. "Three Questions About Sunspot Equilibria in an Explanation of Economic Fluctuations." *American Economic Review* 77: 43–48.

Zarnowitz, V. 1967. *An Appraisal of Short-Term Economic Forecasts*. New York: NBER.

———. 1974. "How Accurate Have the Forecasts Been?" In W.F. Butler, R.A. Kavesh, and R.B. Platt, eds., *Methods and Techniques of Business Forecasting*. Englewood Cliffs, N.J.: Prentice-Hall.

———. 1981. "Business Cycles and Growth: Some Reflections and Measures." In W.J. Mückl and A.E. Ott, eds. *Wirtschaftstheorie und Wirtschaftspolitik: Gedenkschrift für Erich Preiser*. Passau: Passavia Universitätsverlag.

———. 1985. "Recent Work on Business Cycles in Historical Perspective." *Journal of Economic Literature* 23: 523–580.

———. 1987. "The Regularity of Business Cycles." NBER Working Paper no. 2381 (September). Reprinted as Chapter 8 in Zarnowitz (1992).

———. 1990. "Corporate Bond Prices as a Leading Indicator." In G.H. Moore *Leading Indicators for the 1990s*. Homewood, IL: Dow-Jones Irwin.

———. [1989] 1992. "Facts and Factors in the Recent Evolution of Business Cycles in the United States." NBER Working Paper no. 2865. Reprinted as Chapter 3 in Zarnowitz (1992).

———. 1992. *Business Cycles: Theory, History, Indicators, and Forecasting*. Chicago: University of Chicago Press for NBER.

Zarnowitz, V., and C. Boschan. [1975] 1977. "Cyclical Indicators: An Evaluation and New Leading Indexes." *Business Conditions Digest* (May): v–xxii. Reprinted in U.S. Department of Commerce, Bureau of Economic Analysis, *Handbook of Cyclical Indicators*. Washington, D.C.: U.S. Government Printing Office, pp. 170–184.

Zarnowitz, V., and P. Braun. 1990. "Major Macroeconomic Variables and Leading Indexes: Some Estimates of their Interaction." In P.A. Klein, ed., *Analyzing Modern Business Cycles*. Armonk, N.Y.: M.E. Sharpe, pp. 177–205.

Zarnowitz, V., and G.H. Moore. 1982. "Sequential Signals of Recession and Recovery." *Journal of Business* 55: 57–85.

———. 1986. "Major Changes in Cyclical Behavior." In Gordon (1986).

Commentary

by James H. Stock

Victor Zarnowitz has provided us with an authoritative and valuable overview of the business cycle: its definition, the history of thought associated with business cycle analysis, and key facts about the evolution of the business cycle, both in the United States and abroad. His summary at once provides a handy reference for many of the key empirical facts about business cycles and some new comparisons of cycles since World War II across countries.

Given the limited scope of a discussant, it would be impossible to address most of Zarnowitz's points. These comments are therefore limited to two of the main themes in the chapter. The first concerns changes over time in the U.S. business cycle, more precisely the finding that contractions are shorter, and expansions longer, after World War II than before. The second topic is Zarnowitz's observation that there can be no single theory that can explain the business cycle but that rather each cycle can differ in its sources and perhaps even in its propagation mechanisms. This observation in turn implies that careful studies of individual cyclical episodes can in principle yield new insights on the workings of the macroeconomy and its response to various types of shocks. My second set of remarks builds on this observation by considering a concrete example: the lessons that we as macroeconomists can learn from the 1990 recession.

1 The U.S. Business Cycle, Prewar and Postwar

The argument that the U.S. economy has stabilized since World War II has two parts: first, that the volatility of output (say, its standard deviation) has decreased, and second, that postwar contractions are shorter, and expansions longer, than they were before the Depression. The first part of this argument has come under serious attack by Romer (1986, 1989). Her argument is that the prewar output figures were constructed using inherently more volatile series: The available series cover more volatile sectors of the economy. Although the particulars of her findings are still debated, the case for stabilized postwar output is certainly much weaker than previously thought. Zarnowitz lays out the evidence for the second part of the argument. Drawing on previous careful analyses of the dating of certain suspect prewar cycles, he concludes that, even if several prewar recessions were deleted from the chronology, the empirical evidence remains that postwar cycles have longer expansions and shorter contractions.

My purpose in this part of the discussion is to review some recent research by Watson (1991) that questions this conclusion. As Moore and Zarnowitz (1986) point out, different economic time series were used to construct the NBER reference cycle chronology, depending on the historical period. This raises the possibility that systematic differences in the series might induce an apparent shift in the properties of the reference cycles. Watson addresses this possibility in two ways: first, by comparing pre- and postwar phase durations for the same or comparable series and second, by constructing an aggregate postwar index of industrial production that has a similar coverage and definition to the available prewar industrial production (IP) series. He concludes that specific cycles (cycles based on individual series) appear not to have changed when they are computed for series that are consistently defined prewar and postwar.

Selected evidence on this point is presented in table 1C–1. Panel A presents average expansion and contraction lengths for the prewar and postwar data based on the NBER chronology, and also based on the NBER chronology as modified by Zarnowitz by dropping some suspicious early recessions. As Zarnowitz emphasizes, postwar the recessions are shorter and the expansions longer, whether the suspicious early recessions are included or not.

Panel B presents evidence for specific cycles for series with comparable definitions pre- and postwar. The specific cycle dates were computed using the turning point identification algorithm developed by Bry and Boschan (1973).[1] For each series with comparable definitions, the differences in prewar and postwar phase durations are modest or negligible. For example, contractions in stock prices averaged 19 months prewar and 17 months postwar. The most noteworthy results are for industrial production. Prewar contractions and expansions, measured using the historical IP index recently constructed by Miron and Romer (1990), averaged 16 and 22 months, respectively, both shorter but comparable to the average durations based on the official NBER chronology in panel A. Similarly, the postwar expansions and contractions based on the official IP series (produced by the Federal Reserve Board) are essentially the same as those based on the official NBER chronology. To examine the hypothesis that this difference arises because of differences in the composition of series used to construct the FRB and Miron–Romer IP indexes, Watson constructed a postwar extension of the Miron–Romer series. His approach was to apply the Miron–Romer weights to component series that were similar to those used by Miron and Romer. As the results in the final rows of table 1C–1 indicate,

Table 1C–1. Durations of Historical Expansions and Recessions, in Months

A. Durations Based on Reference Cycles

Period	$\bar{E}$	$\bar{C}$	*Dating Method*
1854–1919	27	22	NBER
1854–1919	37	23	Modified NBER*
1945–1990	50	11	NBER

Source: Zarnowitz (1992). $\bar{E}$ and $\bar{C}$ respectively denote average expansion and contraction lengths, in months.

* Modified NBER: drop 1869–1870, 1887–1888, and 1899–1900 recessions.

B. Durations for Selected Individual Series

Series	*Period*	$\bar{E}$	$\bar{C}$
S&P composite	1871–1940	24	19
S&P composite	1945–1990	26	17
Pig iron production	1887–1940	28	13
IP—iron & steel	1947–1990	22	20
Plans for new buildings	1868–1937	19	18
Building permits	1947–1990	20	18
IP—Miron–Romer	1884–1940	22	16
IP—Miron–Romer (approx.)	1947–1990	22	14
IP—FRB	1947–1990	50	13

Source: Watson (1991). Peaks and troughs were dated using the Bry–Boschan (1973) algorithm.

Watson's approximate Miron–Romer IP series has phase durations very close to its prewar counterpart—and in particular has longer recessions and much shorter expansions than those measured using the FRB IP series or the postwar NBER chronology.

These results suggest that the postwar shifts in duration, as measured using the FRB IP series or using the NBER postwar chronology (which itself relies in large part on the specific cycles in IP), are a consequence of the chronologies having been constructed using different series in the two periods. Of course, as Zarnowitz emphasizes, the sectoral composition of the U.S. economy has evolved over this period, so the use of a different mix of series to date turning points might be appropriate. Watson (1991) examines this possibility but argues that it does not really resolve the large differences between the dates obtained from the official IP series and his approximate Miron–Romer series. The reason, it seems, is that the older series were not representative of historical economic activity and emphasized too heavily materials, metals, financial series, and extractive industries.

In summary, this evidence suggests that the postwar shortening of recessions and lengthening of expansions using the NBER chronology can largely be attributed to the use of different mixes of series to date the prewar and postwar recessions; the prewar dating relied on series with more cycles, longer contractions, and shorter expansions than the series used for postwar dating. Whether this imparts a "bias" to the dating chronology is, however, a matter of interpretation. One possibility is that the shifting mix of series accurately reflected compositional changes in the United States; despite Watson's preliminary negative evidence on this point, the issue remains unresolved. A second possibility is that the underlying time series behavior of the U.S. economy has not changed prewar and postwar, but rather the conception of a recession has changed by the NBER dating authorities; that is, the definition of a recession has intentionally changed. This view, however, is at odds with the the NBER researchers' emphasis on continuity and the importance of having a chronology that can be compared over time. A third possibility is that the intent of the NBER has been the same but that the postwar use of a broader set of indicators has spuriously resulted in fewer and shorter recessions being identified. Learning which of these explanations prevails must await further research.

2 The 1990 Recession: Initial Implications for Economic Theory

A second theme in Zarnowitz's chapter is that business cycles can have different causes and propagation mechanisms. The implication is that each business cycle provides new and different information about the workings of the economy and that each cycle therefore merits special study. This general observation is consistent with the behavior of the economy entering and during the 1990 recession. In brief, current evidence suggests that relationships among economic variables that held on average over the postwar period, and held during the recessions of the 1970s and 1980s, did not hold while the economy was entering the 1990 recession. The modest

Table 1C–2. Monthly Percentage Changes in Coincident Economic Indicators, April 1990 to July 1991

Month	*IP*	*Pers Inc*	*Emp-Hours*	*MT Sales*	*XCI*
1990: 4	–.1%	.1%	–.6%	–.9%	–.2%
90: 5	.5	.0	.7	.9	.4
90: 6	.6	.1	.5	.6	.5
90: 7	.3	.2	–.2	–.7	.1
90: 8	.1	–.4	–.3	1.2	.0
90: 9	.1	–.4	.4	–1.8	–.1
90: 10	–.6	–1.1	–1.3	–.2	–.7
90: 11	–1.5	.2	.3	–1.6	–.8
90: 12	–1.0	.4	.4	–2.1	–.5
1991: 1	–.6	–1.6	–1.2	–.9	–.9
91: 2	–.8	.0	.2	.4	–.4
91: 3	–.7	.3	–.4	–.4	–.2
91: 4	.5	–.3	–.5	1.8	.3
91: 5	.8	.3	.6	.8	.7
91: 6	.8	.5	.5	.3	.8
91: 7	.7	–.2	–1.0	.8	.2

Notes: 1990: 4 denotes April 1990, etc.
Series:
IP: Industrial production (total).
Pers Inc: Real personal income less transfer payments.
Emp-Hours: Employee-hours in nonagricultural establishments.
MT Sales: Real manufacturing and trade sales, total.
XCI: Stock–Watson (1991) experimental index of coincident indicators.

purpose of this part of my comments, then, is to illustrate Zarnowitz's general observations by listing some of the characteristics that distinguish the 1990 recession from the preceding three recessions.

Although the NBER dated the cyclical peak as July 1990, overall economic activity was stagnant from June through September. Monthly growth rates of four main economic indicators—industrial production, real personal income less transfers, employee-hours in nonagricultural establishments, and real manufacturing and trade sales—are presented in table 1C–2 for this period. Although employee-hours peaked in June, industrial production did not peak until September. The striking feature in this recession is not the flat growth over the summer but rather the precipitous declines in the main indicators in the fourth quarter of 1990, in particular the sharp drops in IP, personal income, and employee-hours in October.

My argument is that the "explanations" for recent postwar U.S. recessions do not really work for the 1990 experience. The evidence for this is simple (perhaps too simple): A large number of time series forecasting relations that worked over the previous 30 years performed extremely poorly during the fall of 1990. This assertion is documented in detail in Stock and Watson (1991); here, I present some of the key evidence on this matter.

One way to examine whether "typical" behavior was present during the onset of the 1990 recession is to ask whether the correlations between a broad set of leading economic indicators and overall economic activity appeared to be stable during this episode. More concretely, this can be examined by using leading indicators to construct forecasts of coincident indicators or an index of coincident indicators. Such forecasts were constructed in Stock and Watson (1991) by regressing future three-month growth of an experimental index of coincident indicators (the "XCI") on current values and two lags of XCI growth and on current and five lags of a candidate indicator. Such forecasts were constructed for more than 45 leading indicators. The regressions were estimated using data from 1959:1 to 1988:9, and the out-of-sample performance was examined in each of two periods: for forecasts made during 1989:10–1990:4, and forecasts made during 1990:5–1990:8. (The three-month ahead forecast made in 1990:7, say, forecasted growth from July through October 1990.) The performance of the forecasts can be compared by examining the root mean square errors (RMSEs) of the forecasts over the various subsamples.

Selected results from this out-of-sample forecasting exercise are presented in Table 1C–3. Two general sets of observations are apparent. First, the forecasts for most series were seriously off track during the summer and early fall of 1990, with three-month-ahead forecast errors as high as 8.0% at an annual rate, even though the forecasting relations actually performed better during the initial out-of-sample period than during the in-sample period. Only a few leading indicators had performance comparable to the 1959:1–1988:9 sample: real M2, the index of help wanted advertising, building permits, and the index of consumer expectations. Second, those series that had relatively good average performance during the 1962–1988 period, particularly indicators of monetary activity such as the 10–year/1-year Treasury bond spread or the fed funds rate, performed particularly poorly during the 1990 episode.[2] Conversely, the few series that performed well during the summer of 1990 had in fact performed poorly during the 1962–1988 sample. Interestingly, two series that one might think would have performed well during the summer of 1990—stock prices and oil prices—did not produce reliable forecasts when these forecasts were made using the historically estimated forecasting equation.

These observations suggest that the historical correlations between these leading indicators and overall economic activity were not good guides to this episode. More concretely, one can reasonably argue that disinflationary monetary policy was an important proximate cause of the 1975, 1979, and 1981 recessions. The poor performance of the monetary indicators in the 1990 recession suggest that restrictive monetary policy, or an associated credit crunch, played at most a limited role in inducing the sharp contractions of October and November.

The results instead are consistent with an alternative mechanism based on unprecedented shifts in consumer expectations. The timing was right: Expectations dropped precipitously in August; manufacturing and trade sales fell sharply in September; and production, employee-hours, and income all dropped in October. One interpretation is that the recession transpired as a self-fulfilling prophecy. For example, the drop in consumer expectations induced firms to restrict hiring and to expect lower sales; with lower incomes, sales did in fact drop. Another interpretation is that consumer expectations played only a passive role and reflected increased uncertainty in the face of rising oil prices and the threat of war in the Gulf, which together induced consumers to adopt more conservative spending patterns. If these explanations are right, they illustrate Zarnowitz's point that each cycle can have different sources: Over the previous 30 years, consumer expectations had in fact been of only limited forecasting value.[3] Whether or not consumer expectations played a causal role in the contraction, the circumstances of the 1990 downturn differed from their recent predecessors, in which indicators of monetary policy provided reasonably reliable forecasts.

3 Conclusions

These observations only touch on the rich set of facts and theories reviewed in Zarnowitz's chapter. In particular, his work on international business cycles warrants careful reading and raises an interesting set of research questions concerning international phase durations, cyclical stability, and cross-country patterns of growth. One of the implications of this chapter, which I have attempted to illustrate and which I hope is taken up by subsequent researchers, is that there are good reasons to study

Table 1C–3. Performance of Selected Leading Indicators as Forecasts of the XCI Coincident Index During the Onset of the 1990 Recession (three-month-ahead forecast horizon)

	RMSE of Forecasts of XCI Growth Over:		
Series	*62:1–88:9*	*88:10–90:4*	*90:5–90:8*
Financial Indicators			
S&P composite	4.30	2.61	4.72
Real M1	4.28	1.92	5.06
Real M2	4.08	2.02	3.57
Monetary base	4.51	1.68	6.40
Federal funds rate	4.09	1.39	5.67
10-year T-bond rate, smoothed	4.36	2.18	5.47
Commercial paper/T-bill spread, six months	3.66	1.51	8.00
10-year T-bond/1-year T-bond spread	4.12	1.38	6.63
Employment Indicators			
New claims, unemployment insurance	4.46	1.83	5.34
Persons unemployed < five weeks	4.55	2.11	5.95
Index of help wanted ads, newspapers	4.05	2.52	3.07
Part-time work, economic reasons	4.35	2.03	5.38
Average weekly hours, manufacturing production workers	4.54	1.88	5.16

Inventories and Orders			
Real unfilled orders, durable goods industries	4.48	2.01	5.31
Real manufacturing & trade inventories	4.55	2.37	6.21
Additional Indicators			
Real retail sales	4.53	1.82	5.27
Building permits—private housing	4.15	1.56	4.13
Consumer expectations (University of Michigan)	4.27	2.01	3.00
PPI, crude petroleum	4.56	2.04	6.82
Weighted average of nominal exchange rates	4.42	2.10	7.83
Capacity utilization, manufacturing	4.55	1.86	5.08
Index of vendor performance	4.40	1.73	6.57

Notes: All results were computed using the data as revised through 91:02. RMSEs were computed for forecasts of $x_t = \ln(c_{t+3}/c_t)$ on current values plus two lags of $\ln(c_t/c_{t-1})$ and current values plus five lags of the (suitably transformed) individual leading indicator, where c_t is the Kalman smoother estimate of the Stock–Watson (1989) experimental coincident index (the XCI) computed on data revisions through 1991:2. The dates in the column headings are the months in which the three-month forecasts were made. Units are annual rate percent growth rates.

Source: Stock and Watson (1991).

individual cycles in detail. Perhaps because this sort of analysis is antithetical to the econometric methodology developed by the Cowles Commission and taught in modern textbooks, it has had limited applications in recent years and therefore might yield important new insights.

Notes

1. The Bry–Boschan (1973) algorithm is an early computerized expert system developed at the NBER to automate the dating of specific cycles in the large number of series that NBER business cycle researchers have collected over the years. This algorithm succeeded in closely replicating specific cycle dates ascertained by the NBER experts. Watson (1991) demonstrates that the algorithm, applied to the Miron–Romer IP series, closely replicates the prewar NBER chronology.

2. Although real M2 produced relatively small forecast errors, recent research (for example, Bernanke and Blinder, 1991, and Friedman and Kuttner, 1989) suggests that other financial market indicators provide more accurate measures of monetary policy than does M2. These alternative indicators include, in particular, interest rates such as the fed funds rate, the slope of the Treasury bond yield curve, and matched maturity public–private spreads such as that between the commercial paper and the Treasury bill rate. Moreover, forecasts based on M1 and the monetary base during the 1990 episode performed poorly. It is therefore unclear how to interpret the relatively satisfactory performance of M2 during this episode.

3. The poor historical forecasting performance of consumer expectations is supported by its relatively large in-sample root mean squared error (RMSE) in table 1C–3. In a more thorough study, Garner (1991) also found a weak historical relationship between consumer expectations and consumer spending.

References

Bernanke, B., and A. Blinder. Forthcoming. "The Federal Funds Rate and the Channels of Monetary Transmission." *American Economic Review.*

Bry, G., and C. Boschan. 1973. *Cyclical Analysis of Time Series: Selected Computer Procedures and Computer Programs.* New York: Columbia University Press.

Friedman, B.M., and K.N. Kuttner. 1989. "Another Look at the Evidence on Money-Income Causality." Manuscript, Department of Economics, Harvard University. *Journal of Econometrics*, forthcoming.

Garner, C. Alan. 1991. "Forecasting Consumer Spending: Should Economists Pay Attention to Consumer Confidence Surveys?" *Economic Review of the Federal Reserve Bank of Kansas City* (May/June): 57–71.

Miron, J.A., and C.D. Romer. 1990. "A New Index of Industrial Production, 1884–1940." *Journal of Economic History* 50: 321–337.

Moore, G.H., and V. Zarnowitz. 1986. "The Development and Role of the NBER's Business Cycle Chronologies." In R.J. Gordon, ed., *The American Business Cycle: Continuity and Change.* Chicago: University of Chicago Press.

Romer, C.D. 1986. "Spurious Volatility in Historical Unemployment Data." *Journal of Political Economy* 94: 1–37.

———. 1989. "The Prewar Business Cycle Reconsidered: New Estimates of Gross National Product, 1869–1908." *Journal of Political Economy* 97: 1–38.

Stock, James H. and M.W. Watson. 1989. "New Indexes of Coincident and Leading Economic Indicators." *NBER Macroeconomics Annual, 1989*. Cambridge, Mass.: MIT Press, pp. 351–393.

Stock, J.H., and M.W. Watson. 1991. "Predicting Recessions." In J.H. Stock and M.W. Watson, eds., *Business Cycles, Indicators and Forecasting*. Chicago: University of Chicago Press for the NBER.

Watson, M.W. 1991. "Business Cycle Durations and Postwar Stabilization of the U.S. Marcroeconomy." Manuscript, Northwestern University.

Zarnowitz, V. 1992. "What is a Business Cycle?" In M.T. Belongia and M.R. Garfinkel, eds., *The Business Cycle: Theories and Evidence*. Norwell, Mass.: Kluwer Academic Publishers.

2 THE CYCLE BEFORE NEW-CLASSICAL ECONOMICS

David Laidler

If an idea is to be influential in economics, it is not enough that it be a good idea. Economists must also be convinced of its quality, and this is not achieved simply by demonstrating theoretical rigor and empirical relevance. It also involves the persuasive use of language. The formal study of "The Rhetoric of Economics," of which the use of persuasive language is but one component, is of more recent origin than the phenomenon itself. It was, after all, Keynes, not Donald McCloskey (1983) who said, "Words ought to be a little wild—for they are the assault of thought upon the unthinking." Even so, recent developments in business cycle theory provide a striking example of the power of the right words to draw attention to an idea.[1] Who, when all is said and done, could resist the appeal of a "real" theory of the business cycle? How could it fail to be better than, shall we say, a "mythical" theory? And if it wins hands down in this comparison, might it not also prove to be more satisfactory than a "monetary" theory? That is surely Kydland and Prescott's (1990) underlying message, and to judge by the literature built upon their original (1982) work, they have been remarkably successful in getting it across.

But the language used to promote modern business cycle theory is, in the context of this chapter, misleading. The major innovation of Kydland and Prescott has been to build a plausible model of the cycle in which the dominant impulse (to borrow a phrase from Brunner and Meltzer, for example, 1978) arises from shocks to the aggregate production function, rather than to aggregate demand. Though it is true that monetary shocks provide a genuine alternative to those hypothesized by Kydland and Prescott, it is also the case that, except in the literature based on the twin assumptions of (Walrasian) clearing markets and rational expectations, monetary-impulse models have always been something of a minority taste. In the literature of the 1950s and 1960s, and long before that, "real" theories of the cycle predominated, though they were very different from anything that currently carries that label.

Modern business cycle theory is based on Walrasian general equilibrium analysis. In such a system, markets always clear and the distinction between "demand" and "supply" shocks is not all that helpful: Say's law holds, supply creates its own demand, and in general any shock will affect both simultaneously. The demand–supply shock distinction does make sense in a system in which the fact of monetary exchange permits aggregate demand and supply to move independently of each other and in which, therefore, a situation of general excess demand or supply can emerge.[2] The appropriate contrast, then, between Kydland and Prescott's work and that of the 1950s and 1960s is not between "real" and "monetary" models; it is between those that locate the shocks initiating the cycle in the economy's production sector and in which both supply and demand behavior interdependently respond, and those that locate them on the demand side and treat production as passively adjusting to demand fluctuations whose origins can be either real or monetary.

It is also worth noting that some advocates of "real business cycle theory"—for example, Plosser (1991)—have lately taken to classifying anything but a change in the monetary base, including a change in the required reserve ratio, as a "real shock." They cannot be prevented from using the word *real* this way, but they should make it clear to their readers that it is then appropriate to use the adjective *nominal* rather than *monetary* to characterize an alternative approach. This matter is important, because every *monetary* theory of the cycle of which I am aware has paid careful attention to, and indeed usually accorded prime importance to, endogenous fluctuations in money multipliers (and in the case of 1937–1938 to changes in reserve requirements as well) when confronting empirical evidence. No one, to the best of my knowledge, ever advanced a purely *nominal* theory of the cycle as a serious explanation of any actual historical experience.

None of this would matter very much if inability to cope with empirical evidence was a characteristic of all demand side models of the cycle. But in fact the models that found themselves in trouble from the mid-1960s onward were *real* (albeit demand-side) models, and these were already in difficulty as a result of a re-examination of previous empirical evidence. The historical studies of Friedman and Schwartz had, by the mid 1960s, established what we would nowadays call the monetarist explanation of the cycle as something to be taken very seriously. Subsequent experience with inflation and unemployment, which was so damaging to the orthodox Keynesian demand-side macroeconomics of the time, did nothing to undermine monetarism. Nor is the stylized fact that the price level has moved in a generally countercyclical fashion in the postwar years, of which Kydland and Prescott (1990) make so much, damaging to monetarist models of this vintage.

It is indeed true that assertions to the effect that the price level is a procyclical variable are to be found in the literature.[3] It is also true, as Kydland and Prescott (1990, p. 7) remark, that "if these perceptions are not in fact the regularities, then certain lines of research are misguided," and that, as they further suggest, the equilibrium monetary models of the 1970s are vulnerable to such criticism. Monetarist models of the 1960s to early 1970s, however, were not constructed to predict any such fact. Nor, incidentally, did they rely on the postulate that "the money stock, whether measured by the monetary base or by M1, leads the cycle" (1990, p. 5). Hence Kydland and Prescott's exposure of this postulate as yet another "misperception" also leaves monetarist models unscathed.

In the following pages, I shall first give an account of how business cycle theory fit into the macroeconomic consensus of the 1950s and early 1960s, and then discuss monetarism's role in disturbing this aspect (along with many others) of the consensus in question, paying particular attention to the predictions of monetarist models about the cyclical behavior of money and prices. I shall go on to argue that the main strength of later new-classical economics, in the Lucas–Sargent–Wallace mode, was not so much its explanatory power, as its conformity to particular *a priori* methodological criteria, and that modern real business cycle theory also conforms to those criteria, whose appeal is understandable in the light of those earlier debates. I shall argue that the criteria in question are insufficient to establish the superiority of modern real business cycle theory and that it therefore remains open to empirical challenge from an alternative approach to which the monetarist economics of the 1960s made a vital contribution.

1 The Rise and Fall of Multiplier–Accelerator Theory

Before the publication of *The General Theory*, the business cycle occupied a central position in what we would nowadays call macroeconomics.

Though it shared the stage with inflation, the fact that many monetary models of the cycle treated inflation as an integral characteristic of the cycle's upswing meant that divisions here were not sharply marked. The essentially comparative static analysis of *The General Theory*, and of the *IS-LM* model that came to be regarded as embodying its central theoretical contribution, shifted the focus of macroeconomics away from cycle theory, but there was more to the "Keynesian Revolution" than that.[4]

Whatever Keynes may have meant, Keynesian economics downgraded the importance of monetary factors as an explanation of macroeconomic phenomena. The empirical postulates that the demand for money was highly interest elastic, and probably unstable too, and the belief that expenditure, again as an empirical matter, was insensitive to interest rates, implied that the real side of the economy, as described by the *IS* curve, must be the source of economic disturbances. An alleged empirically stable marginal propensity to save underpinned a stable multiplier. Hence fluctuations in investment came to be regarded as the main factor driving movements in real income and employment, with variations in interest rates playing at most a marginal and complicating role in the process.

Although, with the onset of the Keynesian revolution, models of the cycle that located the impulses driving it in the monetary sector therefore vanished from the mainstream of the literature, cycle theory continued to flourish as an important component of the subdiscipline, requiring the inclusion of a chapter or two in any intermediate textbook and the production of supplementary textbooks and collections of readings for more advanced students. The comparative statics of real income determination, embodied in *IS-LM* analysis, had to be grasped as ends in themselves, but, for serious students, mastering them was also an essential preliminary to coming to grips with "multiplier-accelerator" models, which treated the cycle as the outcome of systematic rightward and leftward shifts of the *IS* curve along an essentially horizontal *LM* curve.[5]

The pre-*General Theory* literature had contained a number of "real" theories of the cycle. Jevons' speculations about the importance of fluctuations in agricultural output stemming from sunspot activity continued to attract attention well into the 1920s, operating, in the hands of Pigou, in combination with the notion that business investment was subject to influence from waves of optimism and pessimism. Schumpeter argued that investment fluctuated because of irregularities in the pace of innovation and that the cycle was an integral component of the process of capitalist growth. Though all of these approaches found a role for monetary factors, it was a strictly supporting one; but viewed from the perspective of *IS-LM* analysis, they were analytically uninteresting. In that framework they provided little more than reasons—endogenous to the economy perhaps, but exogenous to the model—why the *IS* curve might shift back and forth over time.

The accelerator hypothesis was also well developed in that earlier literature, usually being deployed to explain the relatively large amplitude of cyclical fluctuations in investment, but it had not found a home in any complete model of endogenous (cyclical) fluctuations. Keynesian economics provided the requisite accommodation, and the accelerator proved to be the perfect partner for the multiplier in a union forged by exponents of the analytic techniques (then newly available to economists) of difference and differential equations. The idea of the accelerator as it appeared in the resulting models was simple enough. Suppose that the economy is characterized by a fixed coefficients production function, that capital is fully utilized, but that labor is freely available. Then any increase in the demand for real output will require firms to acquire new capital equipment to produce it. The rate of investment will thus be linked to the rate of change of output by a parameter given by the capital-output ratio. Investment, however, will have a multiplier effect on output, which in turn will feed back through the accelerator to investment. In discrete time, this interactive process may be made to yield a second-order difference equation, whose dynamic properties might be monotonic, cyclical, damped, explosive, and so on, depending upon the precise values of the parameters of the multiplier and accelerator relationships.[6]

But the incorporation of the accelerator into Keynesian economics was not just a matter of the application of technique for technique's sake. *The General Theory* had made much of the influence of investment on the level of aggregate demand for goods and services but had carefully avoided dealing with its other role in changing the economy's productive capacity. As Harrod (1948) and Domar (1947) each showed, a time path for aggregate demand generated by a particular time path of investment could be an equilibrium path only if investment was simultaneously providing just the right amount of capacity to meet the demand in question. The first of these two relationships involved the multiplier, and the second the economy's capital-output ratio and hence the accelerator relationship. Multiplier–accelerator interaction thus seemed to provide the key to extending Keynesian economics into a system that could deal with both growth and cycles. The economy's growth path would, within a limit given by population growth, be the steady state of the same process driving the cycle, and of course the policy implications of Keynesian analysis pointed to the possibility both of stabilizing the cycle and manipulating the economy's steady state, or *warranted*, growth path so that it coincided with that of the labor force and hence the economy's *natural* growth path.

Now multiplier–accelerator interaction is capable of generating virtually any type of dynamic behavior, depending on the size of the relevant coefficients, but it seemed to some, notably Hicks (1949, 1951), that the accelerator was, as an empirical matter, powerful enough to produce a monotonically explosive time path for income's deviation from its steady state path. This presumption formed the basis of his famous "nonlinear" cycle model, whose qualitative characteristics are easily described. Begin in the middle of an upswing, with output moving along an explosive expansionary path, and note that output must eventually reach a level at which its subsequent rate of growth will be constrained by that of the labor force. When output growth is thus constrained, investment will fall and a downward multiplier effect will set a downswing in motion. Since, with durable capital, the flow of net investment cannot fall below the rate of depreciation of the actual capital stock, the multiplier alone will carry the economy to a floor whose value is determined by some exogenously given level of autonomous expenditure. Once at the floor, existing surplus capital will wear out, and when it eventually does, an injection of replacement investment demand will set an explosive upswing going again.

A number of points are worth making about this model. First, it treats the cycle as an entirely "real" phenomenon, with the demand side of the economy dominating the upswing and downswing phases of the cycle but with supply side phenomena providing the constraints that generate its turning points. Second, the cycle it produces is completely self-generating and poses no questions about what kind of impulse might set it in motion. Third, difficult though it is to defend now, until the mid-1960s this model did dominate the chapters devoted to the cycle in intermediate textbooks. Its demise, however, was not the result of the rise of monetarism. It is more accurate to argue that the popularity of monetarist analysis of the cycle resulted from its ability to fill a gap in macroeconomics created by the fact that the Hicks cycle model, and the many variations on it in the literature, failed to survive developments within mainstream macroeconomics during the 1950s. It will suffice to enumerate these.

First, the "new" theories of the consumption of function of Friedman (1957) and Modigliani and Brumberg (1954) suggested that though the marginal propensity to *consume* out of *permanent*, or *life cycle*, income might be stable, this did not imply that the marginal propensity to *save* out of *current* income, and therefore the multiplier, was also stable. Second, the neo-classical model of Meade (1961), Solow (1956), and Swan (1956) soon took over from the Harrod–Domar model as the centerpiece of growth theory, using a variable proportions production function. Hence the capital–output ratio became an endogenous variable, whose long-run equilibrium value was determined as part of the outcome of a process whereby the economy converged smoothly to a full employment growth path determined by the rate of growth of the labor force. In the light of this analysis it became indefensible to treat it as the key structural parameter linking the growth process to an endogenous cycle. Third, work on the microeconomics of the accelerator, as surveyed by Knox (1952), reduced it to little more than a proposition that investment would be some distributed lag function of the difference between the desired and actual capital stock. Here, too, variable proportions were the order of the day, and in the slightly later work of Jorgenson (e.g., 1963), a variable linking the real and monetary sectors, namely the rate of interest, re-emerged as a component of the cost of capital and hence as a determinant of the desired capital stock and an argument in the investment function.

What came to be called the "flexible accelerator," derived from the capital stock adjustment principle, involved the inclusion of forward-looking variables in investment equations to capture the expected profitability of new capital equipment; and, analytically closely related, the new theories of the consumption function modeled consumer expenditure decisions as being inherently forward looking. But expectations were usually modeled as distributed lag functions of the variables they concerned, while adjustment processes gave rise to similar functional forms. As early as 1962, then, a new textbook (Bailey, 1962), in my view the best (but probably not best selling) of its time, had replaced the obligatory chapter on multiplier–accelerator interaction with one entitled "Expectations and Adjustment to Change: A Key Link in Cumulative Movements of the Economy." But expenditure functions based on these ideas were much less prone to generate explosive behavior. Rather they tended to produce persistent but damped fluctuations that required exogenous shocks to get and keep them going. And models containing them were no longer simple multiplier–accelerator systems.

The aim of modern real business cycle theory is to produce an integrated account of growth and cycles, firmly based on sound microeconomic foundations. We have now seen that the integration of growth and cycle theory was also the aim of multiplier–accelerator theorists. It is ironic, therefore, that their work foundered on the results generated by the first round of efforts to produce more satisfactory microfoundations for macroeconomics. Though multiplier–accelerator models lingered on in many textbooks for another decade or more, they had ceased to be the center of active research effort by the early 1960s. The next round of work on the cycle moved in two directions, at first largely separate and distinct from one another, each dealing with a separate component of Ragnar

Frisch's (1933) agenda for this area. First, the demise of the self-perpetuating cycle models meant that the temporarily suspended search for exogenous impulses had to be taken up again. Second, the study of propagation mechanisms moved away from the analysis of low-order difference and differential equation systems that had characterized multiplier–accelerator theory into the domain of the large econometric models whose complex distributed lag structures required numerical simulation exercises to reveal their dynamic properties.[7] These two endeavors were not logically incompatible with one another, but, as a matter of fact, monetarism came to dominate the first while an eclectic type of Keynesian economics was perpetuated in the second.

2 Monetarism and the Cycle

The literature of what later came to be called monetarism is as complex as its intellectual roots are varied. It dealt with inflation and monetary policy, as well as the business cycle. That part of it dealing with the positive theory of the cycle drew heavily on the National Bureau tradition of Burns and Mitchell (e.g., 1946), whose work Koopmans (1947) disparagingly characterized as "Measurement Without Theory." In this case, though, a more accurate description might be "measurement before theory." Friedman's earliest published studies concentrated on describing certain persistent quantitative relationships among the behavior of the money stock, money income, real income, prices, and so on. Only later, partly in response to critics, did he reveal the theoretical framework in which those observations could be explained and interpreted, a framework, as is by now well understood, differentiated from that of the then-prevailing Keynesian orthodoxy more by its quantitative than its qualitative characteristics.[8]

Friedman's (1958) study for the Joint Economic Committee of Congress was mainly concerned with describing both the secular and cyclical relationships between money and prices revealed in U.S. data, and it was there that he pointed to the fact that the *rate of change (not the level)* of the stock of money displayed "well marked cycles that match closely those in economic activity in general and precede the latter by a long interval" (p. 181). Though Friedman was careful to deny unidirectional causation here—because "the character of our monetary and banking system means that an expansion of income contributes to an expansion of the money stock. . . . Similarly a contraction of income contributes to a reduction or slower rate of rise in the money stock" (p. 179)—he nevertheless insisted that regardless of their source, changes in the rate of money growth would have subsequent effects on economic activity in general and on the time path of prices in particular. Hence, monetary changes affected the economy with a long and variable time lag. Subsequent monetarist work on money and the cycle elaborated these basic themes.

Friedman and Schwartz's (1963*a*) *A Monetary History of the United States*, among many other things, documented the preceding relationships on a cycle-by-cycle basis and established that the predominance of money growth as a causative factor was more easily discerned in the violent fluctuations that marked the interwar years than at other times. Drawing on the then-unpublished work of Phillip Cagan (1965), it also established that changes in the stock of money were predominantly the result of variations usually endogenous, but sometimes, notably in 1937, were the result of regulatory changes in the banking system's demand for reserves relative to deposits, and in the public's currency-to-deposit ratio, hence confirming the cumulative and interactive nature of money's relationship to the cycle. And Friedman (1961) and Friedman and Schwartz (1963*b*) explained the transmission mechanism through which variations in money growth affected the economy, something that had been very much missing from Friedman's first account of this matter, and an omission for which he was frequently criticized long after he had repaired it. Two matters are important here: First, *why* is the rate of money growth, rather than the level of the money stock, the important impulse variable? Second, *how* can such an impulse lead to the fluctuations that we call the cycle?

Friedman stressed more than once that one element in the case for paying attention to money's rate of change was statistical. The stock of nominal money is a heavily trended variable, and its percentage rate of change (log first difference) is not. But the process of first differencing moves the monetary impulse forward in time and, as John Culberston (1961) pointed out, opens up the possibility that the "long and variable" time lag is purely a statistical artifact. The level of the nominal money supply was (as Kydland and Prescott have recently reminded us) not so much a leading as a coincident variable. There was a good theoretical reason for treating changes in nominal money growth as the critical monetary impulse, however, and Friedman's (1961) account of it, offered in response to Culbertson, is worth quoting at some length.

> Consider a hypothetical long-run moving equilibrium in which both output and the stock of money are rising at constant percentage rates, the rise being fully anticipated so that actual, expected, and desired stocks of money are equal. The result would be a roughly constant percentage rate of change of prices. . . . The percentage rate of change of prices itself is the opportunity cost of holding money rather than goods, so a constant rate of change in the stock of money

> corresponds to a constant opportunity cost of holding money. . . . An unanticipated change in the rate of change of the stock of money would then produce a deviation of the actual from the desired stock of money for two reasons: initially, it would make the actual stock deviate from the expected stock and therefore from the desired stock; subsequently, by altering the cost of holding money, it would change the desired stock itself. These discrepancies will set up adjustments that may very well be cyclical. . . . It is therefore theoretically appealing to regard the "normal" or secular monetary base [*sic*] around which cyclical fluctuations occur as described by a constant percentage rate of change in the stock of money and to regard changes in the percentage rate of change as the feature of monetary behavior that contributes to the generation of cycles. [p. 247]

For Friedman, that is to say, a monetary surprise constituted the cyclical impulse, and a change in the rate of nominal money growth marked its occurrence. But, although his monetarism had this much in common with the later new-classical analysis of Lucas and others, its view of the subsequent propagation process, what used to be called the "transmission mechanism," was very different. Indeed, it was very much in line with what we nowadays usually think of as Keynesian economics, as the following summary of Friedman and Schwartz's (1963*b*, pp. 229–234) account of the matter makes clear.[9]

Beginning in precisely the moving long-run equilibrium just described, they postulate a once and for all change in the rate of monetary growth, brought about by "an increased rate of open-market purchases by a central bank." They then point out that "although the initial sellers of the securities . . . were willing sellers, this does not mean that they want to hold the proceeds in money indefinitely." They sold because they were offered a good price, not because their cash balances were deficient, and hence will "seek to readjust their portfolios." To the extent that these original purchasers were commercial banks, moreover, this effort will involve a further round of credit and hence money creation. Be that as it may, "It seems plausible that . . . holders of redundant balances will turn first to securities similar to those which they have sold, say, fixed interest, low-risk obligations;" but this will bring about a rise in the price of such securities which will spread to other assets:

> . . . higher-risk fixed-coupon obligations, equities, real property and so forth. . . . These effects raise demand curves for current productive services, both for producing new capital goods and for purchasing current services. The monetary stimulus is, in this way, spread from the financial markets to the markets for goods and services.

Output and prices will begin to rise, and money income will tend to overshoot its new equilibrium time path because, as higher inflation becomes anticipated, the economy's demand for real balances falls and also because second and subsequent round influences on deposit–currency ratios will affect the behavior of money growth relative to its ultimate equilibrium.

In new-classical analysis, a monetary surprise affects output because, although the price level moves instantaneously to restore *equilibrium between the supply and demand for nominal money*, that movement is misperceived by agents who react by increasing their *supply of goods and services*, and its effects are spread out over time because of costs of adjusting *quantities supplied*. In stark contrast, for Friedman and Schwartz, persistent *portfolio disequilibrium* and its effects on *flows of expenditure* is of the essence:

> The central element in the transmission mechanism . . . is the concept of cyclical fluctuations as the outcome of balance sheet adjustments, as the effects of flows on adjustments between desired and actual stocks. It is this interconnectedness of stocks and flows that stretches the effect of shocks out in time, produces a diffusion over different economic categories, and gives rise to cyclical reaction mechanisms. The stocks serve as buffers or shock absorbers of initial changes in rates of flow, by expanding or contracting from their "normal" or "natural" or "desired" state, and then slowly alter other flows as holders try to regain that state. [p. 234]

Since among the stocks to which Friedman and Schwartz explicitly drew attention were those of consumer durables and fixed capital, there was no reason at all why their view of the monetary impulse could not have been combined with a real propagation mechanism of the type, already referred to, incorporating a flexible accelerator mechanism, to produce an eclectic account of cyclical fluctuations. Matters did not at first develop in this way, however. While the quantitative analysis of these real propagation mechanisms advanced in the context of work on large-scale econometric models, a separate literature debated the monetarist view of the primacy of monetary impulses.

The debate about the monetary origins of the cycle was untidy and drawn out. It touched on general issues concerning the difficulty of deriving conclusions about the direction of causation between variables from data on timing, and about whether Friedman's (1959) view of the empirical nature of the demand for money function as being essentially devoid of significant interest rate effects had led him and his associates to pay insufficient attention to the possibility that nonmonetary impulses might sometimes be important.[10] But when these issues had been settled in favor of the critics—data on timing might indeed be misleading, and velocity was after all interest-sensitive so money income could fluctuate even if money did not—that still left the core of the monetarist case undamaged. It had been advanced, not as a set of theorems that were true of logical necessity under any conceivable circumstances, but as a collection of falsifiable hypotheses about how real-world data had been generated. Much, though not all, of the debate about these hypotheses concentrated upon a particular episode, namely, the Great Depression, and for a number of very good reasons.

First, the episode in question had generated sufficiently large data swings that it seemed likely that they might permit discriminating tests to be carried out. Second, and closely related, Friedman and Schwartz had used their interpretation of the Depression (and of one or two other relatively major fluctuations) to establish an *a priori* presumption of the importance of money for milder cycles, where the data made it much harder to allocate cause and effect. Finally, and decisively, though the actual history is a good deal more complicated, in the mythology of the mainstream economics of the 1950s and 1960s, the Depression was the episode that had given birth to the Keynesian revolution in economic thought. To argue that the causes of the Great Depression were monetary, then, was to mount a challenge to that mythology that could not be ignored by Keynesians, in whose rhetoric it supplied the example *par excellence* of the irrelevance of money in general, and the impotence of monetary policy in particular.

But undermining Friedman and Schwartz's account of the Depression proved to be hard indeed. They attributed some causative significance for the initial downturn, which more or less coincided with the 1929 stock market crash, to a preceding slowdown in the growth of the monetary base and hence of the money supply. However, their key claim was that a sharp recession turned into a major catastrophe because the Federal Reserve failed to prevent a series of bank failures. The first round of these occurred in 1930, precipitating large increases in reserve and currency deposit ratios, which led to a collapse of money growth. In Friedman and Schwartz's view, this collapse was the proximate cause of falling prices and output. From 1931 to 1933 this "great contraction" fed upon the further bank failures, which a continued absence of lender of last resort action on the part of the Federal Reserve permitted to occur. After 1933, the monetary base continued to grow (as it had since late 1930) but was mainly absorbed into bank reserves; and, according to Friedman and Schwartz, this showed not that the Fed was "pushing on a string," but rather that surviving banks had a well-developed, and easily justified, appetite for free reserves. This hypothesis found support in the fact that, when reserve requirements were increased in 1937 to absorb what the Fed believed to be excessive bank liquidity, the banks responded by restoring their free reserve levels, in the process causing a money growth slowdown that brought on the 1938 contraction.[11]

In short, endogenous, cumulative interaction between the quantity of money and the cycle, which the authorities could have, but did not, offset, rather than some mechanical one-way link between exogenous money and endogenous income, was at the heart of Friedman and Schwartz's story. And indeed, in their original exposition, they were careful *not* to identify the mild monetary slowdown that began in 1928 as the only plausible explanation for the initial onset of the contraction. Thus, though other scholars could, and did, point to the Smoot–Hawley tariff, bank failures in Europe, problems in the U.S. housing market, and so forth, as other important contributing factors, such arguments left the core of the monetarist case untouched. Only Peter Temin (1976) attempted to rebut that core. He pointed out that, after the bank failures of 1930, *real* balances continued to grow, and *nominal* interest rates to fall, and argued that these facts were *prima facie* evidence that monetary contraction was a purely passive response to a downturn whose fundamental cause was real, namely, a downward shift of the consumption function.

There is not space here to survey the debate that Temin provoked. Suffice it to note his arguments failed to convince the majority of his colleagues, who wondered, for example, whether the supply of real balances might not have expanded less than the demand for them between 1929 and 1931, or whether nominal rates of interest were a reliable sole measure of the opportunity cost of holding money during a period of great financial uncertainty and rapidly falling prices. Mayer (1978) showed that Temin's postulated downward shift of the consumption function was very sensitive to his choice of data. And this is not to mention the difficulty involved in attempting to reinstate a Keynesian interpretation of the Depression on the basis of instability of the consumption function, of all relationships! All in all, the criticism their work provoked failed to undermine Friedman and Schwartz's reinstatement of the importance (though not the sole importance) of monetary influences on the Great Depression. Certainly, as Karl Brunner (1981, p. 316) remarked, "The story of a powerless Central Bank acting valiantly but in vain in order to contain the economic storm" was effectively disposed of by the controversies of the 1960s and 1970s. The status of the monetary explanation of the cycle was thus considerably enhanced, even though, as Brunner also noted, these controversies stopped well short of establishing monetary shocks as the sole impulse driving the cycle during the 1930s, let alone at other times.

Nor, by and large, did the econometric studies of the time convincingly establish money's dominance during the Depression. Friedman and

Meiselman's celebrated (1963) Commission on Money and Credit paper, whose central thrust was to compare the explanatory power over the time path of nominal consumer spending of variations in autonomous expenditure on the one hand, and the money supply on the other, and which found that the money supply seemed to perform much better on average, nevertheless attributed an important influence to variations in autonomous expenditure during subperiods dominated by the 1930s.[12] And, as Ando and Modigliani (1965) and DePrano and Mayer (1965) soon showed, the apparent dominance of money in other periods was very sensitive to the way in which autonomous expenditure was defined. It is true that Andersen and Jordan's (1968) methodologically closely related study of the relative effects of money and fiscal variables found little role for the latter, but fiscal policy is not quite the same thing as autonomous expenditure in general, and Andersen and Jordan did not study the 1930s, but only the postwar period.

In short, though the debates of the 1960s and early 1970s did re-establish monetary factors as being far more important than the almost exclusively real business cycle models of the preceding two decades had allowed, a dispassionate reading of their outcome surely supports an eclectic, rather than monocausal, monetary interpretation of the cycle.[13] Interest in the work that seemed to be leading to this conclusion faded, however, before such a result became firmly established, as macroeconomics took up and debated a specific relationship that was to be of central importance to the evolution of cycle theory during the 1970s and 1980s. I refer, of course, to the Phillips curve.

3 The Phillips Curve and Sticky Prices

Friedman and Schwartz (1963*b*) were more precise about the way in which monetary changes would affect the nominal demand for goods and services than about how real income and prices would separately react to demand-side shocks. In this their analysis was completely representative of its time. The Keynesian economics of the postwar period was above all an economics of real income determination, and as we have seen the multiplier–accelerator theory of the cycle that went along with it was a completely real model. Though, in their work of the 1950s, Friedman and his associates were far from the Keynesian mainstream in their attention to price level behavior, this was in contexts in which ouput changes could be ignored. The macroeconomics of the 1950s, that is to say, could deal with real output fluctuations, or inflation, but not the two simultaneously and separately.

A.W. Phillips had encountered just this problem in constructing an analytic cycle model for the study of stabilization policy as an application of control theory. He had "solved" it in 1954 with an equation in which the rate of price inflation varied with the excess demand for output. In 1958, in a paper that was essentially a by-product of the already mentioned research agenda, he showed that in almost a century of United Kingdom data there appeared to have existed a rather stable relationship between the rate of money wage inflation on the one hand and the level of unemployment and its rate of change on the other.[14] This "Phillips curve" provided the prototype for equations that could be inserted in econometric models to allocate fluctuations in nominal income between real output and the price level; and in an apparently natural policy application, it also permitted the effects of stabilization policy on the inflation rate, as well as the level of income and employment, to be discussed. It was quickly absorbed into the mainstream of Keynesian macroeconomics, therefore, but remained an object of considerable suspicion among exponents of a monetary approach to cycle theory who were enamored of neither large econometric models nor stabilization policy.

Analysis of the Phillips curve's theoretical foundations soon uncovered difficulties. Richard Lipsey (1961), elaborating on Phillips' own very sketchy suggestions, argued that the unemployment rate should be interpreted as a proxy variable for the excess demand for labor, and wage inflation's responsiveness to it as nothing more than a manifestation of the general tendency of any price to respond to excess demand. As Edmund Phelps (1967) and Friedman (1968) soon pointed out, however, the relevant price here, according to standard economic theory, was the *real* and not the *money* wage; so that the apparently permanent inflation–unemployment tradeoff promised by the Phillips curve ought to be at best a temporary phenomenon, stemming from a tendency for agents' expectations of inflation to lag behind experience. Though this point was quickly and widely accepted as theoretically correct, the apparent weight of empirical evidence to the contrary led many commentators—Solow (1968) and Tobin (1972) provide examples—to argue, as a practical matter, either that agents did not fully adjust their expectations to experience or that the frictions of a less-than-perfect labor market prevented them from acting upon those expectations. Hence the first impact of the Phelps–Friedman critique of the Phillips curve was to persuade its proponents to distinguish between long- and short-run inflation–unemployment tradeoffs and to accept that the former might be less favorable than the latter. It did not, however, convince them that it was nonexistent.

The catastrophic breakdown of large-scale econometric models during the inflation of the 1970s was almost solely due to the fact that they contained equations implying the existence of a long-run inflation–unemployment tradeoff. That the failure of one equation (or block of equations), only recently developed, should lead, as Lucas and Sargent (1978) were later to claim, to the demise of Keynesian economics is surprising. To begin with, there was more to Keynesian economics than large forecasting models. Moreover, the failure of one equation did not logically require the radical transformation of the structure of macroeconomic analysis that the proponents of new-classical economics set in motion. Indeed, the monetary model of the cycle that they proposed as the alternative to the Keynesian analysis embodied in the large econometric models of the 1970s was from the outset empirically suspect in its own way: That model has output fluctuations occurring as a response to misperceived price levels and hence cannot cope with the fact that output fluctuations lead those in the inflation rate at cyclical turning points. The new-classical revolution was, however, brought about more by the attractive elegance of its theoretical models, not to mention its proponents' persuasive use of language, than by the empirical content of their case.

Lucas (1977) argued that the Phelps–Friedman critique of the Phillips curve had amounted to much more than a suggestion that an extra variable, carrying a particular coefficient, should be added to the equation. Rather, he pointed out, that critique had been based on the contention that the equation should be constrained to reflect equilibrium behavior. In this Lucas was quite correct, and as things subsequently transpired, the collapse of the Phillips tradeoff involved a victory for those who had insisted on the validity of equilibrium theory over those who had relied on empirical evidence to discipline their work.[15] Hence the episode seemed to vindicate one methodological criterion and weaken the status of another. In this context, the word *equilibrium* can be construed only to refer to the behavior of maximizing agents whose plans concern real (not nominal) magnitudes and are executed. Since it is hard to see how economics could have any predictive content if the plans of individuals were not executed and therefore did not produce observable consequences, it is difficult to regret that vindication.

It is, however, a nonsequitur to go on to argue that, because macroeconomics is concerned with the economy as a whole, the same methodological criterion requires that it should concern itself only with situations of *general equilibrium* in which the plans of all agents are rendered compatible with one another by the operation of flexible prices. Nevertheless, that is how new-classical economists did, and continue to, argue; and the history of macroeconomics over the past 15 years bears eloquent witness to the persuasiveness of their nonsequitur and to the attractive tractability of the theoretical models which adherence to it enabled them to build.[16] I have written elsewhere (e.g., Laidler 1990*a*, chap. 4) about this more recent history, and at a recent conference it was dealt with by Olivier Blanchard and Robert King. For purposes of this chapter it is sufficient to point out that the practice of treating the expectations-augmented Phillips curve as an aggregate supply relationship, forced upon new-classical economics by its adoption of Walrasian foundations, led it to develop, not a more refined version of an already existing monetary impulse theory of the cycle, but a radically different theory; it is this radically different theory that has been found empirically wanting in the last decade, rather than the general hypothesis that monetary impulses are important.

It was, and is, possible to construct a model that captures the essential insights of a late 1960s monetarist view of macroeconomic processes, including those concerning the absence of any long-run inflation unemployment tradeoff, but that is also compatible with the basic stylized facts of the cycle as summarized by, say, Kydland and Prescott (1990). This author constructed and estimated the prototype of just such a model in 1973. It consisted of three equations: an income velocity formulation of the quantity theory, an expectations-augmented Phillips curve linking price inflation to real output's deviation from trend, and—dare one still mention it—a first-order error-learning characterization of the formation of inflation expectations. It yielded three key predictions: (1) that the critical exogenous monetary variable on the right-hand side of the reduced form equation for output's deviation from trend was indeed, as Friedman had suggested, the rate of growth of the nominal money supply; (2) that it was inflation's *rate of change* that varied with the deviation, and rate of change of that deviation, of output from trend; and (3) that there would be a damped cyclical response to a monetary shock, with *the rate of inflation* lagging a bit less than one-quarter cycle behind output, so that the *price level* was an inherently *countercyclical* variable.

Now the model of which I am here referring was in no sense an outlier in the literature of its time. It was, in fact, a "bare bones" version of a framework that could easily be extended so as to (1) incorporate the kind of financial stock–flow interaction discussed by Friedman and Schwartz (1963*b*) or Karl Brunner (1961), as well as endogenous fluctuations in nominal interest rates; (2) test for, and confirm, the presence of other-than-monetary shocks as a source of real fluctuations; and (3) cope with balance of payments phenomena in an open economy setting.[17] In short, a small monetarist model of early 1970s vintage proved to be a limiting case of a more eclectic Keynesian model. With rather minor extension, moreover, it was capable of tracking some data as well as, and other data better than, say Barro's (1978) new-classical system. From the point of view of the model's mechanics, there is no mystery about why this proved to be so. First, and crucially different from any monetary new-classical model, it incorporated the idea that in response to a monetary shock, ouput changes preceded those in the inflation rate; second, the inclusion of a geometrically declining weighted average of past values of the inflation rate on the right-hand side of the Phillips curve guaranteed considerable inertia to the predicted behavior of inflation. Since these are properties of the data, the model could not help but fit them.[18]

4 The Lessons of the Debates

Two points about the type of model just described are worth stressing. First, it can accommodate the idea that monetary changes are an important cyclical impulse and can simultaneously predict the key stylized facts about the business cycle that readers of Kydland and Prescott (1990) might think disqualify a monetary explanation from serious consideration. Second, its capacity to do so stems from its assuming price stickiness. This assumption ensures that quantities begin to move before prices and that the inflation rate displays inertia. But, of course, in the 1990s price stickiness is the hallmark of so-called "new-Keynesian economics." Monetarism seemed, two decades ago, to provide a distinct approach to understanding the cycle. Nowadays it looks more like a particular version of the very orthodoxy to which it had at one time been diametrically opposed. This appearance is not just a matter of the vantage point from which we now view the macroeconomics of the 1960s and early 1970s. Friedman's debate with his critics, published in Gordon (1974), showed that most of their differences, though deep and important, were nevertheless more quantitative than qualitative and that further movement toward a synthesis of monetarist and Keynesian views was in fact implicit in the debates described earlier in this chapter.

Those debates seemed to establish that monetary impulses had been far more important in generating economic instability than the Keynesian economics of the 1950s would have had it. They also seemed to establish that a long-run inflation–unemployment tradeoff, which could be treated as defining a policy menu, did not exist. Keynesian economics had to absorb these lessons if it was to continue as an empirically viable and policy-relevant body of doctrine—and it did so. But the story is not of the universal triumph of monetarist ideas. To establish monetary instability as an important source of cyclical impulse and propagation mechanisms does not also establish its general dominance in either role. To begin with, any cycle theory has to address the fact of the relatively large amplitude of variations in investment, and a purely monetary approach seems to have little to say about the matter. Moreover, the debates that I have described stopped far short of establishing the unimportance of nonmonetary cyclical impulses. Anyone still in doubt about the lessons of the historical evidence on this matter in the early 1970s was soon confronted with the effects of OPEC's activities on the economy's behavior. Monetarists had to absorb that lesson, as they did the evidence produced in the 1970s about the sensitivity of the demand for money function to institutional change and its implications for the effectiveness of a legislated money growth rule as a built-in stabilizer.[19]

This is not to say that there would have been nothing to argue about by the mid-1970s had new-classical economics not come upon the scene, but it is to say that the differences between that body of theory and what had gone before it were far more profound than any that still needed settling between monetarists and Keynesians. The new-classical economists did not advance an alternative set of empirical hypotheses formulated within an already existing theoretical framework whose validity could bc judged by applying already accepted criteria. Rather they put forward an alternative theoretical framework whose superiority they defended with recourse to alternative methodological criteria. In their hands, cycle theory became an application of general equilibrium analysis, and the approach was defended with reference, not so much to superior empirical content, as to its conformity with the theoretical principles of equilibrium modeling.

Even so, empirical evidence did play a role, if only a subsidiary one, in the literature of new-classical economics. Thus Lucas and Sargent (1978) made much of the breakdown of the permanent inflation–unemployment tradeoff in their premature obituary of Keynesian economics, arguing, misleadingly, that only a model incorporating rational expectations could cope with the evidence of the 1970s. I have already commented on this and on Kydland and Prescott's more recent efforts to use stylized facts as a way of distinguishing between various approaches to cycle theory. The acid test of new-classical economics' methodological priorities arises, however, with respect to its treatment of money wage and price stickiness. That many money wages and prices are subject to contractual arrangements that render them hard to change is beyond question, as it is that the incorporation of such a fact into any macroeconomic model gives it distinctly Keynesian characteristics. If we give priority to the facts in the selection of models, we should let models that assume price stickiness stand or fall by their predictions. But because we do not by any means fully understand the nature of the underlying maximizing behavior that might lead to money wage and price stickiness, new-classical economists refuse to take seriously the predictions of models that assume it.[20] An important theme to emerge from the history recounted in this chapter is, nevertheless, that it is dangerous to ignore microfoundations. We have seen that models of consumption and investment behavior based on maximizing principles undermined multiplier–accelerator analysis in the 1950s and 1960s, and that the application of simple micro theory produced the expectations-augmented Phillips curve, at a time when a simple permanent tradeoff version of the relationship seemed confirmed by the facts. One can understand the attractiveness of equilibrium modeling in the light of this experience. But, to repeat a point made earlier, Walrasian general equilibrium modeling is a rather special case of that approach.

Only someone who believes that Walrasian general equilibrium theory embodies a set of first principles whose correct application will always guarantee the generation of scientific truth would refuse to entertain the possibility that the postulate of wage and price stickiness might not only generate better predictions but might also, at some time in the future, be discovered to be quite compatible with maximizing behavior after all. To insist on explicit microfoundations as a condition for taking an empirical hypothesis seriously is to indulge in what Karl Brunner, who discussed these matters extensively (for example in Brunner, 1989), used to call the "Cartesian Fallacy," namely, the belief that there exist certain fundamental postulates from which scientific truth can be deduced, and, crucially, that we can know when such postulates have been discovered. In the ongoing debate about business cycles, let us hope that this conference will help to reinstate empirical evidence as a factor more important than *a priori* principles reinforced by the deployment of persuasive language.

Acknowledgments

I am grateful for the research support of the Bradley Foundation. I am also grateful to Andreas Hornstein, Peter Howitt, Michael Parkin, and Steve Williamson for comments on an earlier draft.

Appendix A: A Generic Model of Multiplier–Accelerator Interaction

Where A is real autonomous expenditure, C is real consumption, I is real investment, Y is real income, s is the marginal propensity to save, and v is the desired capital–output ratio, we can write

$$Y = C + I = A + (1 - s)Y_{-1} + v(Y_{-1} - Y_{-2}), \tag{1}$$

so that

$$Y = A + (1 - s + v)Y_{-1} - vY_{-2}. \tag{2}$$

Since steady state income, Y^*, is given by

$$Y^* = \frac{1}{1-s}A, \tag{3}$$

the dynamics of income's deviation from this steady state, $\hat{Y}$, are described by

$$\hat{Y} = (1 - s + v)\hat{Y}_{-1} + v\hat{Y}_{-2}. \tag{4}$$

In general, a difference equation of the form

$$x - \alpha_1 x_{-1} + \alpha_2 x_{-2} = 0$$

is stable if and only if

$$\alpha_1 - \alpha_2 - 1 < 0 \qquad -\alpha_1 - \alpha_2 - 1 < 0 \qquad \text{and} \qquad \alpha_2 < 1$$

and will display cyclical characteristics if and only if

$$\alpha_1^2 - 4\alpha_2 < 0.$$

If $v > 1$ and $s < 1$, such a multiplier–accelerator system may or may not generate cycles, but it will be explosive. This is the system that forms the starting point for Hicks' (1951) cycle model.

Appendix B: A Generic Monetarist Model

When m is the log of the nominal money supply, y the deviation of the log of real income from its steady state value y^*, p the log of the price level, and Δp^e the expected inflation rate, we write the quantity theory equation as

$$\Delta m = b\Delta y + b\Delta y^* + \Delta p, \tag{5}$$

the expectations-augmented Phillips curve as

$$\Delta p = gy_{-1} + \Delta p^e_{-1}, \tag{6}$$

and the error-learning hypothesis as

$$\Delta p^e = d\Delta p + (1 - d)\Delta p^e_{-1}. \tag{7}$$

This model yields, as a reduced form for y,

$$y = \frac{1}{b}(\Delta^2 m - \Delta^2 y^*) + \frac{2b - g}{b} y_{-1} - \frac{b - (1 - d)g}{b} y_{-2}. \tag{8}$$

Application of the conditions for stability and cyclical behavior set out in Appendix A will confirm that it is likely to be cycle prone, but that only if g is "large" relative to b will this model fail to converge on its steady state. The relationship between inflation and the cycle may be written as

$$\Delta^2 p = g\Delta y_{-1} + dg\Delta y_{-2}. \tag{9}$$

With the rate of *acceleration* of prices thus a function of the rate of growth of income's deviation from trend and the lagged value of this variable, the price *level* clearly lags well behind income's deviation from trend, and hence the "cycle."

This model is described in detail, and estimated, in Laidler (1973).

Notes

1. The quotation from Keynes comes from a *New Statesman* article of 1933. I have borrowed it from Elizabeth Johnson (1978, p. 20). The reader's attention is drawn to the fact that I do not here use the phrase "persuasive use of language" as synonymous with the word "rhetoric." As readers of McCloskey (1983) will understand, there is much more to the way in which economists converse with one another than their choice of words. This matter is, however, sometimes important—indeed to someone like myself who clings to the rather old-fashioned stance of attaching primary importance to the persuasive power of empirical evidence, it is occasionally too important!

2. Even "real demand side" models—of the multiplier–accelerator variety, for example—require that the monetary system operate so as to prevent the rate of interest moving to equilibrate savings and investment at full employment if they are to generate cyclical fluctuations.

3. But, the data for the first half of this century do show prices to move procyclically. See Haberler (1956, p. 133), Matthews (1959, p. 3), and indeed Lucas (1977, p. 3) for assertions about this characteristic of the data. It is only in the postwar period that this has ceased to be the case. The postwar reversal of the "loops" around the Phillips curve, discussed in note 15, reflects this change in the stylized facts.

4. Haberler (1937) still provides the best available survey of interwar cycle theory. See Patinkin (1990) for a persuasive defense of *IS-LM* as a valid, though simplifying, account of the central theoretical content of *The General Theory*.

5. The American Economic Association produced two sets of readings in the area of business cycles—Haberler (1944) and Gordon and Klein (1965). A random inspection of old intermediate macroeconomics textbooks confirms that those of Day (1957), Dernberg and McDougall (1960), and Brooman (1962) all contained chapters on the cycle. Matthews (1959) was a widely used supplementary text of the same period. There is no reason to believe that this small sample of what students might have been asked to read three decades ago is unrepresentative, and in each case the cycle theory presented was of the multiplier–accelerator type.

6. Harrod (1936) and Samuelson (1939) should be credited with pioneering the analysis of multiplier–accelerator interaction as a key to cycle theory. Curious readers, whose training has been recent enough to leave them unfamiliar with the general nature of this class of models, are referred to Appendix A, where a simple generic example is briefly described.

7. The pioneering paper was surely that of Adelman and Adelman (1959).

8. The relevant papers of Friedman are reprinted as chapters 9–12 in his 1969 collection, *The Optimum Quantity of Money*. See also R.J. Gordon (1974).

9. Though it is convenient to cite and quote Friedman and Schwartz's account of the transmission mechanism here, the reader should not be misled into believing that their account was in any way unique. Johnson (1962) noted that a variety of essentially similar accounts of the mechanism were emerging in the literature at that time, as much from Keynesians as from quantity theorists (as monetarists were then called). He quoted a lengthy section from Brunner (1961) to illustrate its properties.

10. In particular, Friedman's downplaying of the importance of the interest sensitivity of velocity, most notable in (1959) but also apparent in Friedman and Schwartz (1963*b*), attracted much comment before being finally laid to rest as an issue by Laidler (1966) and Friedman himself (1966). The question of interpreting the timing of data was most notably debated by Tobin and Friedman in their 1970 exchange in the *Quarterly Journal of Economics*.

11. Even so, this 1933–1937 episode still seems to me to be the most difficult one for a monetary explanation of the 1930s to cope with. That surviving banks might want to build up free reserves in the wake of the bank failures of 1930–1933 is not surprising, but that they should do so slowly over a four-year period is much harder to understand. Morrison's (1966) explanation of the phenomenon is cast in terms of backward-looking expectations and would be well worth some new analysis. The reader's attention is drawn to the fact that the emphasis of monetarist analysis of the 1930s is on the behavior of the money supply. Other commentators (e.g., Bernanke, 1983), while focusing on events in the banking system, stress the destruction of the information-processing and decision-coordinating capacity of the financial sector, rather than the mere contraction of the money supply, as an important element in the propagation of the Great Depression.

12. And, as Johnson (1962) noted at the time, a Keynesian could take considerable comfort from the fact that a theory designed to explain fluctuations in income during periods of chronic unemployment seemed capable of doing just that.

13. This is the view of Brunner and Meltzer (1987).

14. Two points are worth making about Phillips' contribution. First, the major finding of his research on stabilization policy, which utilized his engineer's knowledge of control mechanisms, was that feedback rules had to be extremely carefully designed and implemented if they were not to be actively destabilizing; so Phillips himself was very nearly as skeptical as Friedman about the feasibility of "fine-tuning." Second, according to Conrad Blyth (1987), the Phillips curve itself began life as an attempt to meet Sir Dennis Robertson's criticism that Phillips' earliest work concentrated too exclusively on real variables. That the analytical centerpiece of the Keynesian econometric models that were later to be so confidently used to design stabilization policies should have such a pedigree is ironic, to say the least.

15. But it should be noted that Phillips' original empirical results still need to be explained. They show procyclical behavior of the inflation rate, rather than the price level, but the presence of counterclockwise loops around the relationship in earlier years (they are clockwise in postwar data) tends to make inflation lead the cycle, and hence to make the price level itself procyclical, thus reflecting the stylized facts referred to in note 3. Presumably the relatively constant inflation expectations existing in Britain under the gold standard, and

under the Bretton Woods system, go a long way toward explaining the appearance of a stable inflation–unemployment tradeoff before 1914 and during the 1950s. The interwar years never did generate so well-defined a relationship. During the 1960s, and with considerable perceptiveness, G.C. Archibald referred to this phenomenon in conversations as "the econometric consequences of Mr. Churchill." And, of course, the disappearance of the Phillips curve in the 1970s came immediately after the breakdown of the Bretton Woods system.

16. This is not the place to rehearse well-known arguments about the appropriateness of assuming price stickiness in the absence of a widely accepted microeconomic explanation of the phenomenon. The argument that the behavior of prices ought to be explained as the outcome of maximizing behavior is unexceptional but does not suffice to defend new-classical analysis, since, in a competitive model, it is well known that all endogenous agents are price-takers and that such a model cannot explain how prices are set. Since I know of no well-articulated microeconomic explanation of money price flexibility, and since stickiness of many money prices does seem to be a well-documented fact, I agree wholeheartedly with Brunner (1989) on the appropriateness of making the assumption in question.

17. The reader interested in the formal properties of this type of model is referred to Appendix B, where these are briefly described. The most complete extension of this line of research into a macroeconometric model is surely to be found in the publications of Peter Jonson and his associates at the Reserve Bank of Australia (see Jonson, Moses, and Wymer, 1976, and Jonson and Trevor, 1980). These models were differentiated from contemporary Keynesian models by their relatively small size (< 30 behavior equations), their emphasis on the importance of monetary impulses, and their lack of a long-run inflation–unemployment tradeoff. With hindsight, their similarities to Keynesian models, which stem from the assumption that wages and prices adjust slowly to market disequilibrium over real time, are more striking than their differences. It is worth noting that these models are not simply systems of independently estimated equations, but incorporate the cross-equation restrictions implied by the theoretical analysis of stock–flow interaction that lies at the heart of the monetarist analysis of the transmission mechanism. It is also worth noting that they represent a product of the research agenda begun by Phillips (1954) and continued by Rex Bergstrom and Clifford Wymer (1974). Finally, it should be pointed out that small empirical models were not a complete monetarist monopoly. Benjamin Friedman (1977), for example, presents a five-equation model of a very Keynesian type.

18. For a small model of the U.S. economy with these characteristics, and results that are directly comparable (and are compared) to those obtained by Barro (1978), see Laidler and Bentley (1983).

19. The relevant literature as far as the United States is concerned was ably surveyed by Judd and Scadding (1982). My own views on the significance of the evidence on the instability of the demand for money function that emerged in the 1970s have most recently been set out in Laidler (1990*b*).

20. And given that, from the 1880s onward, money wage stickiness was the explanation of cyclical unemployment accepted by those whom we would nowadays classify as "classical" economists—for example, Alfred Marshall and A.C. Pigou among others—and that, in Chapter 19 of *The General Theory*, Keynes made it quite clear that he did not believe that his own explanation of the phenomenon depended on such stickiness, the inappropriateness of the current usage of the adjectives "new-classical" and "new-Keynesian" could not be more total. It is, however, far too late to do anything about it.

References

Adelman, I., and F.L. Adelman. 1959. "The Dynamic Properties of the Klein–Goldberger Model." *Econometrica*. Reprinted in Gordon and Klein (1965).

Andersen, L.C., and J.L. Jordan. 1968. "Monetary and Fiscal Actions: A Test of Their Relative Importance in Economic Stabilization." *Federal Reserve Bank of St. Louis Monthly Review* 50: 11–23.

Ando, A., and F. Modigliani. 1965. "The Relative Stability of Monetary Velocity and the Investment Multiplier." *American Economic Review* 55: 693–728.

Bailey, M.J. 1962. *National Income and the Price Level.* New York, McGraw-Hill.

Barro, R.J. 1978. "Unanticipated Money, Output, and the Price Level in the United States." *Journal of Political Economy* 86: 549–581.

Bergstrom, R. and C.R. Wymer. 1974. "A Model of Disequilibrium Neo-Classical Growth and Its Application to the United Kingdom." LSE International Monetary Economics Research Program (mimeo).

Bernanke, B. 1983. "Non-Monetary Effects of the Financial Crisis in the Propagation of the Great Depression." *American Economic Review* 73: 257–276.

Blyth, C. 1987. "A.W. Phillips." In J. Eatwell, M. Millgate, and P. Newman, eds., *The New Palgrave*. London: Macmillan.

Brooman, F. 1962. *Macroeconomics*. London: George Allen and Unwin.

Brunner, K. 1961. "The Report of the Commission on Money and Credit." *Journal of Political Economy* 69: 605–620.

———. 1981. "Epilogue: Understanding the Great Depression." In K. Brunner, ed., *The Great Depression Revisited.* The Hague: Martinus Nijhoff Publishing.

———. 1989. "The Disarray in Macroeconomics." In F. Capie and G.E. Wood, *Monetary Economics in the 1990s*. London: Macmillan.

Brunner, K., and A.H. Meltzer, eds. 1978. *The Problem of Inflation.* Carnegie Rochester Conference Series, vol. 8. Amsterdam: North-Holland.

———. 1987. "Money and the Economy: Issues in Monetary Analysis." The 1987 Raffaele Mattioli Lectures, Carnegie-Mellon University (mimeo).

Burns, A.F., and W.C. Mitchell. 1946. *Measuring Business Cycles.* New York: NBER.

Cagan, P. 1965. *Determinants and Effects of Changes in the Stock of Money 1870–1960.* New York: Columbia University Press for the NBER.

Culbertson, J.M. 1961. "Friedman on the Lag in Effect of Monetary Policy." *Journal of Political Economy* 68: 617–621.

Day, A.C.L. 1957. *Outline of Monetary Economics*. Oxford: Clarendon Press.

DePrano, M., and T. Mayer. 1965. "Tests of the Relative Importance of Autonomous Expenditure and Money." *American Economic Review* 55: 729–752.

Dernberg, T.F., and D.M. McDougall. 1960. *Macroeconomics.* New York: McGraw-Hill.

Domar, E. 1947. "Expansion and Employment." *American Economic Review* 37: 34–55.

Friedman, B.M. 1977. "The Inefficiency of Short-Run Monetary Targets for Monetary Policy." *Brookings Papers on Economic Activity* 2: 293–346.

Friedman, M. 1957. *A Theory of the Consumption Function*. Princeton, N.J.: Princeton University Press for the NBER.

———. 1958. "The Supply of Money and Changes in Prices and Output." JEC of 85th Congress. Reprinted as chap. 9 of Friedman (1969).

———. 1959. "The Demand for Money: Some Theoretical and Empirical Results." *Journal of Political Economy*. Reprinted as chap. 6 of Friedman (1969).

———. 1961. "The Lag in Effect of Monetary Policy." *Journal of Political Economy*. Reprinted as chap. 11 of Friedman (1969).

———. 1966. "Interest Rates and the Demand for Money." *Journal of Law and Economics*. Reprinted as chap. 7 of Friedman (1969).

———. 1968. "The Role of Monetary Policy." *American Economic Review*. Reprinted as chap. 5 of Friedman (1969).

———. 1969. *The Optimum Quantity of Money and Other Essays*. London: Macmillan.

———. 1970. "Comment on Tobin." *Quarterly Journal of Economics* 84: 318–327.

Friedman, M., and D. Meiselman. 1963. "The Relative Stability of Monetary Velocity and the Investment Multiplier in the United States 1898–1958." In Commission on Money and Credit, *Stabilization Policies*. Englewood Cliffs, N.J.: Prentice-Hall.

Friedman, M., and A.J. Schwartz. 1963*a*. *A Monetary History of the United States 1867–1960*. Princeton, N.J.: Princeton University Press for the NBER.

———. 1963*b*. "Money and Business Cycles." *Review of Economics and Statistics*. Reprinted as chap. 10 of Friedman (1969).

Frisch, R. 1933. "Propagation Problems and Impulse Problems in Dynamic Economics." In *Economic Essays in Honour of Gustav Cassel*. Reprinted in Gordon and Klein (1965).

Gordon, R.A., and L.R. Klein, eds. 1965. *Readings in Business Cycles*. Homewood, Ill.: Richard Irwin, for the AEA.

Gordon, R.J., ed. 1974. *Milton Friedman's Monetary Framework*. Chicago: University of Chicago Press.

Haberler, G. 1937. *Prosperity and Depression*. Revised edition reprinted (1964). Cambridge, Mass.: Harvard University Press.

———. ed. 1944. *Readings in Business Cycle Theory*. Homewood, Ill.: Richard Irwin for the AEA.

———. 1956. "Monetary and Real Factors Affecting Economic Stability: A Critique of Certain Tendencies in Modern Economic Theory." *Banca Nazionale del Lavoro Quarterly Review*. Reprinted in Gordon and Klein (1965).

Harrod, R.F. 1936. *The Trade Cycle*. Reprinted 1965. New York: Augusts Kelley.

———. 1948. *Towards a Dynamic Economics*. London: Macmillan.

Hicks, J.R. 1949. "Mr. Harrod's Dynamic Theory." *Economica*. Reprinted in Gordon and Klein (1965).

———. 1951. *A Contribution to the Theory of the Trade Cycle*. London: Oxford University Press.

Johnson, E.S. 1978. "Keynes as a Literary Craftsman." In E.S. Johnson and H.G. Johnson, *The Shadow of Keynes*. Chicago: University of Chicago Press.

Johnson, H.G. 1962. "Monetary Theory and Policy." *American Economic Review* 52: 335–384.

Jonson, P.D., E.R. Moses, and C.R. Wymer. 1976. "A Minimal Model of the Australian Economy." Reserve Bank of Australia Discussion Paper 7601, Sydney (mimeo).

Jonson, P.D., and R.G. Trevor. 1980. "Monetary Rules: A Preliminary Analysis." Reserve Bank of Australia Discussion Paper 7903 (revised 1980), Sydney (mimeo).

Jorgenson, D.W. 1963. "Capital Theory and Investment Behavior." *American Economic Review* 53, Papers and Proceedings, 247–259.

Judd, J., and J. Scadding. 1982. "The Search for a Stable Money Demand Function: A Survey of the Post–1973 Literature." *Journal of Economic Literature* 20: 993–1023.

Knox, A.D. 1952. "The Acceleration Principle and the Theory of Investment: A Survey." *Economica* NS. 19: 269–297.

Koopmans, T.C. 1947. "Measurement Without Theory." Reprinted in Gordon and Klein (1965).

Kydland, F., and E. Prescott. 1982. "Time to Build and Aggregate Fluctuations." *Econometrica* 50: 1345–1370.

———. 1990. "Business Cycles: Real Facts and a Monetary Myth." *Federal Reserve Bank of Minneapolis Quarterly Review* (Spring): 3–18.

Laidler, D. 1966. "The Rate of Interest and the Demand for Money: Some Empirical Evidence." *Journal of Political Economy* 74: 545–555.

———. 1973. "The Influence of Money on Real Income and Inflation: A Simple Model with Some Empirical Tests for the United States 1953–72." *Manchester School* 41: 367–395.

———. 1990*a*. *Taking Money Seriously*. Cambridge, MA: MIT Press.

———. 1990*b*. "Understanding Velocity: New Approaches and Their Policy Relevance—Introduction." *Journal of Policy Modeling* 12: 141–164.

Laidler, D., and B. Bentley. 1983. "A Small Macro-Model of The Post-War United States." *Manchester School* 51: 317–340.

Lipsey, R.G. 1961. "The Relationship Between Unemployment and the Rate of Change of Money Wage Rates in the United Kingdom 1862–1957." *Economica* NS. 27: 115–138.

Lucas, R.E., Jr. 1977. "Understanding Business Cycles." In K. Brunner and A.H. Meltzer, eds., *Stabilization of the Domestic and International Economy*. Carnegie Rochester Conference Series, vol. 5. Amsterdam: North-Holland.

Lucas, R.E. Jr., and T.J. Sargent. 1978. "After Keynesian Economics." In *After the Phillips Curve: Persistence of High Inflation and High Unemployment*. Boston: Federal Reserve Bank of Boston.

Matthews, R.C.O. 1959. *The Business Cycle*. Chicago: University of Chicago Press.

Mayer, T. 1978. "Consumption in the Great Depression." *Journal of Political Economy* 86: 139–146.

McCloskey, D. 1983. "The Rhetoric of Economics." *Journal of Economic Literature* 21: 481–517.

Meade, J.E. 1961. *A Neoclassical Theory of Economic Growth*. London: Allen and Unwin.

Modigliani, F., and R. Brumberg. 1954. "Utility Analysis and the Consumption Function: An Interpretation of the Cross-Section Data." In K. Kurihara. ed., *Post Keynesian Economics*. New Brunswick, N.J: Rutgers University Press.

Morrison, G. 1966. *Liquidity Preferences of Commercial Banks*. Chicago: University of Chicago Press.

Patinkin, D. 1990. "In Defense of IS-LM." *Banca Nazionale del Lavoro Quarterly Review* 172: 119–134.

Phelps, E.S. 1967. "Phillips Curves, Expectations of Inflation, and Optimal Unemployment over Time." *Economica* NS 34: 254–281.

Phillips, A.W. 1954. "Stabilization in a Closed Economy." *Economic Journal* 64 (June): 290–323.

———. 1958. "The Relation Between Unemployment and the Rate of Change of Money Wages Rates in the United Kingdom." *Economica* NS 25: 283–299.

Plosser, C. 1991. "Money and Business Cycles: A Real Business Cycle Interpretation." In M. Belongia, ed., *Monetary Policy on the 75th Anniversary of the Federal Reserve System*. Boston: Kluwer Academic Publishers.

Samuelson, P.A. 1939. "Interactions Between the Multiplier Analysis and the Principle of Acceleration." *Review of Economics and Statistics* 21: 75–78.

Solow, R.M. 1956. "A Contribution to the Theory of Economic Growth." *Quarterly Journal of Economics* 70: 65–94.

———. 1968. "Recent Controversies in the Theory of Inflation: An Eclectic View." In S.W. Rousseas, ed., *Proceedings of a Symposium on Inflation, Its Causes, Consequences and Control*. Wilton, Conn.: Calvin K. Kazanjian Economics Foundation.

Swan, T.W. 1956. "Economic Growth and Capital Accumulation." *Economic Record* 32: 334–361.

Temin, P. 1976. *Did Monetary Forces Cause the Great Depression*? New York: Norton.

Tobin, J. 1970. "Money and Income: Post Hoc Ergo Propter Hoc?" *Quarterly Journal of Economics* 84: 301–317; "Rejoinder," 328–329.

———. 1972. "Inflation and Unemployment." *American Economic Review* 62: 1–18.

Commentary

by Ben S. Bernanke

David Laidler's chapter is a very informative and broad-minded discussion of the traditional Keynesian–monetarist debate—so broad-minded in fact as to make one wonder how, with participants like Laidler, the debate could have been as rancorous as it was. Along the way, Laidler also offers some views on the more recent debate, the controversy between the Keynesian–monetarist synthesis and the so-called real business cycle (RBC) school.

In my commentary I will do two things: First, I will list what I believe to be the principal contributions of monetarism, with a few words about recent developments. Unlike the author, I was not a participant in the Keynesian–monetarist debate as it happened, so perhaps the differences in our perceptions will be sociologically if not economically illuminating. Second, I would like to say a bit about the theme suggested by the chapter's title, namely, the parallels and differences between the monetarist and RBC assaults on the Keynesian paradigm.

In retrospect, I believe monetarism made three major contributions. The first was to establish the empirical importance of money in cyclical fluctuations (Laidler and I agree here). Friedman and Schwartz's *Monetary History* (1963), the first comprehensive documentation of the role of money in the business cycle, is one of the most persuasive books ever written on economics. The findings of the "narrative approach" used by Friedman and Schwartz (as described and updated by Romer and Romer, 1989), in conjunction with postwar episodes such as the Volcker and Thatcher disinflations, are the main reason that purely nonmonetary models of the business cycle remain today a minority taste.

During the last two decades, considerable research has confirmed the empirical importance of money in economic fluctuations, real business cycles notwithstanding. For example, Friedman and Schwartz's monetarist interpretation of the Great Depression has been substantially supported by a developing consensus among economic historians. According to this new consensus, the Depression was caused by the gross mismanagement of the international gold standard, which in turn led to falling money supplies in the gold standard countries (see, for example, Eichengreen and Sachs, 1985; Hamilton, 1987; Temin, 1989; and Bernanke and James, 1991). Much recent research has also found evidence for the role of money in postwar cycles. For example, attempts to measure the effects of monetary policy and its channels of transmission have tended to find that contractionary policy played a role in nearly every recession of the last 30 years (Romer and Romer, 1989; Bernanke and Blinder, forthcoming).[1]

The second central contribution of monetarism that I would point to is the idea that in the long run the unemployment rate equals the natural rate. Laidler does not emphasize this point; however, the natural rate idea was clearly stated by Friedman (for example, in his Presidential Address and Nobel lecture), and it underlies some of his policy recommendations (such as the constant-growth-rate rule for money).

Currently, the notion of a natural rate is an integral part of the macroeconomic orthodoxy, and a vertical long-run Phillips curve is implied by all the leading theories of monetary nonneutrality. It is interesting that, empirically, the natural rate hypothesis may not be on such firm ground, a point that Laidler makes. For example, at least some people interpret the persistence of the Great Depression and the "hysteresis" in European unemployment as evidence against the natural rate view. More narrowly, empirical studies such as that of Romer and Romer (1989) find that the real effects of a monetary shock decay extremely slowly. This issue awaits further research.

The third contribution of monetarism, also not much emphasized by Laidler, was to make the case for nonactivist policy and in particular the use of rules (such as the famous "*k* percent rule" for money growth). The nonactivist conclusion follows from the combination of the natural rate theory, monetarists' empirical findings about long and variable outside lags, and the plausible belief that policy makers may not always have incentives to act in the interest of the society as a whole. The advocacy of rules by monetarists over the years has been an important check on excessive optimism about what stabilization policy could realistically accomplish.

More recent research has found a powerful new theoretical rationale for rules, namely, that the use of rules can help policy makers achieve credibility and avoid the problems of dynamic inconsistency. Nevertheless, in practice, policy making these days seems pretty activist (on the day I write this, the Fed has just lowered the discount rate in response to cyclical conditions). Why does nonactivism seem to be losing out in policy circles? The problem is that we are no longer confident that we can design a rule that can deliver at least reasonable macroeconomic performance almost all of the time. Without such confidence, policy makers cannot commit credibly to a rule. In particular, money growth rules are perceived as having failed to be robust in situations where there is significant financial innovation or other instability in money demand.

Having reviewed the very substantial contributions of monetarism, I turn now to a discussion of the current "cycle" in macroeconomics—the competition between the Keynesian–monetarist synthesis and the RBC approach. In his chapter, Laidler vacillates to some degree both in his assessment of RBC contributions and in his explanation of why this approach has had significant success at winning adherents among researchers. In the end, I suspect that the following three statements, which describe my own views, are not too far from what Laidler is suggesting in his chapter:

1. The principal criteria that determine whether a new approach is accepted in any scientific field are demonstrated empirical success, theoretical or methodological advantages, and persuasive rhetoric.
2. In varying degrees, the monetarist approach of the 1950s and 1960s met all three of these criteria and thus became part of the mainstream synthesis.
3. The real business cycle approach has some clear methodological attractions and some effective rhetoric to commend it. What is missing at this point—and this is the reason that Laidler is less than enthusiastic—is a demonstration that the RBC models produce better empirical fits.

Ray Fair's chapter goes into more detail about the empirical shortcomings of the RBC approach. Here I would like to focus on the question of methodology. What exactly is distinctive and appealing about the RBC methodology, enough so to bring the approach a considerable following even in the absence of convincing empirical successes?

Let me start by listing some features of RBC models that are often pointed to but are *not*, in my view, the defining aspects of those models. First, although much has been made of the productivity or supply shock aspect of early RBC models, the focus on supply shocks is not essential to that approach. Witness, for example, the recent work on fiscal and monetary shocks in an RBC context. Nor is the emphasis on the representative agent, the attempt to base behavior on rigorous microfoundations, or even the assumption of instantaneous market-clearing essential. It is not difficult to find recent examples of RBC-style research missing each of these characteristics.

Rather, what is distinctive and attractive about the RBC methodology is its emphasis on *general equilibrium modeling* as the right way to do macroeconomics. The strict adherence to general equilibrium modeling has a number of advantages. Greatest among these is logical coherence—the general equilibrium approach helps us see how the various aspects of the economy fit together. For example, in his chapter Ben Friedman correctly points out the difficulty of isolating "pure" demand or supply shocks to the macroeconomy. Rather than being an argument against the RBC approach, however, Friedman's observation is an argument in favor of it: It is precisely a general equilibrium approach that is needed to work out both the demand and supply implications of, for example, a rise in the price of imported oil.

In principle, the general equilibrium approach also has important empirical advantages. At a minimum, the general equilibrium approach eliminates the spectacle of independent research teams working on the different equations of the macro model, each with its own set of mutually inconsistent identifying assumptions. More positively, the full-information estimation of a general equilibrium model increases our ability to identify parameters or test specifications, since each paramenter value or specification choice has implications for the behavior of the entire model, not just its "own" equation.

Given these advantages, why hasn't the RBC approach produced more solid empirical results? The main problem, it seems to me, is the computational complexity associated with solving general equilibrium models that embody even modest degrees of realism. At this point the cost and technical difficulty of working with these models are too great for them to be the workhorses of quantitative macroeconomic analysis that their proponents would like them to be. This may change in the future, of course, as we learn more about how to work with these models and as computing costs continue to decline.

This brief discussion helps clarify, I hope, the difference between the monetarist and RBC attacks on the Keynesian paradigm—the old cycle and the new cycle. While the monetarist approach involved a methodological component, its main contributions—the empirical relevance of money to the business cycle, the natural rate hypothesis, and the case for nonactivism—are straightforward propositions about how the world works. In contrast, the RBC innovation is to introduce an appealing but—at this point—not fully developed methodology for systematically studying macroeconomic questions. This methodology has not delivered very much so far, it is true; but would we rule out further investigation of superconductivity (for example) because of its limited practical value thus far? I think a fair evaluation of the RBC approach will have to wait a few more years. In the meantime, the practical knowledge delivered by the Keynesian–monetarist synthesis will continue to be of great value in practical debates about the economy and economic policy.

Note

1. However, these authors do not necessarily equate tight monetary policy with slow money growth *per se*. Romer and Romer use the minutes of FOMC meetings to try to measure policy intentions, while Bernanke and Blinder use interest rate indicators of monetary policy.

References

Bernanke, Ben, and Alan Blinder. Forthcoming. "The Federal Funds Rate and the Channels of Monetary Transmission." *American Economic Review*.

Bernanke, Ben, and Harold James. 1991. "The Gold Standard, Deflation, and Financial Crisis in the Great Depression: An International Comparison." In R. Glenn Hubbard, ed., *Financial Markets and Financial Crises*. Chicago: University of Chicago Press for NBER.

Eichengreen, Barry, and Jeffrey Sachs. 1985. "Exchange Rates and Economic Recovery in the 1930s." *Journal of Economic History* 45: 925–946.

Friedman, Milton, and Anna J. Schwartz. 1963. *A Monetary History of the United States, 1867–1960*. Princeton, N.J.: Princeton University Press for NBER.

Hamilton, James. 1987. "Monetary Factors in the Great Depression." *Journal of Monetary Economics* 19: 145–169.

Romer, C. and Romer, D. 1989. "Does Monetary Policy Matter? A New Test in the Spirit of Friedman and Schwartz." *NBER Macroeconomics Annual 1989*. Cambridge, MA: MIT Press, pp. 121–170.

Temin, Peter. 1989. *Lessons from the Great Depression*. Cambridge, MA: MIT Press.

SESSION II

3 FOR A RETURN TO PRAGMATISM

Olivier Jean Blanchard

For the last 20 years, mainstream macroeconomics has been facing a strong challenge. For a while, it looked as though it would not survive, as though it would be reconstructed along drastically new lines. As the challenge is now clearly fading, it is a good time to assess what has been done and where to go from here. This is what this chapter does. The message is not one of self-congratulation. There has been progress but also much time wasted. Put simply, to capitalize on what we have done, we need to return to pragmatism.

1 Macroeconomics, Circa 1970

Behind the heated exchanges between Keynesians and monetarists, there was, by 1970, a largely common view both of the structure of the economy and of the sources and nature of fluctuations: Shocks were seen to come mostly from shifts in aggregate demand, from either *IS* or *LM* shifts. The adjustment process, which required the adjustment of nominal prices and wages, was slow and unreliable, with both stabilizing and destabilizing mechanisms at work. Without policy, the effects of shocks were prolonged.

Policy could in principle reduce their effects and their duration. But given the realities of the political process, and the lags in the transmission process, whether fiscal and monetary policies were likely to actually improve things was very much a matter of debate.

This common view of structure and basic mechanisms allowed for division of labor, with work on the parts proceeding in parallel with work on an integrated structure. Work on the pieces—consumption, investment, and so on—was proceeding through the simultaneous development and interaction of theoretical models, construction of the appropriate aggregates, and estimation of aggregate relations. Those making the theoretical breakthroughs—Modigliani, Friedman, Jorgenson and Hall—were often those making empirical progress as well. But the empirical specifications were inspired from, rather than dictated by, theoretical work. The belief was that aggregation problems were such that individual microoptimizing relations should serve as a guide, not as a corset to the estimation of aggregate relations.

Work on an integrated structure was proceeding in parallel. Small analytical models, with an *IS-LM* backbone, but paying attention to a particular aspect of general equilibrium, were used to identify channels and strengthen the intuition. The strength of the best ones, those built by the likes of Tobin and Mundell, came from the smart shortcuts they used to deliver a high ratio of relevant insights to machinery. At the same time, larger empirical models such as the MPS provided, by integrating the different estimated components, a much richer dynamic structure. They gave a sense of the time dimension of the relevant dynamics, something small analytical structures could not do. When simulated, they would often reveal unexpected dynamics; if those dynamics appeared implausible, research would identify their source and possibly modify the models. The models could be used to study medium-run issues, which were hard to handle analytically. Most importantly, they provided a common practical and mental structure in which the implications of new contributions could be assessed, alternative formalizations compared, and so on.

Not everything was perfect. There were two main problems. The first would trigger the crisis and the new-classical challenge. The second would become obvious only in retrospect.

While optimization was heavily used to think about the behavior of consumers and firms, from consumption to investment to portfolio decisions, this reliance on optimization did not carry over to the explanation of price and wage determination. This was not based on the belief that markets could be thought of as perfectly competitive, so that there was no need to think about who was setting prices and how. Indeed, a central aspect of the adjustment to shocks was the small and slow adjustment of nominal prices and wages. And the belief was that goods markets were largely oligopolistic, that complex bargaining was taking place in the labor market, and that credit rationing was a pervasive feature of credit markets. Nevertheless, descriptions of price and wage evolutions were mostly data determined, and theories were used rather casually to justify the presence of a variable in an equation. For example, imperfect competition was used to justify markup over standard cost in the "price equation." Labor markets were in effect treated as a black box, with Phillips curve relations providing an empirical, atheoretical "wage equation."

The second problem was that the basic model, and U.S. macroeconomic thinking in general, was very much that of a closed economy. While perhaps a decent approximation for the U.S. economy at that time, this was already a serious problem in thinking about fluctuations in other countries. More importantly, these models were very much "one-sector," "one-country" models, leaving U.S. macroeconomists with little training in thinking about "two-sector/two-country models" and thus about such issues as changes in the prices of imported raw materials, changes in competitiveness, and the like, issues that were to dominate the macroeconomic scene for the following 20 years.

2 1970–1990: Back to Basics

In 1970 the main claim to success of macroeconomics was success itself, the ability to explain events and help policy through progressively more sophisticated conceptual and empirical models. But in the early 1970s macroeconomics, finding itself confronted with issues it had not thought about, from supply shocks to stagflation, was having a tough empricial time. The challenge posed by the new-classical attack, and their argument that empirical failure stemmed directly from theoretical flaws, was thus a tough one to counter. The challenge was met badly at first. Initial fights were about the appropriateness of the assumption of rational expectations, as the assumption seemed so damaging to mainstream macroeconomics. But, by the late 1970s, regrouping had occurred, and progress happened in two phases:

2.1 *Integrating Supply Shocks and Rational Expectations*

The first phase, in the late 1970s and early 1980s, was based on the realization that supply shocks and rational expectations could be fruitfully integrated in mainstream macroeconomics. The development of a richer supply side and the analysis of the effects of changes in the price of oil were major research projects of the late 1970s. And by the early 1980s, books such as those by Bruno and Sachs showed how it could be done. How one could reconcile rational expectations and slow adjustment of prices and wages to changes in nominal demand was shown in contributions by Fischer and Taylor. With the techniques required to solve models under rational expectations now available, small and large models were expanded to allow for a richer role of expectations in consumption, investment, and portfolio choices, to study the implications of forward-looking prices in asset markets and slowly adjusting prices and wages in other markets. And empirical models with rational expectations were quickly developed and used by Fair, Taylor, and others to forecast as well as to study policy choices and implications.

2.2 Looking at the Structure of Markets

These developments were important. But they were the easy part. The hard part was to understand the structure of markets, to understand how prices and wages were set. This is where most of the work in U.S. mainstream macroeconomics has taken place for the last ten years. Much progress has been made.

We have shown how small individual delays in changing prices or wages can be individually rational yet lead to substantial aggregate price inertia and lasting effects of demand on output. In the process, we have learned about the trickiness of aggregation issues, about how, for example, individual price inertia can disappear or instead be amplified in the process of aggregation from individual prices to the price level. We have learned about the effects of inflation on the distribution and the information content of prices and clarified the allocation costs of inflation. I feel that this part of the research agenda has largely been fulfilled and that decreasing returns are setting in. But there is no longer any doubt that slow adjustment of the price level could be given and has been given solid foundations.

We have explored alternative theories of wage setting, with the primary purpose of explaining how fluctuations in labor demand lead to fluctuations in unemployment rather than in wages. We have explored various structures of individual and collective bargaining, asking what role the unemployed play in the process and how they affect the outcome. Following up on work that had started with the Phelps volume, we have explored models of "efficiency wages," models in which firms use wages to elicit effort, motivate workers, or recruit better workers. All these models can explain the presence of unemployed workers who would rather be working at the prevailing wage. I do not believe that they yet provide very convincing reasons why fluctuations in labor demand translate mostly in employment variations rather than in wages. I return to this later.

We have explored alternative theories of imperfect competition and price setting in the goods markets, with the aim of explaining why firms are willing to satisfy changes in demand at roughly constant markups over wages. We have examined the most natural explanation, that marginal cost is flat, and concluded it probably is not. Following again lines first drawn in the Phelps volume, we have explored the idea that firms concerned about customers may decide not to increase their prices in response to an increase in demand. Using developments from industrial organization and game theory, we have examined whether oligopolists are also likely to smooth prices relative to marginal cost. On these issues, I believe, we still have a long way to go; I also return to this later.

We have explored the role of asymmetric information, moral hazard, and adverse selection in credit markets, with the purpose of understanding the interactions among money, credit, and activity. We have looked at the role of banks and made progress in thinking about credit rationing. We have studied the role of internal finance and thus the role of current cash flow in investment decisions. In other financial markets, Shiller nearly single-handedly has forced us to think about deviations from arbitrage and the efficient market hypothesis. This has led to work on how interactions of speculators and noise traders in asset markets can generate large deviations from fundamentals, which can in turn feed back on consumption and investment decisions.

2.3 Why All Is Not Well

The preceding description of progress sounds impressive, and to a large extent it is. But all is not well. From closer, these developments look more scattershot, a point made recently by Barro in his critique of "new-Keynesian" macroeconomics. An analogy here may be to a team of engineers asked to build a new car, spending their time designing many new state-of-the-art catalytic converters, disk brake systems, and so on, but never bothering to check which one works best and whether and how the car will run. In labor markets, for example, a bewildering array of theories, efficiency wages, and insider-outsiders search, coexist side by side, with few systematic attempts to relate them or even to explore whether they can explain the large set of cyclical facts that characterize labor markets. The point goes beyond labor markets. We have developed a large collection of theories or, more often, sketches of theories; we have not explored whether and how they add up to a macro theory. This failure can be traced to two causes. The first has been our "back to basics" mode. The second has been our too frequent adoption of the wrong methodology.

Going "back to basics" meant going away from complex issues and returning to the study of the basic elements of our models. It also meant keeping an open mind and exploring whatever new directions the models we were developing to shore up foundations would lead us. Thus confrontation with broad sets of facts and integration were clearly not at the top of the list of priorities. What was a healthy intellectual attitude at the beginning has now become a disease. And part of the reason we never proceeded to the next step—namely, systematic empirical exploration and integration—is that along the way we got stuck with the wrong methodology.

While we were rejecting the new-classical view of the world, we have too often adopted one of its methodological ukases, namely, the quasi-religious insistence on micro foundations and the derivation of results from "tastes and technology." (This point echoes a theme developed by Larry Summers a few years back, in which he denounced the dangers of "scientific illusion" in macroeconomics.) In doing so, we have constructed too many monsters, too many heavy models with few interesting results. But, worse than that, those rules have *de facto* prevented both systematic empirical exploration and integration. Exploring how a theory of the labor market can explain not the time series behavior of one or two specific time series but rather the broad set of facts about the cyclical behavior of the structure of wages, the composition of unemployment, and so on, just cannot be done when one plays by such rules: The taste and technology machine that would be required would be monstrous, if it could be built at all. Exploring how various theories of labor, goods, and asset markets combine into a macro theory also requires shortcuts, the ability to capture the essence and ignore the details of the various theories. Deciding what is of the essence is neither easy nor uncontroversial, but this is precisely what shortcuts are about. Absent the willingness to take them, systematic empirical explorations and integration have simply not happened.

What we have seen instead of smart new Tobin–Mundell-like machines has been an explosion of "fully articulated" one-explanation-models of "the business cycle." The premium has too often been on intellectual excitement *per se*, on *epater les bourgeois* rather than on relating a model to the facts and to the existing body of knowledge. Think of the typical

NBER Economic Fluctuations conference, circa 1990, in which six papers, all starting from scratch, would present six unrelated explanations of the business cycle. Excesses have been made worse by the nature of what we were exploring: Imperfect competition, increasing returns, externalities, can all easily lead to multiple equilibria, limit cycles, and so on. It is all the more crucial to confront the assumptions and implications of those models with the data. Think of the many models of multiple equilibria that depend crucially on a testable, but untested, nonlinearity in the data.

Lack of systematic exploration and of integration has not been the only cost. Another has been an increasing separation between research and actual macroeconomic developments and policy issues. By being in the "back to basics" mode, the field has developed mostly according to its own internal logic, and we have shunned external stimulus too much. Too many of us have a knowledge of the economy reduced to a number of correlations and statistical regularities. And, unfortunately, one of the aspects that we have borrowed from the pre-1970 mode of thinking has been a nearly complete ignorance of the open economy, sharply reducing our field of vision.

For all these reasons—ignorance of the world and of the policy issues, reluctance or inability to handle messy issues—we have missed on many if not most of the important macro policy events, debates, and decisions of the past decade. Events elsewhere in the world, or events with a clear open economy aspect, the hyperinflations of Latin America, European integration—what labor economists would call "natural experiments" and examine eagerly—have been left to international macroeconomists, who were not embarrassed at the idea of using variations of Mundell–Fleming, Cagan, and the like. They have not done badly, but it is clearly a suicidal strategy for U.S. macroeconomists to follow. Complex happenings, such as the determinants of worldwide interest rates, prolonged unemployment in Western Europe, the macroeconomics of transition in Eastern Europe, which require pragmatic analysis, have also been left largely untouched by U.S. macroeconomists. (Or, more precisely, in the case of Eastern Europe, those macroeconomists who have been most involved are among those who questioned the evolution of macro research in the 1980s and have followed a more applied, policy-oriented, research agenda.) And even with respect to the worldwide shift in macroeconomic policy away from activism and toward simple rules, an evolution to which we would have had a lot to contribute, our contributions have often been of little direct use. Our debates about extreme forms of Ricardian equivalence, for example, have provided little intellectual help to governments trying to chart a path of debt and deficits or thinking about the best path for fiscal consolidation.

3 Where We Should Go from Here

Much of what I believe we should do is obvious from the preceding discussion. The main order of business is, I believe, to identify both what we have and have not explained and to see what macro theory has emerged from our research. And to do so, we must adopt a more flexible, more pragmatic appoach to research.

Let me sketch my preferred path, starting with my view of fluctuations and moving on to a number of specific research topics.

1. We should get rid of another new-classical heritage, the focus on "business cycles." "Business cycles" is too reductionist a view of what short- and medium-term macroeconomics should be about. Most of the time, economies are indeed subject to regular fluctuations. Understanding those, and thinking about the role of policy in that context, is obviously desirable. But there are too many other "irregular" fluctuations, from which we can learn much and for which the issue of whether and how policy can help is often of crucial political and social importance. The list is a long one, from those without an obvious trigger, such as the Great Depression, the long period of high unemployment in Europe, and the inability of Latin American countries to stabilize, to those with clear triggers, such as the integration of Germany and the stabilization and restructuring process in Eastern Europe. Focusing on "business cycles" has led too many of us to think of those as freak events and to leave them aside. We should go back to using "fluctuations": Words do matter.

2. The view of fluctuations pre-1975 was one of dominant demand shocks and weak stabilizing mechanisms. This view is still fundamentally right. The deep U.K. and U.S. recessions of the early 1980s are testimony to the real effects of monetary contraction. But the nature of the shocks has changed and is likely to keep changing in the future. And so have changed and will change the relevant stabilizing mechanisms.

The traditional view emphasized the importance of shifts in domestic demand, such as shifts in the propensity to save coming from changes in consumer confidence. Of increasing importance, however, are shifts in the demand for domestic goods. As countries become more open and integrated, they also become more specialized, and there is an increasing discrepancy between the basket of goods they produce and the basket they consume. The relative importance of the two types of shocks obviously varies from country to country, depending on their degree of specialization. U.S. states, European countries, and the United States nicely cover the range. U.S. states produce and consume very different baskets of goods. In the medium run, the evolution of their employment is dominated by the relative demand for the particular basket of goods they produce. European countries are, for the moment, much less specialized than U.S. regions, but Europe 1992 is likely to lead to higher specialization. The United States as an economy is still much less specialized, so that shocks to domestic demand still dominate. But even the United States is becoming increasingly specialized. Like most OECD countries, it is specializing in products using skilled labor while consuming products which we both skilled and unskilled labor.

The natures of these two shocks are quite different. While consumer confidence, for example, can swiftly reverse direction, consumers who shift their demand from one product to another are unlikely to make a quick turnaround. And the adjustment mechanisms are also quite different. With respect to shifts in aggregate demand, the basic stabilizing mechanism involves the effects of changes in employment on nominal prices and wages and in turn on real money balances. Of central importance in the process are "nominal rigidities," to which we have devoted so much work. But for employment to return to normal in the face of shifts in relative demand, relative prices, and thus real consumption wages must adjust, or over a longer horizon, factors must move, or the basket of goods produced must change. "Real rigidities," in particular the speed and strength of the effect of unemployment on real wages, are central to that process; even absent nominal rigidities, changes in relative demand can generate sustained fluctuations in unemployment. And, indeed, in a number of European countries, nominal rigidities appear to play only a small role in generating fluctuations in unemployment. In a rather ironic twist, what we are observing are increasingly "real business cycles," or, following my semantic edict, "real fluctuations."

3. One aspect of those fluctuations is the set of interactions among recessions, technological change, and unemployment. I am struck at how these issues keep coming up and how primitive our thinking about them is. Do recessions trigger or hinder technological progress and the introduction of new products? Do they leave permanent scars on the labor force? Or do they instead lead to cleansing, to the elimination of weak firms, to the elimination of fat in others? From the work on the apparent disenfranchising of the long-term unemployed in Europe to the work on the cyclical behavior of job creation and destruction in the United States, we have tantalizing hints of the presence of both sets of effects. Will the politics of austerity followed by many governments in Western Europe make or break their economies, will they lead to rationalization and improved competitiveness, or will they lead instead to inefficient bankruptcies and prolonged unemployment? Closely related issues are also at the center of discussions in

Eastern Europe. How much unemployment will the transition to market economies involve, and how much unemployment should those countries accept? It is clear that, on these issues, help will come from the resurgence of growth theory, from the work on trade and growth, from the models that formalize the introduction of new products, the process of creation and destruction. They are too sketchy yet to be of direct use, but they will eventually help.

4. Within that general framework, we should go back to our work on labor, goods, and credit markets; take stock of what we have and have not explained; and see how the pieces may fit. Having not worked on credit markets, I shall limit myself here to labor and goods markets. In so doing, I shall develop themes I touched on earlier.

First, in *labor markets*, we should go beyond sketches. We have a large number of good sketches, all of them probably relevant, and all with the basic implication that the wage exceeds the marginal utility of not working and that the wedge depends on the state of the labor market. But we have not explored seriously whether those theories can explain the observed dynamic relation between wages and unemployment, in unusual times as in Europe in the 1980s, but even in more normal times as in the United States during the same decade. As a result, our empirical specifications have remained embryonic. We also have not explored the theories in sufficient detail to explore their more micro implications, for the distribution of unemployment, the dynamics of unemployment duration, the cyclical movement of relative wages, and the like. On those issues, there is a large body of work by labor economists on both sides of the Atlantic that is highly relevant and has largely gone unexploited by U.S. macroeconomists. The returns to making contact with those findings are high.

In *goods markets*, the problem is not one of excess of good theories. More than 20 years after the Nordhaus survey and its conclusion that we did not have a clue about pricing behavior, we are still not very far from ground zero, theoretically and empirically. The basic fact to be explained there is why firms, which appear to face upward-sloping marginal cost, reduce their markup as demand expands. The two main fully articulated theories we have—customer markets and supergames between oligopolists—have a strong air of implausibility as general explanations of price behavior. And the price setting behavior of firms during regular fluctuations is not the only thing we do not understand. There has been a very large increase in profit shares in many OECD countries since the mid-1980s. We have few clues as to why. Goods markets may be the exception to my earlier proposition that what we do not need are new theories. Alternative theories, more directly aimed at explaining cross-sectional differences and similarities in behavior among types of firms, across sectors, and across countries, are very much needed here.

5. I have emphasized work on the functioning of markets because this is where we must capitalize on the work of the past decade. But the pieces of the old agenda—consumption, investment, the transmission mechanisms of monetary policy, and fiscal policy—are also ready for a thorough going over. An encyclopedic review would be boring. Let me pick a few topics I believe to have high social and private returns. Some are primarily empirical, requiring either panel or aggregate data. Others are primarily synthetic, requiring the development of simple analytical machines, a new generation of Mundell–Tobin models.

We have worked hard on consumption. But we still have a very poor idea of how much foresight people use in making consumption/saving decisions. Separating decisions about retirement income from others, taking into account the increasing importance of pension plans in allowing people to in effect delegate their retirement saving decisions, may be a productive way to go. On investment, we have shown that aggregate time series for investment do not satisfy the tight constraints imposed by any of our standard theories, but, in the end, the rejections have not been very informative. Despite useful work using panel data, we still do not know how much of the strong relation between aggregate profit and investment comes from profit as an internal source of funds rather than as a signal of future profitability. We also suspect that some of the variations in investment spending come from changes in uncertainty and the changing option value of waiting to invest. But we have little idea of the importance of those effects. Our belief that user costs affect investment is still very much based on faith rather than on hard evidence. All these issues should be high priority items. Recent theoretical work on irreversibility and aggregation may prove of much value here.

The transmission mechanism of monetary policy, as summarized by Modigliani, had many parts. We have worked on many of those, from the behavior of financial intermediaries, to the role of internal finance and bank credit, to the behavior of the term structure of interest rates. It is time to see how the parts fit. Many of the pieces we have worked on, from price setting to the behavior of financial intermediaries, suggest asymmetric effects of monetary expansions and recessions. This is a topic just ripe for new research. Finally, while we have become much more aware of some of the medium-term costs of deficit finance, we have not taken the analysis to the point of deciding whether, when, and how much governments should rely on deficit finance.

6. Let me end on an optimistic note. Mainstream macroeconomics, circa

1970, was not perfect. But it had solid foundations and was basically right. Because of that, it has survived the new-classical challenge. Much progress has been made; much of it, however, is still latent. Realizing that progress will require more systematic confrontation with the data and more systematic integration. This task is far from impossible. But it will require a return to more pragmatic, data-oriented research than we have relied on for the past decade.

Acknowledgments

I thank Larry Ball, Robert Barro, Roland Benabou, Ricardo Caballero, Peter Diamond, Stanley Fischer, Bob Gordon, Herschel Grossman, Chad Jones, Anil Kashyap, Bob Solow, Philippe Weil, and especially Rudiger Dornbusch and Julio Rotemberg, for comments, suggestions, and objections.

4 THE COWLES COMMISSION APPROACH, REAL BUSINESS CYCLE THEORIES, AND NEW-KEYNESIAN ECONOMICS

Ray C. Fair

I have been given the daunting task of discussing how the debate among the various schools of business cycle theorists might be resolved. People obviously differ in how they think the macroeconomy works. Will there ever be a winner? I am optimistic enough to think so, although I view the last two decades as making only modest progress in this direction. One problem is that there is too little testing of alternative models. There has been no systematic attempt to find the model that best approximates the macroeconomy. As disturbing, however, is the fact that macroeconomic research appears to be moving away from its traditional empirical emphasis. I will elaborate on both points in this chapter.

From Tinbergen's (1939) model building in the late 1930s through the 1960s, the dominant methodology of macroeconomics was what I will call the "Cowles Commission" approach.[1] Structural econometric models were specified, estimated, and then analyzed and tested in various ways. One of the major macroeconometric efforts of the 1960s, building on the earlier work of Klein (1950) and Klein and Goldberger (1955), was the Brookings model (Duesenberry et al., 1965, 1969). This model was a joint effort of many individuals, peaking at nearly 400 equations. Although much was learned from this exercise, the model never achieved the success initially expected and was laid to rest around 1972.

Two important events in the 1970s contributed to the decline in popularity of the Cowles Commission approach. The first was the commercialization of macroeconometric models.[2] This changed the focus of research on the models. Basic research gave way to the day-to-day needs of updating the models, of subjectively adjusting the forecasts to make them "reasonable," and of meeting the special needs of clients. The second event was Lucas's (1976) critique, which argued that the models are not likely to be useful for policy purposes.

The Lucas critique led to a line of research that has cumulated in the real business cycle (RBC) theories. This in turn has generated a counter response in the form of new-Keynesian economics. I will argue that neither the RBC approach nor new-Keynesian economics is in the spirit of the Cowles Commission approach and that this is a step backward. The Cowles Commission approach is discussed in section 1; the RBC approach, in section 2; and new-Keynesian economics, in section 3. Suggestions for the future are then presented.

1 The Cowles Commission Approach

1.1 Specification

Some of the early macroeconometric models were linear, but this soon gave way to the specification of nonlinear models. Consequently, only the nonlinear case will be considered here. The model will be written as

$$f_i(y_t, x_t, \alpha_i) = u_{it} \qquad (i = 1, \ldots, n) \qquad (t = 1, \ldots, T), \tag{1}$$

where y_t is an n-dimensional vector of endogenous variables, x_t is a vector of predetermined variables (including lagged endogenous variables), α_i is a vector of unknown coefficients, and u_{it} is the error term for equation i for period t. For equations that are identities, u_{it} is identically zero for all t.

Specification consists of choosing (1) the variables that appear in each equation with nonzero coefficients, (2) the functional form of each equation, and (3) the probability structure for u_{it}. (In modern times one has to make sufficient stationarity assumptions about the variables to make the time series econometricians happy. The assumption, either explicit or implicit, of most macroeconometric model building work is that the variables are trend stationary.) Economic theory is used to guide the choice of variables. In most cases there is an obvious left-side variable for the equation, where the normalization used is to set the coefficient of this variable equal to one. This is the variable considered to be "explained" by the equation.

It will be useful to consider an example of how theory is used to specify an equation. Consider the following maximization problem for a representative household. Maximize

$$E_0U(C_1, \ldots, C_T, L_1, \ldots, L_T), \tag{2}$$

subject to

$$\begin{aligned} S_t &= W_t(H - L_t) + r_tA_{t-1} - P_tC_t \\ A_t &= A_{t-1} + S_t \\ A_T &= \bar{A}, \end{aligned} \tag{3}$$

where C is consumption, L is leisure, S is saving, W is the wage rate, H is the total number of hours in the period, r is the one-period interest rate, A is the level of assets, P is the price level, $\bar{A}$ is the terminal value of assets, and $t = 1, \ldots, T$. E_0 is the expectations operator conditional on information available through time 0. Given A_0 and the conditional distributions of the future values of W, P, and r, it is possible in principle to solve for the optimal values of C and L for period 1, denoted C_1^* and L_1^*. In general, however, this problem is not analytically tractable. In other words, it is not generally possible to find analytic expressions for C_1^* and L_1^*.

The approach that I am calling the Cowles Commission approach can be thought of as specifying and estimating *approximations* of the decision equations. In the context of the present example, this approach is as follows. First, the random variables, W_t, P_t, and r_t, $t = 1, \ldots, T$, are replaced by their expected values, E_0W_t, E_0P_t, and E_0r_t, $t = 1, \ldots, T$. Given this replacement, one can write the expressions for C_1^* and L_1^* as

$$C_1^* = g_1(A_0, \bar{A}, E_0W_1, \ldots, E_0W_T, E_0P_1, \ldots, E_0P_T, E_0r_1, \ldots, E_0r_T, \beta) \tag{4}$$

$$L_1^* = g_2(A_0, \bar{A}, E_0W_1, \ldots, E_0W_T, E_0P_1, \ldots, E_0P_1, E_0r_1, \ldots, E_0r_T, \beta), \tag{5}$$

where β is the vector of parameters of the utility function. Equations (4) and (5) simply state that the optimal values for the first period are a function of (1) the initial and terminal values of assets; (2) the expected future values of the wage rate, the price level, and the interest rate; and (3) the parameters of the utility function.[3] The functional forms of equations (4) and (5) are not in general known. The aim of the empirical work is to try to estimate equations that are approximations of equations (4) and (5). Experimentation consists in trying different functional forms and in trying different assumptions about how expectations are formed. Because of the large number of expected values in equations (4) and (5), the expectational assumptions usually restrict the number of free parameters to be estimated. For example, the parameters for $E_0W_1, \ldots, E_0W_T$ might be assumed to lie on a low-order polynomial or to be geometrically declining. The error terms are usually assumed to be additive, as specified in equation (1), and they can be interpreted as approximation errors.

It is often the case when equations like (4) and (5) are estimated that lagged dependent variables are used as explanatory variables. Since C_0 and L_0 do not appear in equations (4) and (5), how can one justify the use of lagged dependent variables? A common procedure is to assume that C_1^* in equation (4) and L_1^* in equation (5) are long-run "desired" values. It is then assumed that because of adjustment costs, there is only a partial adjustment of actual to desired values. The usual adjustment equation for consumption would be

$$C_1 - C_0 = \lambda(C_1^* - C_0) \qquad 0 < \lambda < 1, \tag{6}$$

which adds C_0 to the estimated equation. This procedure is *ad hoc* in the sense that the adjustment equation is not explicitly derived from utility maximization. One can, however, assume that there are utility costs to large changes in consumption and leisure and thus put terms like $(C_1 - C_0)^2$, $(C_2 - C_1)^2$, $(L_1 - L_0)^2$, $(L_2 - L_1)^2, \ldots$ in the utility function, equation (2). This would add the variables C_0 and L_0 to the right-hand side of equations (4) and (5), which would justify the use of lagged dependent variables in the empirical approximating equations for (4) and (5).

This setup can handle the assumption of rational expectations in the following sense. Let $E_{t-1}y_{2t+1}$ denote the expected value of y_{2t+1}, where the expectation is based on information through period $t - 1$, and assume that $E_{t-1}y_{2t+1}$ appears as an explanatory variable in equation (1). (Equation 1 might be the equation explaining consumption, and y_2 might be the wage rate.) If expectations are assumed to be rational, equation (1) can be estimated by either a limited information or a full information technique. In the limited information case $E_{t-1}y_{2t+1}$ is replaced by y_{2t+1}, and the equation is estimated by Hansen's (1982) generalized method of moments (GMM) procedure. In the full information case the entire model is estimated at the same time by full information maximum likelihood, where the restriction is imposed that the expectations of future values of variables are equal to the model's predictions of the future values.[4] Again, the parameters of the expected future values might be restricted to lessen the number of free parameters to be estimated.

The specification just outlined does not allow the estimation of "deep structural parameters," such as the parameters of utility functions, even under the assumption of rational expectations. Only approximations of the decision equations are being estimated. The specification is thus subject to the Lucas (1976) critique. More will be said about this later. The specification also uses the certainty equivalence procedure, which is strictly valid only in the linear-quadratic setup.

1.2 Estimation

A typical macroeconometric model is dynamic, nonlinear, simultaneous, and has error terms that may be correlated across equations and with their lagged values. A number of techniques have been developed for the estimation of such models. Techniques that do not consider the correlation of the error terms across equations (limited information techniques) include limited information maximum likelihood and two-stage least squares. Techniques that do account for this correlation (full information techniques) include full information maximum likelihood and three-stage least squares. It is straightforward to modify these techniques to handle the case in which the error terms follow autoregressive processes. Also, as already noted, the techniques can be modified to handle the assumption of rational expectations.

Computational advances, both in hardware and software, have made the application of these techniques fairly routine. Even full information maximum likelihood when expectations are assumed to be rational appears computationally feasible for most models.

1.3 Testing

Testing has always played a major role in applied econometrics. When an equation is estimated, one examines how well it fits the data, if its coefficient estimates are significant and of the expected sign, if the properties of the estimated residuals are as expected, and so on. Equations are discarded or modified if they do not seem to approximate very well the process that generated the data.

Complete models can also be tested, but here things are more complicated. Given (1) a set of coefficient estimates, (2) values of the exogenous variables, (3) values of the error terms, and (4) lagged values of the endogenous variables, a model can be solved for the endogenous variables. If the solution (simulation) is "static," the actual values of the lagged endogenous variables are used for each period solved; if the solution is "dynamic," the values of the lagged endogenous variables are taken to be the predicted values of the endogenous variables from the previous periods. If one set of values of the error terms is used, the simulation is said to be "deterministic." The expected values of the error terms are usually assumed to be zero, and so in most cases the error terms are set to zero for the solution. A "stochastic" simulation is one in which (1) the error terms are drawn from estimated distributions, (2) the model is solved for each set of draws, and (3) the predicted value of each endogenous variable is taken to be the average of the solution values across the sets of draws.

A standard procedure for evaluating how well a model fits the data is to solve the model by performing a dynamic, deterministic simulation and then compare the predicted values of the endogenous variables with the actual values using the root mean squared error (RMSE) criterion. Other criteria include mean absolute error and Theil's inequality coefficient. If two models are being compared and model A has lower RMSEs for most of the variables than model B, this is evidence in favor of model A over model B.

There is always a danger in this business of "data mining," which means specifying and estimating different versions of a model until a good fit has been achieved (say in terms of the RMSE criterion). The danger with this type of searching is that one finds a model that fits well within the estimation period but is in fact a poor approximation of the economy. To guard against this, predictions are many times taken to be outside of the estimation period. If a model is poorly specified, if should not predict well outside the period for which it was estimated, even though it may fit well within the period.[5]

One problem with the RMSE criterion is that it does not take account of the fact that forecast-error variances vary across time. Forecast-error variances vary across time because of nonlinearities in the model and because of variation in the exogenous variables. Although RMSEs are in some loose sense estimates of the averages of the variances across time, no rigorous statistical interpretation can be placed on them: They are not estimates of any parameters of a model.

A more serious problem with the RMSE criterion as a means of comparing models is that models may be based on different sets of exogenous variables. If one model takes investment as exogenous and a second does not, the first model has an unfair advantage when computing RMSEs.

I have developed a method, based on stochastic simulation, that accounts for the RMSE difficulties (Fair, 1980). The method accounts for the four main sources of uncertainty of a forecast from a model: uncertainty due to (1) the error terms, (2) the coefficient estimates, (3) the exogenous variables, and (4) the possible misspecification of the model. The forecast-error variance for each variable and each period estimated by the method accounts for all four sources of uncertainty, and so it can be compared across models. The estimated variances from different structural models can be compared, or the estimated variances from one structural model can be compared to those from an autoregressive or vector autoregressive model. If a particular model's estimated variances are in general smaller than estimated variances from other models, this is evidence in favor of the particular model.

A by-product of the method is an estimate of the degree of misspecification of a model for each endogenous variable. Any model is likely to be somewhat misspecified, and the method can estimate the quantitative importance of the misspecification.

The method can handle a variety of assumptions about exogenous-variable uncertainty. One polar assumption is that there is no uncertainty attached to the exogenous variables. This might be true, for example, of some policy variables. The other polar assumption is that the exogenous variables are in some sense as uncertain as the endogenous variables. One can, for example, estimate autoregressive equations for each exogenous variable and add these equations to the model. This would produce a model with no exogenous variables, which could then be tested. An in-between case would include estimating the variance of an exogenous-variable forecast error from actual forecasting errors made by a forecasting service—say the errors made by DRI in forecasting defense spending.

Another method comparing models is to regress the actual value of an endogenous variable on a constant and forecasts of the variable from two or more models. This procedure is explained in Fair and Shiller (1990) and is related to the literature on encompassing tests—see, for example, Davidson and MacKinnon (1981), Hendry and Richard (1982), and Chong and Hendry (1986). Again, one can use autoregressive or vector autoregressive models as comparisons for structural models using these tests.

Testing models in the ways described here seems clearly in the spirit of the Cowles Commission approach. A model to the Cowles Commission was a null hypothesis to be tested.

1.4 A Digression on Monetarism

Laidler (1992) has written an interesting and useful chapter on the history of monetarism. From the perspective of the Cowles Commission approach, I have no complaints about this chapter. The Laidler and Bentley (1983) model, for example, is a standard macroeconometric model and can be tested in the ways already discussed. In fact, in Laidler's last sentence he states that he hopes to "reinstate empirical evidence as a factor more important than *a priori* principles" in the debate about business cycles. I would interpret this as an argument for the Cowles Commission approach.

This is not to say, however, that I would argue in favor of the Laidler and Bentley model. Although in simple tests the model does about the same as Barro's (1978) model, I doubt that it would hold up well against larger structural models or even against autoregressive and vector autoregressive models. But the main point is that the model can be tested. The debate is simply between which macroeconometric model—a model in the monetarist spirit or some other model—best explains the data.

2 The Real Business Cycle Approach

In discussing the RBC approach, it will be useful to begin with the utility maximization model already considered. The RBC approach to this model would be to specify a particular functional form for the utility function in equation (2). The parameters of this function would then be either estimated or simply chosen ("calibrated") to be in line with parameters estimated in the literature.

Although there is some parameter estimation in the RBC literature, most of the studies calibrate rather than estimate, in the spirit of the seminal article by Kydland and Prescott (1982). If the parameters are estimated, they are estimated from the first-order conditions. A recent example is Christiano and Eichenbaum (1990), where the parameters of their model are estimated using Hansen's (1982) GMM procedure. Altug (1989) estimates the parameters of her model using a likelihood procedure. Chow (1991) and Canova, Finn, and Pagan (1991) contain interesting discussions of the estimation of RBC models. There is also a slightly earlier literature in which the parameters of a utility function, as in equation (2), were estimated from the first-order conditions—see, for example, Hall (1978), Hansen and Singleton (1982), and Mankiw, Rotemberg, and Summers (1985).

The RBC approach meets the Lucas critique; deep structural parameters are being estimated (or calibrated). It is hard to overestimate the appeal this has to many people. Anyone who doubts this appeal should read Lucas's 1985 Jahnsson lectures (Lucas, 1987), which is an elegant argument for dynamic economic theory. The tone of these lectures is an exciting sense of progress in macroeconomics and hope that in the end there will be essentially no distinction between microeconomics and macroeconomics. There will simply be economic theory applied to different problems.

Once the coefficients are chosen, by whatever means, the overall model can be solved. In the earlier example, one could solve the utility maximization problem for the optimal consumption and leisure paths. The properties of the computed paths of the decision variables are then compared to the properties of the actual paths of the variables. If the computed paths have similar properties to the actual paths (for example, similar variances, covariances, and autocovariances), this is judged to be a positive sign for the model. If the parameters are chosen by calibration, there is usually some searching over parameters to find that set that gives good results in matching the computed paths to the actual paths in terms of the particular criterion used. In this sense the calibrated parameters are also estimated.

Is the RBC approach a good way of testing models? At first glance it might seem so, since computed paths are being compared to actual paths. But the paths are being compared in a very limited way in contrast to the way that the Cowles Commission approach would compare them. Take the simple RMSE procedure. This procedure would compute a prediction error for a given variable for each period and then calculate the RMSE from these prediction errors. This RMSE might then be compared to the RMSE from another structural model or from an autoregressive or vector autoregressive model.

I have never seen this type of comparison done for a RBC model. How would, say, the currently best-fitting RBC model compare to a simple first-order autoregressive equation for real GNP in terms of the RMSE criterion? My guess is very poorly. Having the computed path mimic the actual path for a few selected moments is a far cry from beating even a first-order autoregressive equation (let alone a structural model) in terms of fitting the observations well according to the RMSE criterion. The disturbing feature of the RBC literature is there seems to be no interest in computing RMSEs and the like. People generally seem to realize that the RBC models do not fit well in this sense, but they proceed anyway.

If this literature proceeds anyway, it has in my view dropped out of the race. The literature may take a long time to play itself out, but it will eventually reach a dead end unless it comes around to developing models that can compete with other models in explaining the economy *observation by observation*.

One of the main reasons that individuals proceed anyway is undoubtedly the Lucas critique and the general excitement about deep structural parameters. Why waste one's time in working with models whose coefficients change over time as policy rules and other things change? The logic of the Lucas critique is certainly correct, but the key question for empirical work is the quantitative importance of this critique. Even the best econometric model is only an approximation of how the economy works. Another potential source of coefficient change is the use of aggregate data. As the age and income distributions of the population change, the coefficients in aggregate equations are likely to change, and this is a source of error in the estimated equations. This problem may be quantitatively much more important than the problem raised by Lucas. Put another way, the representative agent model that is used so much in macroeconomics has serious problems of its own, which may completely swamp the problem of coefficients changing when policy rules change. The RBC literature has focused so much on solving one problem that it is likely in the process to have exacerbated the effects of a number of others.

There are a number of reasons the RBC models probably do not fit the data well. The RBC approach requires that a particular functional form for, say, the utility function be chosen, and errors made in this choice may lead to large prediction errors. Remember that this function represents the average of the utility functions of all the households in the economy, and it is unlikely that one is going to get this quite right. The advantage of estimating approximations of the decision equations, as discussed in section 1, is that it allows more flexibility in estimating functional forms. The data are allowed more play, if you will. Using the approach of estimating approximations of decision equations, one trades off estimating deep structural parameters for less sensitivity to functional-form errors and the like.

When deep structural parameters have been estimated from the first-order conditions, the results have not always been very good even when judged by themselves. The results in Mankiw, Rotemberg, and Summers (1985) for the utility parameters are not supportive of the approach. In a completely different literature—the estimation of production-smoothing equations—Krane and Braun (1989), whose study is based on quite good data, report that their attempts to estimate first-order conditions was unsuccessful. It may be that one is asking too much of the aggregate data to force them into estimating what one thinks are parameters from some postulated function.

Finally, one encouraging feature regarding the Lucas critique is that it can be tested. Assume that for an equation or set of equations the parameters change considerably when a given policy variable changes. Assume also that the policy variable changes frequently. In this case the model is obviously misspecified, and so methods like that discussed in section 1 should be able to pick up this misspecification if the policy variable has changed frequently. If the policy variable has not changed or changed very little, the model will be misspecified but the misspecification will not be given a chance to be picked up in the data. But otherwise, models that suffer in an important way from the Lucas critique ought to be weeded out by various tests.

3 The New-Keynesian Economics

After reading or rereading a number of new-Keynesian articles for this chapter, I came away feeling uneasy. It's like coming out of a play that many of your friends liked and feeling that you did not really like it, but not knowing quite why. Given my views of how the economy works, many of the results of the new-Keynesian literature seem reasonable, but something seemed missing. One problem is that it is hard to get a big picture. There are many small stories, and it's hard to remember each one. In addition, many of the conclusions do not seem robust to small changes in the models.

On further reflection, however, I do not think this was my main source of uneasiness. The main problem is that this literature is not really empirical in the Cowles Commission sense. *This literature has moved macroeconomics away from its econometric base.* Consider, for example, the articles in the two volumes of *New Keynesian Economics*, edited by Mankiw and Romer (1991). By my count, of the 34 chapters in these two volumes, only 8 have anything to do with data.[6] Of these 8, one (Carlton, "The Rigidity of Prices") is more industrial organization than macro and one (Krueger and Summers, "Efficiency Wages and the Interindustry Wage Structure") is more labor than macro. These two studies provide some interesting insights that might be of help to macroeconomists, but they are not really empirical macroeconomics.

It has been pointed out to me[7] that the Mankiw and Romer volumes may be biased against empirical papers because of space constraints imposed by the publisher. Nevertheless, it seems clear that there is very little in the new-Keynesian literature in the nature of structural modeling of the kind outlined in section 1. As in the RBC literature, one does not see, say, predictions of real GNP from some new-Keynesian model compared to predictions of real GNP from an autoregressive equation using a criterion like RMSE. But here one does not see it because no econometric models of real GNP are constructred! So this literature has dropped out of the race not because it is necessarily uninterested in serious tests but because it is uninterested in constructing econometric models.

I should hasten to add that I do not mean by these criticisms that there is no interesting empirical work going on in macroeconomics. For example, the literature on production smoothing, which is largely empirical, has produced some important results and insights. It is simply that literature of this type is not generally classified as new-Keynesian. Even if one wanted to be generous and put some of this empirical work in the new-Keynesian literature, it is surely not the essence of new-Keynesian economics.

One might argue that new-Keynesian economics is just getting started and that the big picture (model) will eventually emerge to rival existing models of the economy. This is probably an excessively generous interpretation, given the focus of this literature on small theoretical models, but unless the literature does move in a more econometric and larger-model direction, it is not likely to have much long-run impact.

4 Looking Ahead

So I see the RBC and new-Keynesian literatures passing each other like two runners in the night, both having left the original path laid out by the Cowles Commission and its predecessors. To answer the question posed to me at the conference, I see no way to resolve the debates between these two literatures. The RBC literature is only interested in testing in a very limited way, and the new-Keynesian literature is not econometric enough to even talk about serious testing.

But I argue there is hope. Models can be tested, and there are procedures for weeding out inferior models. The RBC literature should entertain the possibility of testing models based on estimating deep structural parameters against models based on estimating approximations of decision equations. Also, the tests should be more than just observing whether a computed path mimics the actual path in a few ways. The new-Keynesian literature should entertain the possibility of putting its various ideas together to specify, estimate, and test structural macroeconometric models.

Finally, both literatures ought to consider bigger models. I have always thought it ironic that one of the consequences of the Lucas critique was to narrow the number of endogenous variables in a model from many (say a hundred or more) to generally no more than three or four. If one is worried about coefficients in structural equations changing, it seems unlikely that getting rid of the structural detail in large-scale models is going to get one closer to deep structural parameters.

Acknowledgments

I am indebted to my discussant, Arnold Zellner, and other participants at the conference for many helpful comments.

Notes

1. See Arrow (1991) and Malinvaud (1991) for interesting historical discussions of econometric research at the Cowles Commission (later Cowles Foundation) and its antecedents.

2. It should be noted that the commercialization of models has been less of a problem in the United Kingdom than in the United States. In 1983 the Macroeconomic Modeling Bureau of the Economic and Social Research Council was established at the University of Warwick under the direction of Kenneth F. Wallis. Various U.K. models and their associated databases are made available to academic researchers through the bureau.

3. If information for period 1 is available at the time the decisions are made, then E_0W_1, E_0P_1, and E_0r_1 should be replaced by the actual values in equations (4) and (5).

4. See Fair and Taylor (1983) for a description of this procedure. This procedure is based on the assumption of certainty equivalence, which is only an approximation for nonlinear models.

5. This is assuming that one does not search by (1) estimating a model up to a certain point, (2) solving the model for a period beyond this point, and (3) choosing the version that best fits the period beyond the point. If this were done, then one would have to wait for more observations to provide a good test of the model. Even if this type of searching is not formally done, it may be that information beyond the estimation period has been implicitly used in specifying a model. This might then lead to a better-fitting model beyond the estimation period than is warranted. In this case, one would also have to wait for more observations to see how accurate the model in fact is.

6. One might argue nine. Okun's article, "Inflation: Its Mechanics and Welfare Costs," which I did not count in the eight, presents and briefly discusses data in one figure.

7. By Olivier Blanchard.

References

Altug, Sumru 1989. "Time-to-Build and Aggregate Fluctuations: Some New Evidence." *International Economic Review* 30: 889–920.

Arrow, Kenneth J. 1991. "Cowles in the History of Economic Thought." In *Cowles Fiftieth Anniversary*. New Haven, Conn.: Yale University.

Barro, Robert J. 1978. "Unanticipated Money, Output, and the Price Level in the United States." *Journal of Political Economy* 86: 549–581.

Canova, F., M. Finn, and A.R. Pagan. 1991. "Econometric Issues in the Analysis of Equilibrium Models." Paper given at the Canadian Econometric Study Group meeting, Quebec City, September.

Chong, Yock Y., and David F. Hendry. 1986. "Econometric Evauation of Linear Macro-Econometric Models." *Review of Economic Studies* 53: 671–690.

Chow, Gregory C. 1991. "Statistical Estimation and Testing of a Real Business Cycle Model" August 30, mimeo.

Christiano, Lawrence J., and Martin Eichenbaum, 1990. "Current Real Business Cycle Theories and Aggregate Labor Market Fluctuations." Discussion Paper 24, Institute for Empirical Macroeconomics, January.

Davidson, Russell, and James G. MacKinnon. 1981. "Several Tests of Model Specification in the Presence of Alternative Hypotheses." *Econometrica* 40: 781–793.

Duesenberry, James S., Gary Fromm, Lawrence R. Klein, and Edwin Kuh, eds. 1965. *The Brookings Quarterly Econometric Model of the United States*. Chicago: Rand McNally & Company.

———. 1969. *The Brookings Model: Some Further Results*. Chicago: Rand McNally & Company.

Fair, Ray C. 1980. "Estimating the Expected Predictive Accuracy of Econometric Models." *International Economic Review* 21: 355–378.

Fair, Ray C., and Robert J. Shiller. 1990. "Comparing Information in Forecasts from Econometric Models." *American Economic Review* 80: 375–389.

Fair, Ray C., and John Taylor. 1983. "Solution and Maximum Likelihood Estimation of Dynamic Rational Expectations Models." *Econometrica* 51: 1169–1185.

Hall, Robert E. 1978. "Stochastic Implications of the Life-Cycle Permanent Income Hypothesis: Theory and Evidence." *Journal of Political Economy* 86: 971–989.

Hansen, Lars Peter. 1982. "Large Sample Properties of Generalized Method of Moments Estimators." *Econometrica* 50: 1029–1054.

Hansen, Lars Peter, and Kenneth Singleton. 1982. "Generalized Instrumental Variables Estimation of Nonlinear Rational Expectations Models." *Econometrica* 50: 1269–1286.

Hendry, David F., and Jean-Francois Richard. 1982. "On the Formulation of Empirical Models in Dynamic Economics." *Journal of Econometrics* 20: 3–33.

Klein, Lawrence R. 1950. *Economic Fluctuations in the United States, 1921–1941*. New York: Wiley, Cowles Monograph No. 11.

Klein, Lawrence R., and Arthur S. Goldberger. 1955. *An Econometric Model of the United States 1929–1952*. Amsterdam: North-Holland.

Krane, Spencer D., and Steven N. Braun. 1989. "Production Smoothing Evidence from Physical-Product Data," mimeo.

Kydland, F.E., and E.C. Prescott. 1982. "Time to Build and Aggregate Fluctuations." *Econometrica* 50: 1345–1370.

Laidler, David. 1992. "The Cycle Before New-Classical Economics." In M.T. Belongia and M.R. Garfinkel, eds., *The Business Cycle: Theories and Evidence*. Boston: Kluwer Academic Publishers.

Laidler, David, and B. Bentley. 1983. "A Small Macro-Model of the Post-War United States." *Manchester School* 51: 317–340.

Lucas, Robert E., Jr. 1976. "Econometric Policy Evaluation: A Critique." In K. Brunner and A.H. Meltzer, eds., *The Phillips Curve and Labor Markets*. Amsterdam: North-Holland.

———. 1987. *Models of Business Cycles*. New York: Blackwell.

Malinvaud, Edmond. 1991. "Econometric Methodology at the Cowles Commission: Rise and Maturity." In *Cowles Fiftieth Anniversary*. New Haven, Conn.: Yale University.

Mankiw, N. Gregory, and David Romer, eds. 1991. *New Keynesian Economics*, vols. 1 and 2. Cambridge, MA: MIT Press.

Mankiw, N. Gregory, Julio J. Rotemberg, and Laurence H. Summers. 1985. "Intertemporal Substitution in Macroeconomics." *Quarterly Journal of Economics* 100: 225–251.

Tinbergen, J. 1939. *Statistical Testing of Business Cycle Theories*. Geneva: League of Nations.

Commentary

by Arnold Zellner

Ray Fair is to be congratulated for his thoughtful discussion not only on how the debate between the real business cycle (RBC) and new-Keynesian (NK) theories might be resolved but also on how macroeconomic research can be made more productive. I am in agreement with much that he has written but, as is to be expected in such a controversial area, I have several points of disagreement and shall put forward a different prescription in the last paragraphs of my comment, one that we are actively pursuing.

Fair cogently observes, "I view the last two decades as making only modest progress in this direction [of resolving the debate among various business cycle theorists]. One problem is that there is too little testing of alternative models. There has been no systematic attempt to find the model that best approximates the macroeconomy. As disturbing, however, is the fact that macroeconomic research appears to be moving away from its traditional empirical emphasis" (p. 133). There can be no doubt but that Fair is correct in these observations. He could even be more critical by pointing to mystical elements in recent business cycle terminology, namely, "laws of motion" to denote autoregressive processes, "deep structural underlying parameters" to denote alphas and betas, "stylized facts" to denote uncertain facts, "new-Keynesian" to invoke images of Keynes' approval from the grave, and so on.

Fair's chapter starts with an introduction in which he points to modest progress in the last two decades and a movement away from an empirical emphasis, as indicated in the preceding quotation. He then describes the Cowles Commission approach and the reasons for its decline. In section 1, a modern version of the Cowles Commission approach is presented along with a discussion of selected technical issues and a digression on monetarism. In section 2 attention is directed at the RBC approach, while section 3 treats the NK approach. Finally, in section 4 he appraises the future by looking ahead. In this section he suggests that "there is hope" if all parties were to become involved in serious comparative testing of alternative theories and if they were "to consider bigger models." While the proposition that bigger is necessarily better is controversial (see a later consideration of this issue), it is hard to disagree with the need for more strenuous, empirical testing of alternative theories. However, here the issue is how to approach the testing problem most fruitfully.

Perhaps the most depressing aspect of Fair's chapter is that after all these years of research on the business cycle, we still do not have a dependable, thoroughly tested model that explains the past well, predicts satisfactorily, and is useful for policy purposes. He recognizes this fact but is still optimistic, as am I. However, I believe that what is missing is an honest admission of our ignorance in important areas. Let's be frank and admit that we don't know enough to formulate the n nonlinear equations in Fair's equation (1) with much confidence. The forms of consumption equations, investment equations, production functions, and many other equations are highly uncertain. Further, it is not at all clear that the parameter vectors, the α_i's, are constant for reasons given by Fair—namely, Lucas effects and aggregation effects—and, I add, adaptive optimization on the part of firms, consumers, and policy makers, changes in production techniques induced by large-factor price changes, wars, oil crises, and consumer changes in tastes. It is shocking that the underlying deep structural parameters may be variable. Further, who knows how to prove that this n-equation nonlinear system has a unique solution and what its global dynamic properties are? With a large n, there is a substantial probability that equations, error term properties, restrictions, and the like are incorrectly formulated. And with all of these problems, who knows how to estimate parameters well and test hypotheses with confidence? Frank answers to these questions are not reassuring. And indeed, simulation experiments reported by the Adelmans (1959), Hickman (1972), Zellner and Peck (1973), and others have revealed important, unusual properties of existent models unknown to the model builders and users. Further, various forecasting tests of Christ (1951), Cooper (1972), Nelson (1972), Litterman (1986), and McNees (1986) reveal that Cowles Commission–type model forecasts have not been satisfactory. Results such as these and the poor performance of these models led McNees (1986, p. 15) to state in the last paragraph of his paper that "macroeconometric models may have been 'oversold' in the 1960s and early 1970s, leading to disappointment and rejection in the late 1970s and 1980s."

Let's admit that the economic theory underlying the equations and overall structure of macroeconometric models, be they RBC or NK models, is at best tentative and probably inadequate. Fair's chapter gives a reasonable overview of how economic theory has been employed in model building. Let me add a few critical remarks to indicate how shaky this theoretical structure may be. First, with respect to equation (2), there is an expectation operator E in the equation with no remarks on the underlying probability measure. Knight might say, in view of the near ignorance of experts, that consumers face uncertainty, not risk, and the difficulty in formulating a probability measure in this circumstance is formidable. However, if we go along with Savage and Friedman, who disagree with Knight's distinction, and give the typical consumer a probability measure, what is it and what axiom system supports the rationality of dynamic maximization of expected utility? I know of none. But even if we allow the consumer an appropriate probability measure, an exact solution to the consumer's dynamic optimization problem is difficult to compute, as Fair points out. He opts for a "certainty equivalent" approximation by replacing random variables by their means. This "solution" has been shown to be a poor approximation even in very simple problems by Fisher (1962), Zellner (1971), and others. Further, the "solution" of a typical consumer, who is endowed by the rational expectations hypothesis with a knowledge of the "true" model, seems quite irrelevant to situations in which there is model uncertainty and dispersion of beliefs. Also, Lovell's (1986) summary of the empirical evidence relating to the rational expectations hypothesis indicates that it is not as strong as could be desired.

To patch up the approximate equations of theory, a partial adjustment equation is introduced in equation (6). Fair comments that "the adjustment equation is not explicitly derived from utility maximization" (p. 136). Thus it could and probably is at odds with the expected utility maximization solution, theoretically quite disturbing. But more practically, equations such as (6) probably reflect discreteness in durable goods and other types of investment expenditures. Studies of panel data indicate that not everyone buys a car or other large durables each period. On aggregation over buyers and nonbuyers, the aggregate data appear to be generated by an equation like (6) with the parameter lambda not a constant but intimately related to the proportion of individuals making a purchase in a given period. For analyses of such problems involving discreteness for consumers and firms, see, for example, Chau (1967), Levedahl (1969), Laub (1971, 1972), and Peck (1973, 1974).

Further, models such as those described by Fair are deficient in that they don't allow firms to shut down. Indeed in Muth's (1961) fundamental paper on rational expectations, he modeled a competitive industry under the assumption that the number of firms is constant, that is, no net entry or exit. Marshall probably turned over in his grave on learning of this assumption. See Veloce and Zellner (1984, 1985) for analysis of a demand, supply, and entry model for a competitive industry. In most RBC, NK, and other aggregate models, there does not appear to be allowance for shutdowns and startups by plants and firms, a phenomenon extremely important in major recessions and depressions. In RBC models, if the "representative firm" shuts down, does the whole economy shut down? No firm heterogeneity has been introduced to determine which firms shut down, and most models furthermore only indirectly and probably inaccurately predict the number of plants and firms in operation in a given period. Shutdowns and startups involve discrete changes and behavior on the part of entrepreneurs and labor that are different from behavior in "normal" times, another reason for parameters to change over the business cycle. Also, in the latter part of expansions, when firms' profits are abnormally high, there may be systematic inefficiencies afflicting production, another reason for production parameters to vary over the cycle. Some of these effects are being analyzed by Min (1991) in the context of a generalized real business cycle model.

Add to these problems the problem of modeling policy-makers' behavior, and one indeed becomes humble in connection with the theoretical underpinnings of current macroeconometric models. Faced with so much ignorance on the theoretical side, there appears to be a tendency for workers to follow Arrow's analysis of rational behavior under ignorance, namely, to take extreme positions. One is that one or another of the current theories, involving "laws of motion," "deep underlying structural parameters," "rational" expectations, "true" data-generating processes, Keynesian "truths," and so on, is "obviously" correct. Only ignorant barbarians such as Ray Fair, Milton Friedman, and other misguided individuals fail to believe the beautiful truths embodied in these theories and suggest the crass need to test them empirically. At the other extreme are those who reject all theories and retreat to a position of extreme empiricism—this includes almost all of the time series statisticians and many applied forecasters who have trouble understanding the current jargon. The best of them, along with some econometricians, recognize that multivariate time series models, including VARs, have too many free parameters, which means that usually estimates and forecasts are imprecise and tests of hypotheses have low power. Subject matter judgment and theoretical knowledge are needed to restrict the number of free parameters, just as Fair indicates in discussion of his equation (1). However, if the subject matter theory and knowledge isn't there, what's to be done? This problem is irritating to both economic theorists and econometricians. A suggested approach in this situation is described later. Before discussing this problem, let me take up a few technical statistical issues that Fair has raised.

In discussing statistical issues, I'm going to be as frank as I was in discussing economic theory. First of all, the aggregate quarterly data are afflicted with all kinds of systematic and random measurement errors and then subjected to mysterious, horrendous seasonal adjustment procedures with their peculiar assumptions about seasonal, cyclical, trend, and noise components. All of these problems, which are swept under the rug in most econometric studies, not only can vitally affect statistical estimation, testing, and predictive procedures but also undermine the economic rationale underlying statistical tests. Yet they are rarely mentioned. Perhaps engineers' state space models involving measurement equations, reflecting both systematic and random measurement errors and state equations with state equation errors, are worth considering. Also, when error-ridden, current preliminary estimates of GNP and other variables are employed, who knows what results?

Abstracting from these serious measurement error and seasonal adjustment problems, what are we to make of a model with n uncertain nonlinear equations to be implemented with one set of data? There are issues of parameter identification, testing overidentifying restrictions, estimation, diagnostic checking, and prediction. In all of these areas there are serious problems as I discussed years ago (Zellner, 1979). I shall just remark here that there are, as yet, no secure and tested statistical methods for formulating an n-equation nonlinear model from a single set of data. Formulation of such a model is still an art. In the process, the data is often used over and over again in tests of alternative variants of equations, and thus subsequent estimates are afflicted with pretest biases and standard errors are hardly satisfactory. Also, there is the well-known problem of data mining, overfitting, and the like. For example in testing a valid null hypothesis at the 10% level in independent trials, the probability of accepting the null on one try is .9; on two, .81; on three, .73; and so on. Thus after just three tests, the probability is .27 of rejecting the true null hypothesis. Effects like this are well known to be present when a single set of data is employed to screen many hypotheses—for a discussion of how to correct for such "selection" effects in a simple case, see Jeffreys (1967, p. 253). Also, the discussion in Friedman and Schwartz (1991) is relevant. When many alternative hypotheses are considered with a single set of data, conclusive results are hard to obtain, a fact that is probably well known. Getting more data is helpful in such situations as is out-of-sample predictive testing, as Fair indicates.

Fair remarks, perhaps in jest, "In modern times one has to make sufficient stationarity assumptions about the variables to make time series econometricians happy." With the presence of Lucas effects, regime changes, aggregation effects, adaptive optimization, and so on, it is probably the case that the stationarity assumptions, which can be tested, underlying most macroeconometric analyses are violated. These include spectral and cross-spectral analyses, impulse response function analyses, method of moments analyses, and many analyses based on the assumption of fixed parameters. There is a need to utilize flexible time-varying parameter models that can adapt quickly to sudden parameter changes or gradually to more gradual parameter changes. Also, theorists who theorize in terms of fixed parameter models probably have to broaden their sights.

In our past work (Min and Zellner, 1990) we have developed and applied posterior odds for fixed versus time-varying parameter versions of a forecasting equation for the growth rate of real output. The posterior odds are useful not only for model selection and/or combination purposes but also for forecast selection and/or combination purposes—see Palm and Zellner (1990) for further discussion of these issues. Posterior odds reflect relative predictive performance and other factors—see Poirier (1991) for a number of applications of posterior odds to various problems as well as references to the earlier literature, which includes Geisel (1974), who used posterior odds to compare simple Quantity Theory and Keynesian models. The posterior odds approach to model selection deserves more attention in macroeconometrics as does the Bayesian estimation and testing procedures for equations of structural econometric models in Zellner, Bauwens, and van Dijk (1988). These procedures yield finite sample posterior densities for parameters and finite-sample analogues of Wu–Hausman specification error tests. Also, Bayesian predictive densities have been found useful in general forecasting and turning-point forecasting problems—see, for example, Zellner, Hong, and Min (1991), in which good turning-point forecasts were obtained using a relatively simple "autoregressive-leading indicator" (ARLI) model in the form of a simple transfer function equation.

Now to return to the difficult problem of initial model formulation, in earlier work Zellner and Palm (1974, 1975) and Zellner (1979), a *s*tructural *e*conometric *m*odelling, *t*ime *s*eries *a*nalysis, (SEMTSA) approach has been described. In this approach, a tentative structural equation model may be formulated. Then the model's transfer functions can be derived, along with other equation systems. The transfer functions so derived are usually highly restricted and can be estimated and evaluated in extensive forecasting testing. One by one the transfer functions or the components can be evaluated. Once the components have been tested and found to perform well, the problem of finding structural models compatible with the transfer functions can be addressed. Here, rather than start with some fully specified system of n-equations, we construct individual transfer functions that forecast reasonably well and then consider structural equation systems compatible with them that can be tested further in forecasting experiments using as much new data as possible. Currently, we are using data for 18 countries in our work and data for many more are available.

On the issue of how many equations to employ, of course the objectives of an analysis are important in this regard. If our objectives are just to explain and forecast broad aggregates, then probably a small, sophisticatedly simple model will suffice. On the other hand, if our objectives involve explaining the behavior of many markets and sectors in detail, a large, hopefully sophisticatedly simple, model will be needed. In either case, the advice KISS, *k*eep *i*t *s*ophisticatedly *s*imple, is recommended. In U.S. industry, KISS denotes *k*eep it *s*imple *s*tupid. Since some simple models are stupid, I prefer the first interpretation. Many scientists emphasize the importance of sophisticated simplicity in science—see, for example, the "simplicity postulate" in Jeffreys (1967).

On forecasting aggregates, one can model an aggregate variable in a transfer function and forecast it. On the other hand, it is possible to break the aggregate variable up into its components, forecast the components, and add up the forecasts to obtain a forecast of the aggregate variable. Many times, but not always, the latter procedure works better according to some analyses that Enrique de Alba and I have underway. Further, too much disaggregation can obviously lead to diminishing returns.

To illustrate some of the above points, suppose that our tentative structural equation system is given by $H_1 \underset{\sim}{y}_t = H_2 \underset{\sim}{x}_t + F\underset{\sim}{\varepsilon}_t$, where H_1, H_2, and F are matrix lag operators, $\underset{\sim}{y}_t$ is a vector of endogenous variables, $\underset{\sim}{x}_t$ a vector of exogenous variables, and $\underset{\sim}{\varepsilon}_t$ a zero-mean white noise error vector. Given that H_1 is invertible, $\underset{\sim}{y}_t = H_1^{-1}H_2\underset{\sim}{x}_t + H_1^{-1}F\underset{\sim}{\varepsilon}_t$ or with $H_1^{-1} = H_1^*/|H_1|$, where H_1^* is the adjoint matrix,

$$|H_1|\underset{\sim}{y}_t = H_1^*H_2\underset{\sim}{x}_t + H_1^*F\underset{\sim}{\varepsilon}_t \tag{1}$$

is the transfer equation system. Note that the same polynomial operator, $|H_1|$, hits each element of $\underset{\sim}{y}_t$. Let $y_t^A = y_{1t} + y_{2t} + \cdots + y_{mt} = \underset{\sim}{\iota}'\underset{\sim}{y}_t$, where $\underset{\sim}{\iota}' = (1, 1, \ldots, 1)$. Then from equation (1),

$$|H_{11}|y_t^A = \underset{\sim}{\iota}'H_1^*H_2\underset{\sim}{x}_t + \underset{\sim}{\iota}'H_1^*F\underset{\sim}{\varepsilon}_t. \tag{2}$$

It is possible to estimate equation (2) and use it for forecasting or to estimate the equations in (1), forecast the components, and add up the forecasts to obtain a forecast of y_t^A.

Further, the equations actually fitted in (1) should be compatible with a restricted version of the structural equation system. Thus we work back and forth between the structural formulation and the transfer functions that have been found to be successful in forecasting using as much data as possible, that is, data for many countries and reasonably long time periods. See, for example, Hong (1989), who has compared the predictive performance of transfer function (TF) models for the rate of growth of real output incorporating lagged leading indicator variables with that of a version of Barro's monetary surprise model, the Nelson–Plosser (0,1,1) ARIMA model, and various naive models using data for 18 countries, 1951–1973 for fitting and 1974–1984 for forecasting. Hong found that the TF or autoregressive-leading indicator (ARLI) model performs best. He has also rationalized the ARLI model by showing that it can be obtained as a relation implied by a simple structural econometric model. By having relations like equation (1) or equation (2), or time-varying parametric versions of them, implemented with data for many countries, it is possible to use modern shrinkage estimation and prediction procedures to get improved results.

In our recent work, we have been pursuing this approach, which differs in important respects from the Cowles and VAR approaches, both of which involve linking results to tenuous, complicated maintained models, say a large highly restricted simultaneous equation model or a high-order VAR. Since these maintained models are often untried and untested, there is no assurance that results based on them are reliable, an obvious point. Our SEMTSA approach involves testing the components of models thoroughly and then putting them together sensibly to form a model that can then be tested further in simulation experiments, forecasting, and other uses using as much new data as possible. Hopefully, the SEMTSA approach will yield a model capable of explaining the main features of business cycles and of predicting future outcomes with satisfactory precision.

References

Adelman, I., and F.L. Adelman. 1959. "The Dynamic Properties of the Klein–Goldberger Model." *Econometrica* 27: 569–625.

Chau, L.C. 1967. "Stock Adjustment, Liquidity, and Normal Income in the Determination of Household Expenditures on Durable Goods." Doctoral dissertation, University of Wisconsin, Madison.

Christ, C.F. 1951. "A Test of an Econometric Model for the United States, 1921–1947." In *Conference on Business Cycles*. New York: National Bureau of Economic Research, pp. 35–107.

Cooper, R.L. 1972. "The Predictive Performance of Quarterly Econometric Models of the United States." In B.G. Hickman, ed., *Econometric Models of Cyclical Behavior*. New York: Columbia University Press, pp. 813–926.

Fisher, W.D. 1962. "Estimation in the Linear Decision Model." *International Economic Review* 3: 1–29.

Friedman, M., and A.J. Schwartz. 1991. "Alternative Approaches to Analyzing Economic Data." *American Economic Review* 81: 39–49.

Geisel, M.S. 1974. "Bayesian Comparisons of Simple Macroeconomic Models." In S.E. Fienberg and A. Zellner, eds., *Studies in Bayesian Econometrics and Statistics in Honor of Leonard J. Savage*. Amsterdam: North-Holland, pp. 227–256.

Hickman, B.G., ed. 1972. *Econometric Models of Cyclical Behavior*. New York: Columbia University Press.

Hong, C. 1989. "Forecasting Real Output Growth Rates and Cyclical Properties of Models: A Bayesian Approach." Doctoral dissertation, Department of Economics, University of Chicago.

Jeffreys, H. 1967. *Theory of Probability* (3rd ed.). Oxford: Oxford University Press.

Laub, P.M. 1971. "The Dividend-Earning Relationship: A Study of Corporate Quarterly Panel Data, 1947–65." Doctoral dissertation, Graduate School of Business, University of Chicago.

———. 1972. "Some Aspects of the Aggregation Problem in the Dividend-Earning Relationship." *Journal of the American Statistical Association* 67: 552–559.

Levedahl, W.J. 1969. "The Effects of Households' Permanent and Transitory Income on Both Their Timing of Automobile Purchases and Their Net Outlay for Automobile Services for 1968, with Predictions for 1969." Doctoral dissertation, University of Chicago.

Litterman, R.B. 1986. "A Statistical Approach to Economic Forecasting." *Journal of Business and Economic Statistics* 4: 1–4.

Lovell, M.C. 1986. "Tests of the Rational Expectations Hypothesis." *American Economic Review* 76: 110–124.

McNees, S.K. 1986. "Forecasting Accuracy of Alternative Techniques: A Comparison of U.S. Macroeconomic Forecasts." *Journal of Business and Economic Statistics* 4: 5–15.

Min, C. 1991. "Economic Analysis and Forecasting of International Growth Rates Using a Bayesian Approach." Thesis proposal, Department of Economics, University of Chicago.

Min, C., and A. Zellner. 1990. "Bayesian and Non-Bayesian Methods for Combining Models and Forecasts with Applications to Forecasting International Growth Rates." *Journal of Econometrics, Annals*.

Muth, J. 1961. "Rational Expectations and the Theory of Price Movements." *Econometrica* 29: 315–335.

Nelson, C.R. 1972. "The Prediction Performance of the FRB-MIT-Penn Model of the U.S. Economy." *American Economic Review* 62: 902–917.

Palm, F.C., and A. Zellner. 1990. "To Combine or Not to Combine? Issues of Combining Forecasts." *Journal of Forecasting*.

Peck, S. 1973. "A Test of Alternative Theories of Investment Using Data from the Electric Utilities Industry." Doctoral dissertation, Graduate School of Business, University of Chicago.

———. 1974. "Alternative Investment Models for Firms in the Electric Utilities Industry." *Bell Journal of Economics and Management Science* 5: 420–458.

Poirier, D.J., ed. 1991. *Bayesian Empirical Studies in Economics and Finance, Journal of Econometrics, Annals* 49 (July/August).

Veloce, W., and A. Zellner. 1984. "Modeling a Competitive Industry with Entry." *Economics Letters* 16: 71–75.

———. 1985. "Entry and Empirical Demand and Supply Analysis for Competitive Industries." *Journal of Econometrics* 30: 459–471.

Zellner, A. 1971. *An Introduction to Bayesian Inference in Econometrics*. New York: John Wiley and Sons, reprinted by Krieger Publishing Co., 1987.

———. 1979. "Statistical Analysis of Econometric Models." *Journal of the American Statistical Association* 74: 628–651.

Zellner, A., L. Bauwens, and H.K. van Dijk. 1988. "Bayesian Specification Analysis and Estimation of Simultaneous Equation Models Using Monte Carlo Methods." *Journal of Econometrics* 38: 39–72.

Zellner, A., C. Hong, and C. Min. 1991. "Forecasting Turning Points in International Output Growth Rates Using Bayesian Exponentially Weighted Autoregression, Time-Varying Parameter, and Pooling Techniques." *Journal of Econometrics* 49: 275–304.

Zellner, A., and F.C. Palm. 1974. "Time Series Analysis and Simultaneous Equation Econometric Models." *Journal of Econometrics* 2: 17–54.

———. 1975. "Time Series Analysis of Structural Monetary Models of the U.S. Economy." *Sankhya* 37 (Series C): 12–56.

Zellner, A., and S. Peck. 1973. "Simulation Experiments with a Quarterly Macroeconometric Model of the U.S. Economy." In A.A. Powell and R.A. Williams, eds., *Econometric Studies of Macro and Monetary Relations*. Amsterdam: North-Holland, pp. 149–168; reprinted in A. Zellner. *Basic Issues in Econometrics*. Chicago: University of Chicago Press, 1984.

SESSION III

5 HOW DOES IT MATTER?

Benjamin M. Friedman

Making economic policy typically requires positive as well as ethical judgments. Any kind of public policy inevitably involves fundamental presumptions that classify some aspects of human experience as desirable and others not, and that value some of these desirables more highly than others. (It is no accident that "policy" has the same root as "politics.") At the same time, if the actions taken are to be at all effective in promoting the ends sought, they must reflect a not wholly inaccurate perception of how they relate to the aspects of experience they are supposed to influence. In the case of economics, an essentially behavioral field of inquiry, the central question for policy purposes is how (if at all) individuals and institutions will alter the conduct of their affairs in response to any of the vast variety of changes that economic policy can bring about in the environments they face.

Macroeconomic policy is certainly no exception in this regard. Here, too, the notion of which outcomes are desirable and which are not—most obviously, the inherent desirability of a higher rather than lower standard of living, appropriately defined, over time—must ultimately be assumed, not established. And here, too, positive questions about the connection between public policy actions and specific developments bearing on the achievement of these objectives—Do large government deficits depress private capital formation? Does tight monetary policy dampen overall economic activity?—are central.

Moreover, many of the positive questions that bear most importantly on policy making in the macroeconomic sphere are inherently quantitative, and not merely in the sense that empirical evidence is necessary to judge among competing theories of the same phenomenon. Simply asking which theory "explains" unemployment, for example, misses the point that with anywhere from 6 to 11 million people unemployed at any given time (in the United States, during the last decade), there is ample room for different sets of circumstances and responses to underlie the condition of different would-be workers. But conversely, simply asking whether any specific theory of unemployment is "true," in the sense that it accounts for the condition of at least some empirically detectable number of would-be workers, also misses what policy making is, or ought to be, all about. The right question from a policy perspective is which theory or theories, if any, can account for enough of the observed unemployment to serve as a plausible guide to useful policy.

Business cycles—the subject of this conference, and hence of this chapter—have traditionally figured prominently in macroeconomic research, although it is important not to confound the study of business cycles with the entirety of policy-relevant macroeconomics. Price inflation often varies with the business cycle, to be sure; but inflation also can and does occur on a time scale different from that which defines most business cycle research, and inflation can and does arise from causes not directly related to the business cycle. Economists have also recently taken up with renewed vigor the question of what makes economies grow and whether countries that start out either richer or poorer than one another will converge economically, over even longer spans of time. These matters are also part of macroeconomics, and they too bear importantly on key issues of public policy.

Even so, the study of business cycles—what accounts for the irregularities surrounding whatever growth trend aggregate economic activity follows, and in particular what causes occasional episodes of apparent underutilization of the society's available economic resources—is the heart of macroeconomics. After all, macroeconomics, as a distinguishable subfield within the discipline, was born of economists' perplexity at the events of the 1930s, which not only challenged existing economic orthodoxies but also, for a time, threatened the integrity of several countries' democratic political structures. The positive question of why so many people were out of work and factories idle, and the corollary issue of what public policy could or should do to ameliorate the resulting human hardship, were, in the first instance, what the subject was all about. Although the aggregate-level fluctuations observed in the world's advanced industrialized economies in the post-Depression era have been both less severe and less distressing, in human as well as political terms, the same questions have largely framed this line of study ever since.

Modern research on business cycles revolves around several important distinctions, distinctions that appear to correspond to policy prescriptions no less than to positive economics. The line of research that grew most directly out of the Depression experience, and that dominated the first quarter-century of thought on the subject following World War II, emphasized fluctuations in the public's demand for goods and services. The implicit assumption behind this focus on demand was either that the economy's ability to produce goods and services was highly elastic or that that ability, if less elastic, at least did not experience sharp movements over business cycle horizons. The remaining question was then why the demand for goods and services fluctuated, including fluctuations that at times carried demand in the aggregate below what the available resources could readily supply. The main distinction this line of research came to emphasize was that between "monetary" disturbances, which disrupted the equilibrium between the public's desire to hold cash balances and the banks' ability to create those balances, and such nonmonetary factors as changes in government spending and revenues or "autonomous" shifts in households' desire to consume or in firms' desire to invest. (See chapter 2.)

The economic events of the 1960s and 1970s, however, undermined confidence in the assumptions behind this exclusive focus on disturbances to the demand for goods and services as the source of business fluctuations. First, the emergence of rapid price inflation, as a by-product of the effort in many countries to stimulate demand so as to achieve ever higher levels of employment, made the corresponding supply appear less elastic than policy makers in those countries had hoped. Then the quadrupling of petroleum prices by the OPEC cartel (and subsequent redoubling, several years later) showed that aggregate supply could be not only inelastic but also subject to disturbances just as abrupt, and apparently just as important for business fluctuations, as those highlighted in the earlier demand-oriented research. The emergence of a new set of business cycle theories primarily emphasizing disturbances to aggregate supply, in contrast to either strand of the earlier demand-based theories, framed yet another important distinction from which continuing research drew normative as well as positive conclusions. Over time, the ensuing "real business cycle" approach came to encompass not merely disturbances to aggregate supply but also those disturbances to aggregate demand that entered the story in an analytically parallel fashion. (See chapter 3.)

The object of this chapter is to question whether the distinctions among different theories of the business cycle actually have the force usually assumed in their behalf in contemporary discussions of macroeconomic policy. To anticipate, these distinctions do carry important implications about which macroeconomic policies are likely to be more efficacious than others in a business cycle context and about how best to carry out these policies. The distinction most popularly associated with the debate over "real business cycle" theories, however—that is, the distinction between aggregate demand and aggregate supply as the principal location of the disturbances that drive business cycles—is, from a policy perspective, less important than is commonly believed. The policy prescriptions that follow from most "real business cycle" models have more to do with the kinds of assumptions that these models incorporate about how markets function than with whether the chief disturbances to which the economy is subject work through demand or supply. At the same time, a further set of distinctions not customarily addressed in the business cycle literature, mostly revolving around the definition of "income," turns out to be surprisingly important. Finally, yet further issues, which traditionally receive too little attention from economists, arise from the fact that the people and the business institutions that make up the private sector of a modern industrialized economy are vastly heterogeneous and that democratic forms of government, for all their virtues, have not been very effective in arranging appropriate transfers from one group to others as the need arises.

1 Aggregate Supply Versus Aggregate Demand: A Conventional View

In analysis along the lines of the earlier postwar business cycle literature, in which the focus is on aggregate demand and the question at issue amounts to whether the chief disturbances to that demand are monetary or nonmonetary, the analysis nearly always points to at least the potential usefulness of one or another kind of corrective policy intervention. If increased concerns about the risks embodied in nonmoney assets lead investors to want to hold a larger share of their portfolios in money balances, the central bank in a fractional reserve banking system should expand the quantity of bank reserves, so that banks can accommodate the larger demand for deposit creation. If a decline in stock prices leads households to want to cut back on their consumption spending, the fiscal authority should either increase its own spending or stimulate private spending by reducing taxes, or the central bank should stimulate interest-sensitive elements of private spending, such as home building or automobile purchases, by increasing the quantity of bank reserves sufficiently to reduce market interest rates. And so the story goes.

Needless to say, a host of assumptions about the behavior of households and businesses, and about the economic environment that they face, underlies these policy inferences. As is well known, a nonaccommodated disturbance to the demand for money—or, in the same vein, an action by the central bank to increase the supply of bank reserves—would not affect real economic activity if prices and wages were perfectly flexible, if credit markets were subject to neither ordinary frictions nor failures due to asymmetric information, and if none of the other familiar sources of monetary nonneutrality were present. Increased government spending would not stimulate real economic activity if whatever the government purchased were perfectly substitutable for private consumables. Nor would tax changes affect economic activity if all taxes were lump-sum, if credit markets were perfect (so that, for example, no one faced liquidity constraints), and if no such factors as childlessness or immigration or uncertainty over future incomes rendered the appropriately discounted value of taxes to be levied at some undefined future date less than that of taxes to be paid forthwith. But in light of the readily apparent gulf between these sets of rarified conditions and the economies in which actual households and businesses carry out their affairs, the assumption that money is not neutral, or that government spending and tax changes do affect economic activity, is certainly plausible enough.

Within the demand-oriented approach, the distinction between policy interventions that are likely to be useful versus only potentially useful turns importantly on assumptions about how much knowledge policy makers have. Early contributions to this literature established that uncertainty about forces or events that will affect the economy in the same way regardless of what actions policy makers take need not impair the effectiveness of policy interventions. By contrast, uncertainty about the magnitude and timing of the consequences of policy actions themselves clearly blunts the ability of such interventions to do any good at all. Indeed, without at least some minimum knowledge about the how and when of such effects, an interventionist policy might well be destabilizing. These concerns are especially relevant for monetary policy in light of the familiar finding that the lags by which central bank actions affect economic activity are both long and variable. As a result, much of the debate within this literature over the relative merits of a more versus less activist stance for monetary policy has in fact hinged on the uncertainty issue, more so than on any disagreement over such behavioral questions as whether money might be neutral.

Given the assumption that macroeconomic policy actions can stimulate or retard aggregate demand with at least some modicum of reliability on average over time, the guiding presumption of the demand-oriented business cycle literature is that policy actions should do so in such a manner as to even out, insofar as possible, disturbances affecting aggregate demand. The rationale underlying this presumption is simply that in the best of all worlds—which by the economist's standard assumption is, of course, a world free of all impediments to market-clearing equilibrium, so that all relevant marginal this's always equaled the appropriate marginal that's—disturbances to aggregate demand would not affect real economic outcomes anyway. In that world the allocation of all economic resources would depend solely on considerations associated with aggregate supply (and on more fundamental aspects of demand, like the prevailing economy-wide rate of time preference, which are unlikely to vary much over business cycle horizons). In an actual economy not blessedly free of all such imperfections, the role of macroeconomic policy is therefore to nullify the impact of disturbances to aggregate demand whenever possible and thus to restore real economic activity to its pristine supply-determined equilibrium.

Against the background of this general philosophy of the demand-oriented approach to business fluctuations, the realization that aggregate supply also might be subject to sudden disturbances naturally created the appearance of a sharp analytical contrast. Unusually good or bad harvests, new technologies that increase productivity, or changes in an open economy's terms of international trade, all imply changes in just the marginal this's and that's that are ideally supposed to determine how the society deploys its resources. When supply considerations shift, therefore, the standard presumption is not to offset their impact on real activity but instead to interpret that impact as the requisite movement to a fresh supply-determined equilibrium. This new equilibrium may be either superior or inferior to the one that preceded it, depending on whether the disturbance that brought about the change was favorable or adverse, but in either case it is superior to any other allocation available in the new post-disturbance environment.

Hence the chief policy implication of the view that the business cycles actually observed in modern industrialized economies are "real business cycles," in the sense of movements driven by disturbances to aggregate supply (or, less likely for short-run fluctuations, disturbances to the fundamental underpinnings of aggregate demand), is that no macroeconomic policy response is needed or appropriate. Indeed, any effort by policy makers to resist such a "real business cycle" would only impede the economy's progress toward its newly appropriate optimal allocation of resources.

This general philosophy—in an important but usually unstated sense, a direct corollary of that underlying the earlier demand-oriented research —also was well understood, at least implicitly, in that earlier literature. What was new from this perspective in the "real business cycle" approach was simply the idea that disturbances to aggregate supply might play a major role in short-run business fluctuations, as distinct from phenomena observed on a more secular time scale. After the experience of 1973–1975, however, in which the then-largest decline in U.S. output and employment since the 1930s quickly followed a fourfold increase in the price of a major input to industrial production, and other oil-importing economies around the world experienced analogous problems, the possibility of business cycles caused by supply disturbances no longer seemed remote.

2 Aggregate Supply and Aggregate Demand: A Closer Look

Notwithstanding its intuitive attractiveness, the practical usefulness of this supply-versus-demand dichotomy as an organizing principle for macroeconomic policy making is less than the underlying logic suggests, and for several reasons. The most straightforward of these is the difficulty, in an actual policy-making context, of drawing the requisite distinction. Many occurrences that initially seem to represent disturbances to aggregate supply likewise cause disturbances to aggregate demand, and vice versa.

For example, if the United States used only domestically produced oil, an oil cartel's sudden decision to restrict production (in the spirit of the Texas Railroad Commission of earlier days) would simply correspond to an adverse shock to the economy's ability to supply the many goods, such as petrochemicals and services, such as transportation and heating, that use oil as inputs. From a demand perspective, the incomes of oil users facing higher prices would initially fall by just the amount that the incomes of oil producers rose, so that aggregate demand would not shift. The economy's new equilibrium would represent the intersection of the adversely shifted aggregate supply schedule and the same aggregate demand schedule that prevailed beforehand. To resist the decline in overall real output by stimulative monetary or fiscal policy would only generate inflation.

In the actual circumstances surrounding the OPEC price increases of 1973 and 1979, however—circumstances that persist today and are likely to do so for years to come—the United States imports one-half or more of its petroleum. An increase in price imposed by a *foreign* cartel constitutes a disturbance to both aggregate supply and aggregate demand. With U.S. oil imports running at some 7.5 million barrels per day (as of the time of writing), a doubling of the current price of $21 per barrel would immediately impose on American oil users the equivalent of an excise tax of $57 billion per year, or about 1% of the national income, to be paid to foreigners. It is always possible, of course, that the right choice for macroeconomic policy would be to make no response, and so to accept the equilibrium represented by the intersection of the economy's adversely shifted aggregate supply schedule and the dampened aggregate demand schedule. But there is no reason why that need always be so.

A second, more fundamental reason why the distinction between supply disturbances and demand disturbances is of less value than meets the eye is that in many circumstances the dichotomy breaks down for reasons not of institutional fact (like reliance on foreign oil) but basic economic logic. A standard example of a contractionary disturbance to aggregate demand is a decline in households' willingness to spend on consumables at a given price, caused by any of a variety of trauma to consumer confidence. A standard example of an adverse disturbance to aggregate supply is a decline in workers' willingness to sell their labor at a given wage, caused by any of a variety of perceived changes in working conditions. But are these two disturbances really distinct?

An analogy to a different application of economic analysis might clarify the answer. In analysis of portfolio behavior, it is customary to take explicit account of the interrelationships among any investor's demands for different assets (or supplies, if the investor can also issue assets—say, by borrowing). The root of these interrelationships is a balance sheet constraint that allows the investor at any given time to hold assets that sum to no more, and in most familiar circumstances no less, than the value of the portfolio to be invested. At a given moment, therefore, increased demand for one asset necessarily means reduced demand for (or, if the investor can borrow, increased supply of) at least one other asset. The point is not just that a change in expected returns that induces an investor to hold less of one asset means he can then hold more of another. More important, anything that shifts the investor's entire demand schedule for one asset must also shift the demand schedule for at least one other asset. In the absence of special assumptions, a shift in the demand schedule for any one asset will shift the demand schedules for all other assets.

In the case of household behavior determining flows such as consumption demand and labor supply, the analog to the balance sheet constraint in the portfolio case is a budget constraint. People earn incomes, by working and from other sources, and they either spend their incomes on consumables or save them. The sum of incomes earned from all sources must equal the sum of incomes spent and incomes saved. If some change in circumstances leads to a shift in the supply of labor, therefore, the budget constraint implies that it must also shift either the demand for consumables or the demand for saving, or both. Here, too, the point is not merely that a wage change that leads someone to work less will then reduce the amount that individual consumes or saves. More important, anything that shifts a workers's entire labor supply schedule will necessarily shift either that person's consumption demand schedule or saving schedule—or, in general, both.

In principle, it is still possible to distinguish supply shocks from demand shocks by pushing the analysis back still further, to focus not on shifts in labor supply schedules or consumption demand schedules but on the specific events that trigger those shifts. For example, if a new President chose not to enforce the regulations protecting the safety and healthfulness of the workplace, and large numbers of Americans therefore became less willing to work at any given real wage, the resulting shift in both labor supply and consumer demand schedules might plausibly be attributed to a supply disturbance. It is not clear what would be gained from that labelling, however, and in any case the resulting distinction would not fully correspond to the more conventional supply-versus-demand dichotomy with its powerful ability to support inferences about the circumstances under which macroeconomic policy should or should not attempt to counteract business fluctuations.

There is yet a third reason, however, why even the conventional supply-versus-demand dichotomy—and even when the identification of a supply or demand disturbance is completely unambiguous—does not have the force commonly associated with it in contemporary discussions of macroeconomic policy. From a policy perspective, what most importantly distinguishes the "real business cycle" approach from the more traditional analysis of either monetary or nonmonetary influences on aggregate demand is not so much whether the relevant disturbance in the first instance affects the supply or demand side of the economy (again, on the assumption that it is possible to draw such a line), but whether the analysis takes account of either the non-Walrasian market mechanisms or the non-Pigouvian tax systems that characterize actual economies. The standard presumption that the equilibrium allocation of resources established by supply considerations is "right," and conversely that movements of aggregate demand should not be left to interfere with it, rests on the assumption that there are no impediments to the clearing of all markets via the price mechanism and that the tax system embodies a set of penalties and subsidies sufficient to internalize all relevant externalities. By contrast, if wages and prices are not perfectly flexible, or if markets are subject to frictions, or if the tax system leaves some externalities uncorrected, then there is room for macroeconomic policy to respond to even the purest of "supply" shocks.

For example, consider the circumstances ("imagine" might be more appropriate in this case) if OPEC's leaders had been sincere in their protestations throughout the 1970s that they were merely using a higher price to encourage the world to economize on a scarce nonrenewable resource, and thus had compensated each oil-importing country by remitting the extra revenue that the cartel received, to be distributed on a lump-sum basis to that country's population. At least in conventional analyses—that is, abstracting from the prior discussion of inherent interrelationships among such aspects of behavior as labor supply and consumption demand—this situation would strictly correspond to an adverse supply disturbance. The higher price of a key imported input would reduce the economy's overall ability to produce goods and services, but the lump-sum distribution of remitted proceeds would restore the demand for goods and services (in aggregate) to its prior level. In the face of a decline in productivity, the economy's new equilibrium would presumably call for a lower real wage. As long as labor supply exhibits at least some positive elasticity, this new equilibrium would therefore involve lower levels of both output and employment.

But can an economy characterized by sticky nominal wages reach that new equilibrium without some assist from macroeconomic policy? Suppose that in this circumstance the central bank simply kept the supply of bank reserves fixed and that no further disturbance affected either the public's demand for money balances or banks' willingness to create them from a given reserve base. The adverse aggregate supply shift would involve both reduced output and higher prices. The higher prices in turn would imply lower real wages. So far, so good. But in general there is no reason why the reduction of real wages brought about by the price rise needed to clear the market for goods and services would be proportional to the reduction of real wages required to clear the labor market. A plausible role for monetary policy in that case would be to deliver either a greater or a smaller price rise than would occur otherwise, so as to achieve whatever decline in real wages were necessary to reach the new equilibrium despite the rigidity of nominal wages.

The fact that monetary policy *can* play such a role, of course, does not mean that it actually should do so. The implications of uncertainty, as emphasized earlier in the context of disturbances to aggregate demand, are pertinent here as well. In addition, inflation and deflation presumably impose costs too, and these need to be weighed against the costs of the incorrect allocation of resources that would ensue from too high or too low a real wage. But like the analysis of the relevant uncertainty, that comparison would remain to be carried out and would require not only some explicit conceptual view of the costs of price movements but also some ability to quantify these costs (relative to the costs of continuing product and labor market disequilibrium)—on neither of which fronts has the economics profession achieved much progress. In any case, the *prima facie* presumption that there would be no role for macroeconomic policy in these events, simply because the initiating disturbance was a "supply shock," does not withstand scrutiny.

It is a merit of the real business cycle approach that most of the leading contributions to it have been consistent and even explicit in this regard. The models used to carry out the analysis typically describe explicitly Walrasian market mechanisms with perfectly flexible wages and prices. For the most part, they also assume away such other potential impediments to optimal Walrasian outcomes as transactions costs, information asymmetries in credit markets, behavioral nonlinearities, multiple equilibria (and hence the possibility of self-fulfiling expectations), and heterogeneities that might explain the existence of "inside" financial assets (importantly including most of what is conventionally called "money"). Of such assumptions are sharp policy conclusions made.

By contrast, the demand-oriented approach has been neither explicit nor consistent. To recall, the notion that macroeconomic policy *should* change aggregate demand, to counteract disturbances to it, stems from the presumption that the supply-determined equilibrium is always the right one. But macroeconomic policy *can* affect aggregate demand only if some kind of price rigidity or market imperfection (or incompleteness) renders monetary policy nonneutral and fiscal policy non-Ricardian. Whatever combination of rigidities and imperfections accounts for the potency of macroeconomic policy therefore vitiates the automatic presumption in favor of the optimality of the supply-determined equilibrium.

In the end, the dichotomy that remains genuinely compelling in its implications for macroeconomic policy in a business cycle context is not whether the disturbances underlying the fluctuations that confront policy makers predominantly affect aggregate supply or aggregate demand, but whether non-Walrasian rigidities and imperfections importantly characterize the individual behaviors and market mechanisms that collectively constitute "the economy." But that idea is harddly new.

3 Macro Policy for a Heterogeneous Economy

A large part of what distinguishes the modern world from the primitive is its incredible richness of texture. Individuals differ along an infinity of dimensions, of which many probably do not bear on economic behavior but many probably do. People have not only different preferences for this good or that, or for working more or less, but also whole different approaches to organizing their existence in this world. People also differ in what they bring to the economic table in ways that go far beyond such familiar distinctions as who has had how much formal education or on-the-job training or who owns what tradable assets. Institutions, to the extent that they take on an organic aspect and therefore reflect more than just the collective attributes of the individuals associated with them, likewise exhibit enormous differences among one another.

Standard theories of the business cycle, be they of the aggregate demand or real business cycle type, mostly ignore this heterogeneity. Most familiar models at best distinguish the "representative household" from the "representative firm," although some demand-oriented models also distinguish those households that face liquidity constraints from those that do not. Financial intermediaries usually exist in these models only in the form of banks, which except for a stochastic element, unrelated to anything else in the analysis, amount to no more than an extension of the central bank. Much of the demand-oriented literature simply proceeds from mathematical statements describing the behavior of economywide aggregates, with no explicit representation of either households or firms.

Simplification and categorization are both essential, of course, to fruitful study of complex phenomena. Nevertheless, they also bear costs. From the perspective of macroeconomic policy, one of the costs of the level of abstraction at which the standard theories analyze business cycles is the blurring, if not total elimination, of distinctions that experience suggests matter importantly for actual policy decisions.

A hypothetical example can illustrate this point. In 1991, the government of Japan made a $9 billion cash payment to the U.S. government in consideration for the American role in the Persian Gulf War. (For purposes of this discussion it is irrelevant whether one construes this transaction as a cost-sharing contribution in a joint endeavor or as a simple fee paid for services rendered.) It is widely reported that this payment aroused substantial political antipathy among Japanese voters. Suppose, therefore, that instead of remitting $9 billion in cash, the government of Japan had delivered 1 million Japanese-made automobiles, suggesting that the U.S. government then sell them at an average price of $9,000 each.

The arrival in the United States of a million new foreign-made automobiles, free of charge to the economy as a whole, would probably have a readily visible impact at the macroeconomic level. Moreover, because that impact would presumably be short-lived, the resulting macroeconomic disturbance would be of the sort commonly addressed in the business cycle literature. But would this event constitute a "supply shock" or a "demand shock" in the context of the standard theories?

Although it is perhaps conceivable to argue that the U.S. economy's ability to supply automobiles had thus been augmented by 1 million units, any such argument would inevitably hinge on arbitrary conventions of timing. If the gift cars all arrived in 1991, then this line of thinking would hold that 1991 aggregate supply had received a favorable shock and that aggregate supply in 1992 and beyond would remain unaffected. In a model based on monthly time aggregation, however, the shock may have occurred only in July. This kind of awkwardness is inevitable in trying to relate discrete one-time quantities to concepts like production, which properly represent flows per unit time, and they are one indication that in this case the "supply shock" designation is inadequate. Instead, the receipt of the million cars would more plausibly represent a one-time change in the economy's stock of consumer durables, which under most standard theories of consumption behavior would shift aggregate demand.

Given the identification of this event as a disturbance to aggregate demand, the standard presumption is that macroeconomic policy should respond. But how? Should the objective be to maintain levels of aggregate spending, inclusive of consumers' purchase from the government of the million Japanese-made automobiles? Should it be to maintain levels of aggregate output (which would be like maintaining aggregate spending exclusive of the new cars)? And what, if anything, should policy do about the shift in the *composition* of demand for U.S. output, which would involve a sizable decline in demand for American-made automobiles?

If the U.S. economy consisted entirely of "representative agents," these matters would be either straightforward or irrelevant. The appropriate new equilibrium would involve a higher level of U.S. consumption and spending (inclusive of the million gift cars), and a lower level of U.S. production and value added, than would otherwise be the case. The fact that demand for American-made cars in particular would decline, while demand for other consumer goods and services would rise, would not matter. Each "representative agent" would be better off.

In the actual world of American economic policy making, these questions would also be irrelevant, but for a different reason: The U.S.

government would decline the gift. The point is not merely that the government would prefer the cash to the cars. If the cash were simply not in the picture, and the only choice were to take the cars or receive nothing from the Japanese in consideration of the American war effort, the U.S. government would still decline the gift of the cars.

The reason why the actual policy choice would no doubt be to reject a gift that would make the "representative agent" in the American economy better off sheds light on two shortcomings of standard macroeconomic analysis. To begin, the models used do not adequately distinguish between income and output. In the hypothetical case under discussion, the heart of the matter is that aggregate income should rise while aggregate output should decline. If everyone in the economy were a "representative agent," with an equal share in aggregate income and aggregate output alike, there would be no reason to focus macroeconomic policy on maintaining output as distinct from income. Income is what would matter. (In fact, there are good reasons why output matters along with income, but they arise from dynamic considerations of international competition rather than economic fluctuations in the ordinary sense.) But in an economy made up of heterogeneous elements, many people's ability to earn income depends directly on their opportunity to contribute to output. If output falls, *their* income falls too, even if aggregate income rises.

Moreover—and from a practical perspective, more importantly—many people's ability to earn income depends on their opportunity to contribute to the output of a specific good or service. In the hypothetical example of the Japanese gift cars, even if macroeconomic policy managed to maintain aggregate U.S. output unchanged (so that aggregate U.S. spending rose by the value of the million cars), the output of the American automobile industry would be smaller and the output of many if not most other American industries would be greater. This shift, even within a given level of aggregate output, would leave some people worse off even if the "representative agent" were better off.

To the extent that macroeconomic models address such issues at all, as opposed to burying them under the abstraction of the "representative agent," they typically do so in two ways. One is to assume that factors of production, including labor as well as capital, are mobile among alternative uses. The other is to assume that appropriate redistributions from those individuals initially made better off by any change to those initially made worse off can, in the end, leave everyone better off as long as the change is welfare-improving in the aggregate. Both of these responses fall short, at least in terms of what is relevant to macroeconomic policy in a business cycle context.

It is readily apparent that both labor and capital are far from fully mobile, even over horizons longer than any standard business cycle. Individuals possess both industry-specific and employer-specific human capital. Machines and buildings have limited functional adaptability or geographical mobility. Institutions, including conventional businesses as well as many in the "not for profit" sector, likewise acquire vested interests in the continuation or expansion of quite specific economic activities. Even people with no direct participation in a company or industry may acquire analogous interests, in that the elimination of a business (or, for the same reasons, a military base) would reduce the demand for their own services or the market value of their nearby property. The costs of adjustment that induce people and institutions to strive so hard to continue in their economic activity rather than move to deployment elsewhere—witness the 1991 Washington "summit" meeting of some one hundred American corporations to coordinate lobbying strategies to prevent the downscaling or possible elimination of the B2 bomber project, for which each was a supplier—are clearly great enough to preclude the immediate and full transfer of resources in the wake of some kind of supply disturbance.

The absence of transfers by which the "winners" can so compensate the "losers" as to leave everyone better off after a change that would be welfare-improving in the aggregate also involves, conceptually, a kind of transactions or adjustment cost. Here, however, the costs precluding what the standard theory simply assumes will take place are not economic but political. For all their virtues, the democratic political institutions that govern the world's advanced industrialized economies have not been very successful at compensating those individuals or businesses, or other institutions, that are adversely affected by changes that benefit many others. The economist's notion of a Pareto improvement (a change that leaves at least some people better off and no one worse off) therefore loses its practical relevance. Given the combination of enormous heterogeneity and limited mobility that characterizes the modern economy, few changes are likely to be Pareto-improving on initial impact. And given the inability of the prevailing political institutions to achieve the requisite transfers, the winners cannot compensate the losers so as to turn a change that is merely welfare-improving in the aggregate into a Pareto improvement. Hence "policy," including macroeconomic policy, becomes a matter of "politics" in the classic sense.

A different example may further sharpen the point. Unlike the hypothetical receipt of gift cars from Japan, the currently proposed free trade agreement between the United States and Mexico would, if instituted, alter considerations bearing on production in ways that properly constitute a "supply shock." Most obviously, the agreement would expand opportunities to produce goods, for sale in U.S. markets, from American capital and Mexican labor. Like a rise or fall in oil prices, these changes in supply considerations would persist over time. But also like a rise or fall in oil prices, they would have a short-run impact that bears analysis in a business cycle context.

That analysis suggests that the new equilibrium would—as in the case of the gift cars—involve higher aggregate U.S. income and spending and lower aggregate U.S. output and value added. For just the reasons already discussed, this change would be welfare-improving in the aggregate. (That is why economists typically favor free trade.) But here again, heterogeneity importantly enters the story. The reason why U.S. income would be higher despite lower U.S. output is that the additional income earned on American-owned capital deployed in Mexico would outweigh the loss of income earned at home by American workers. In this case, therefore, the relevant distinction is not who works (or owns stock) in the automobile industry and who works elsewhere, but who earns income from selling labor and who earns income from owning capital.

The fact that the free trade agreement would be welfare-improving in the aggregate for the United States means that owners of capital could, in principle, compensate workers so as to render everyone better off. But because there is little prospect that those transfers will occur, organizations representing U.S. labor strongly oppose the free trade agreement. If the agreement is enacted, the same groups will no doubt seek macroeconomic policy action to offset the loss of U.S. employment. (The more than 10% unemployment that developed in Canada following the implementation of a parallel U.S.–Canadian free trade agreement elicited widespread calls for monetary and fiscal expansion there.) Explaining that what has happened constitutes a straightforward supply shock—and a favorable one, at that—and that conventional business cycle theories therefore mandate simply allowing the economy to go to its new (in the aggregate, preferred) equilibrium, would be of little practical import.

The point of all this is that, for reasons wholly apart from the questions of rigidities and market imperfections discussed earlier on, standard business cycle theories fail to address issues that importantly bear on the making of macroeconomic policy in a business cycle context. The upshot is, again, to blunt the force of whatever policy implications these models have to offer.

4 Concluding Thoughts

The main line of argument in this chapter has been that recent developments in business cycle theory—specifically, the emergence of "real business cycle" theories—offer less in the way of practical guidance to macroeconomic policy than what the usual discussion of them normally conveys. One set of reasons involves the difficulty, either practical or conceptual, of drawing the required distinctions between aggregate supply and aggregate demand as the focal point of any given disturbance to the economy. Another stems from the dependence of these theories' policy implications on the absence of price rigidities or other impediments to fully Walrasian market outcomes, a key set of issues mostly resolved by assumption (and, to judge by the evidence, counterfactual assumptions at that) rather than analysis. A third set of reasons reflects the tension between the aggegate level at which these theories study economies and the rich heterogeneity characterizing actual economic behavior and interests in the modern world.

While each of these three arguments is relevant to macroeconomic policy in general, and therefore also to monetary policy in particular, there is yet an additional difficulty in attempting to apply lessons from the real business cycle approach to the practical conduct of monetary policy. The injunction to leave monetary policy unchanged in the face of business fluctuations, because they are presumed to reflect disturbances to aggregate supply, is relevant in practice only when it is possible to define, recognize, and implement the "no change" monetary policy in the first place. Does it mean maintaining growth of the money stock at some previously established rate? If so, which measure of the money stock is that? Moreover, a straightforward extension of the argument drawn earlier about the interdependence between supply shocks and consumption demand suggests that there is no guarantee that supply shocks necessarily leave portfolio demands unchanged—including demand for whatever is the chosen measure of money. Is the "no change" monetary policy that real business cycle models warrant then to make the money stock grow along some new, appropriately adjusted path? If so, is monetary policy conducted in this way really distinguishable from the kind of actively interventionist policy that real business cycle models supposedly reject?

Questions like these are hardly unfamiliar, of course. They have traditionally stood at the core of the debate over the proper role of activist monetary policy within the demand-oriented approach. That they emerge once more, even in the context of real business cycle models, shows that this supply-oriented analysis, even with its full panoply of restrictive Walrasian assumptions, still does not resolve the long-standing issues at the cutting edge of how to conduct actual monetary policy. In the end, there is no easy way to avoid grappling with such hard problems as which measure(s) of money (or reserves, or credit, or interest rates) provides the best guide to the effect of monetary policy on economic activity, and how these quantitative relationships change over time in response to business cycle phenomena as well as other influences.

Finally, one last issue also merits attention. Expectations have always stood close to the center of thinking about business cycles. No reader of Keynes' *General Theory* could miss the persistent emphasis on the role of expectations, and in particular the role of changing expectations, as the source of the "autonomous" shifts that play such a major role in demand-oriented models of business fluctuations. The more recent real business cycle models incorporate expectations in a more up-to-date, and therefore more explicit, way.

Although early work with models of "rational" expectations appeared not only to incorporate expectational elements explicitly but also to restrict them so as to preclude the kinds of randomly shifting sentiments to which previous work had attributed much of the observed aggregate fluctuation, the development of models exhibiting multiple equilibria has shown that this contrast was more one of style than of substance. In these models an economy can have a high- or a low-activity equilibrium, either of which its inhabitants may "rationally" expect. Moreover, in a manner strongly reminiscent of the earlier literature of "animal spirits" that caused "autonomous" shifts in demand, these expectations can be self-fulfilling. Whichever equilibrium people expect will prevail, and so they are "rational" to expect it.

What all this leaves open, of course, is the role that macroeconomic policies can or should play in influencing those expectations. Such a role for authority is well established in other areas relevant to public policy. No one any longer seriously suggests that the right to free speech includes the right to shout "fire" in a crowded theater in which no danger is present but the shout itself, and if somebody were to do that, no one would deny the responsibility of the management to take whatever steps it could to restore order. Similarly, the role of public policy institutions in arresting bank runs that arise from no source other than the spread of false information is also well accepted. Is there then a parallel role for macroeconomic policy in fostering expectations that correspond to high-activity equilibria and resisting the development of low-activity expectations? If there is, how can either monetary or fiscal policy go about playing that role? Perhaps the next wave of research on the business cycle will say.

Acknowledgments

I am grateful to Michael Belongia for helpful comments on an earlier draft.

Commentary: Whatever Happened to Contracyclical Policy?

by Michael R. Darby

One of the few advantages of reaching a certain age is the ability to put things into the perspective of the history and breadth of one's science. Obviously, I envy Ben Friedman's assignment to do just that, and I will embroider my own license along the same lines.

I want to leave aside the issues of appropriate research agendas—we all make our views clear in the agendas we pursue. Instead I want to focus on the policy debate. Ben has challenged the now almost conventional wisdom that the monetary authority's central goal should be price-level stability and that it should eschew both contracyclical policy and unintentional destabilization policy. He also challenges the view that fiscal policy is pretty much hopeless. Finally, he proposes an agenda for future research needed to better choose the correct set of policy instruments to address particular business cycle phenomena. It is my intention to defend the conventional views—a personally novel experience but perhaps that too comes with middle age. Although I must differ with Ben on the desirability of contracyclical policy, I applaud the clarity and vigor of his argument in its favor.

Until living through the recent recession in a policy-making position in Washington, I believed that, by and large, the economics profession had outgrown its fascination with contracyclical policy and fine-tuning economic growth. Obviously I was wrong, and Ben is far from alone in arguing for an activist approach to macroeconomic policy. Nonetheless, after having seen the theory and practice of contracyclical policy thoroughly tested in the 1960s and 1970s, the bulk of the academic segment of the profession has—in my opinion—come to share the view that fine-tuning the economy is beyond our collective wisdom and institutional capacity. Still the urge to do good is strong; so I plan to devote the main portion of my comments to explaining why that urge should properly be resisted.

These remarks will differ sharply from Ben's chapter in that I shall not assume this shift or that shift as necessary to illustrate a particular quandary—instead I shall try to present a bare-bones framework for looking at policy strategies in the face of an economy in which macroeconomic shocks occur randomly and with no clear, timely indication of their size and direction. I shall concentrate on shocks to aggregate demand. The real business cycle theorists do point to stochastic growth in equilibrium real income which is largely orthogonal to the conduct of macroeconomic policy, as will become apparent.

1 Three Approaches to Contracyclical Policy

Let me begin here by stating that by "contracyclical policy" I mean policy aimed at offsetting those demand shocks that move the economy away from its secular equilibrium. I should add that I am using the terms *contracyclical* and *stabilization* interchangeably. The goal of such policy is to attenuate the business cycle, that is, to reduce fluctuations in real income and unemployment.

Economists clearly disagree about the theoretical validity and practical utility of contracyclical policy. The profession boasts at least three major schools of thought on the subject. At the risk of oversimplification, I will label these schools Keynesian, monetarist, and new-classical.

Keynesians and monetarists seem to agree, in theory, that contracyclical policies *can* stabilize the economy. They disagree, however, on the extent of variance reduction possible and on whether government has the tools or the knowledge to implement such policies effectively and without aggravating the conditions they are meant to correct. In contrast, the new-classicals contend that contracyclical policy cannot stabilize the economy because it is either systematic and thus has no effect on the economy at all or is random and hence destabilizing.

The question is: Whose theory provides the most constructive basis for economic policy? One way to address this question is to focus on how the three schools view the effects of stabilization policies on the variance of real income.

In a simplified example, two types of shocks—autonomous shocks and policy-induced shocks—can perturb real income. Autonomous shocks arise from any number of factors, such as shifts in money demand or shifts in investment demand, which in turn can arise from things like war in the Persian Gulf, political unrest in the former Soviet Union, or sunspots. Policy shocks, of course, are man-made changes in either monetary or fiscal policy.

Changes in real income (due to demand shocks) can be represented by the sum of autonomous and policy disturbances. If no shocks were affecting the system, real income would continually equal its growing equilibrium value, leaving aside any adjustments to unexpected supply shocks. Government policies would influence this secular equilibrium through the saving rate, aggregate production function, and the level, quality, and growth of the labor force. These policies have long-run rather than contracyclical aims. Deviations from equilibrium real income due to demand shocks —which I shall term *cyclical income*—would be zero if any autonomous disturbance to the system were offset by a policy disturbance of equal magnitude and opposite sign.

In the absence of stabilization policy, the variance in cyclical income is equal to the variance of the autonomous disturbance. But, if we implement stabilization policy, the variance of cyclical income equals the sum of the variances of autonomous and policy shocks plus twice their covariance. Thus a reduction in the variance of cyclical income is possible only if a negative covariance between autonomous disturbances and policy disturbances can be achieved. This means that when autonomous disturbances are moving cyclical income in one direction, policy disturbances on average are moving cyclical income in the opposite direction.

Where a negative covariance in the values of autonomous and policy disturbances can be demonstrated, contracyclical policy may indeed be stabilizing. There is no certainty, however, that this will be the case. The assumed negative covariance has two components: First, a negative correlation reflects the average ability of policy makers to move in an offsetting direction. Second, a scale factor indicates the magnitude or forcefulness of the policy moves taken. At the optimal scale factor, the variance of cyclical income is reduced by the square of the correlation coefficient. For example, if the correlation between autonomous and policy shocks were -0.2, then *at best* the variance of cyclical income could be reduced by 0.04, or 4%. If the scale of policy shocks supplied by government were too small, the reduction in variance of cyclical income would be less than this amount. If the policy shocks were too large, the result would be either a smaller decrease or an actual increase in the variance of cyclical income.

We are now at the heart of the policy problem. If stabilization policy is to be effective, policy makers must be able to determine the appropriate direction, magnitude, and timing for the required policy shock. If direction and timing can be determined so as to achieve a negative correlation, restraint on the scale of policy is necessary for the policy to be stabilizing rather than destabilizing. Conversely, a correlation of zero would indicate that any active policy can only increase the variance of cyclical income and hence destabilize the economy.

1.1 What Keynesians Believe

Keynesians typically believe that the correlation between autonomous and policy disturbances is substantially less than zero and therefore that the potential gains from stabilization policy are substantial. This is implicit in Ben's presentation, in which it is simply assumed that we can know what shifts will occur in time for an offsetting policy to be implemented and have an effect on the economy. Keynesians may acknowledge that contracyclical policies have often been destabilizing in the past. But they believe that better data and better techniques of analyzing data, as well as the seasoning influence of past mistakes, have made us more adept at implementing stabilization policy in the present.

1.2 What the New-Classicals Believe

In contrast to Keynesians, a group that I shall term new-classicals believes that the correlation between autonomous and policy disturbances is zero. They argue that if policy makers react to autonomous disturbances in a regular and predictable way, the public will learn to anticipate the policy actions and thus they will have no effect on cyclical income. Therefore, only random changes in policy will affect real income.

Furthermore, random policies—policies that are unrelated to the state of the economy—are certain on average to destabilize the economy. Thus their theory leaves no room at all for contracyclical policy. For new-classicals, contracyclical policy is a null set.

1.3 What Monetarists Believe

The monetarist approach to contracyclical policy lies somewhere between the approaches of the Keynesians and the new-classicals on the negative correlation condition, but it argues that contracyclical monetary policy is likely to be destabilizing except as it stabilizes growth in monetary aggregates.

Monetarists believe there can be some negative correlation between autonomous disturbances and policy disturbances. Even in the new-classical paradigm such a negative correlation could be related to superior information or costly indexing. However, if the correlation is small in magnitude, then the optimal scale of policy actions must be quite small. The kind of bold actions that would be popularly acclaimed would also destabilize the economy. As a result, monetarists have traditionally argued that policy makers must tie their hands in advance to avoid intense political pressure to oversteer.

A few decades ago, when the debate was limited to Keynesians and monetarists—aren't the terms quaint to today's ears—I believed that framing the debate in terms of slopes of *IS* and *LM* curves was completely misleading. Here I have proposed a framework first presented by Milton Friedman (1953) some four decades ago and hope that you will find it more to the point.

Now let me summarize the points of view in terms of correlation and scale: On correlation, Keynesians believe that they are able to recognize autonomous shocks and take offsetting actions rapidly enough to achieve a substantial negative correlation. New-classicals, at the other extreme, believe that systematic actions are ineffective and therefore that only random policy shocks uncorrelated with the state of the economy are possible. Monetarists fall in between, allowing for some effects of systematic policy but emphasizing lags of recognition, decision, and effect so that the correlation between autonomous and policy shocks is necessarily small in absolute magnitude. On scale, Keynesians tend not to worry about finding the right setting as well as direction, monetarists fear that political pressures will lead to an overzealous and hence destabilizing scale of policy actions, while any scale of random actions is destabilizing for the new-classicals.

So what has happened to contracyclical policy? First, Keynesian optimism has not fared at all well in the academic community and little better in the practical world. By and large the 1960s and 1970s have been read as demonstrating that the Keynesian policy means well but is badly destabilizing. I must say that the theoretical arguments against contracyclical policy, which Ben challenges, may be used to explain why it didn't work, but have not been *per se* fatal to the Keynesian agenda. Second, and perhaps as importantly, neither monetary nor fiscal policy has really been available for attempting sophisticated contracyclical fine-tuning. Fiscal policy has been dominated by longer-term clashes over the scale of taxes and spending while the monetary authorities were facing a daunting task just to avoid doing harm.

2 Monetary Policy

Monetary policy early in the Reagan administration can be characterized as anti-inflation shock therapy that reduced the 13% inflation rate by one-third. There was no contracyclical intent, and the resulting recession was accepted by the monetary authorities and much of the public as the unfortunate side effect of long overdue medicine. As we emerged from that recession, regulatory changes in the financial service industry led to real uncertainty as to what effect monetary policy actions would have on the economy. Parametric uncertainty works to reduce the absolute magnitude of the expected correlation of policy and autonomous actions, so there was little scope for stabilizing monetary policy and a stable monetary policy was a considerable achievement.

I have argued that both M1A (M1 less other checkable deposits) and M2 continued in the 1980s to be good indicators of the effect of monetary policy on real income and inflation (Darby, Mascaro, and Marlow, 1989). Knowing either monetary aggregate does not make one a perfect forecaster, but it does seem that either may serve as a reasonable indicator of future effects of monetary policy. Chairman Greenspan's recent remarks suggest that the Federal Reserve System's reading of the evidence has come to correspond more closely with ours at least with respect to the M2 aggregate. Thus the recent lowering of interest rate targets can be understood in terms of M2 growth persistently below Federal reserve targets. I would characterize this as avoiding unintentional destabilizing as opposed to contracyclical policy in the conventional sense.

Should we expect that the reemergence of usable monetary aggregates will lead the monetary authorities to undertake an active contracyclical policy again? Probably not. Much has been learned since 1980, and it seems clear that the current Federal Reserve believes it cannot stabilize real income to any significant extent and should instead focus on an achievable goal of price stability. In that world view, usable monetary aggregates make it easier to avoid unintended policy shocks.

3 Fiscal Policy

Fiscal policy actions do not generate nearly as long-lasting effects on real income as does monetary policy. This tends to increase the absolute magnitude of any negative correlation between policy and autonomous effects on cyclical income. Despite this favorable comparison on the effect lag, even two decades ago fiscalists faced a daunting problem trying to reduce the decision and implementation lag to manageable proportions. The autonomous shocks affecting the economy when the fiscal changes finally took effect were unlikely to be the ones originally targeted and were, therefore, unlikely to be appropriately offset by the fiscal actions.

In the 1980s, conflicts between the administration and Congress have led to even longer decision and implementation lags. Fiscal policy too must be inevitably aimed at long-term goals.

4 Conclusion

Stabilization policy was tried in the 1960s and 1970s. It failed. I believe that it is that failure, and not any literal belief in the assumptions to which Ben points, that explains its current disrepute. That does not mean that the Federal Reserve's move since 1988 toward price stability did not affect the real economy. Rather, those effects were viewed as a temporary side effect of a long-run shift to a better equilibrium. While clearly there have been internal and external differences of opinion about the speed with which the Fed has moved toward price stability, those debates have not been in the context of contracyclical policy.

I believe that the passing of contracyclical policy as a strategy is a good thing for economists as a group. First, we are no longer promising a cure that in actuality makes things worse. Second, as concentration shifts to medium- and longer-term strategies, the systematic forces that economists understand become more important relative to the random shocks that elude us. It is perhaps inevitable that during what appears to be the early stages of recovery from a recession, the siren song of contracyclical policy might sound good. But nostalgia for a past which wasn't must not blind us to the present reality. While I applaud the Fed's efforts to get M2 growing again, that falls under eschewing procyclical policy or automatic destabilizers. That, I think, we can all agree is a good idea.

References

Darby, Michael R., Angelo R. Mascaro, and Michael L. Marlow. 1989. "The Empirical Reliability of Monetary Aggregates as Indicators: 1983–1987." *Economic Inquiry* 27: 555–585.

Friedman, Milton. 1953. "The Effects of a Full-Employment Policy on Economic Stability: A Formal Analysis." In *Essays in Positive Economics*. Chicago: University of Chicago Press.

CONFERENCE OVERVIEW

Commentary: DéjàVu All Over Again

by Alan S. Blinder

Often, conferences acquire nicknames. I suggest we name this one either the Michael J. Fox conference or the Yogi Berra conference, for it has provided the most reminiscences since my high school reunion. The analogy is an apt one because the way David Laidler and Olivier Blanchard review the two "debates"—a polite word for cockfights—reminds me of puberty: It isn't much fun when you are going through it, but you look back at it fondly—though inaccurately—as "the good old days."

Permit me a brief biographical detour. I received my undergraduate and graduate educations in economics between 1963 and 1971, just the years when the Keynesian–monetarist debate was in full swing, and began my career as a macroeconomist on the eve of the new-classical counter-revolution. In 1971, when I joined the cadre of practicing macroeconomists —thereby Granger-causing the subsequent arrival of both Olivier Blanchard and Bob King—I believed myself to be joining a process of Kuhnian "normal science." Those of us trained in the 1960s knew there were problems with both the empirics and, especially, the theoretical foundations of the standard consumption, investment, and money-demand functions—not to mention the wobbly Phillips curve. We also knew that the treatment of inflationary expectations was a major problem for the latter. But progress was being made. The macroeconomics of 1971 was noticeably better than the macroeconomics of 1961 and 1951. And we had every reason to think that the macroeconomics of 1981 would be better yet.

But those expectations were far from rational. What has happened since has been neither normal nor science. Who would say that the macroeconomics of 1991 is demonstrably better than the macroeconomics of 1972?[1] Not I, nor, I surmise, Blanchard. It turned out that we macroeconomists spent the better part of two decades arguing—often from behind ideological barricades (a point the authors in this volume delicately ignore) —whether wages and prices move instantly to clear all markets. Not *why* they do not, which is a good question, but *whether* they do. That, in retrospect, and probably even in prospect, was ridiculous.

1 The Conference Theme

Laidler, Blanchard, and Fair articulate a fairly clear, common theme in their chapters. Their message is that we wasted a great deal of time and energy arguing about theoretical basics (Blanchard) and that it is high time we got back to empirics (Laidler, Fair).

Blanchard writes (p. 127) that "by being in the 'back to basics' mode, the field has developed mostly according to its own internal logic, and we have shunned external stimulus too much."

Laidler observes (p. 103) that "the new-classical economists did not advance an alternative set of empirical hypotheses. . . . Rather they put forward an alternative theoretical framework whose superiority they defended . . . with reference, not so much to superior empirical content, as to its conformity with the theoretical principles of equilibrium modeling."

There is no point in providing a similar quotation from Fair, for Ray's entire chapter carries this message. Let me just state, instead, that I agree entirely.

However, those who endorse the pre-eminence of empirical evidence over theory, as I do, must reckon with the Phillips curve episode of the 1960s. Laidler described it exactly correctly. The position of mainstream Keynesian economists in, say, 1969 was that the Friedman–Phelps arguments for a vertical long-run Phillips curve were theoretically correct but that the empirical evidence said otherwise—and we should stick with the empirical evidence until it was proven wrong. We did; and it was. So those who placed their bets on *a priori* theorizing over empirics won that round. Advocates of real business cycle theory maintain that its eventual triumph will be a second case in point. Blanchard, Laidler, Fair, and I implicitly take the other side of this bet. (In fact, I'll give odds.) But we should remember that it's a bet and duly note that our side was wrong once before.

There is another aspect of these debates—in addition to and related to the ideological component—that should be brought out; but none of the chapters have done so. Once a few positive issues (like the interest elasticity of money demand) were resolved, the Keynesian–monetarist debate was largely over normative, policy-related issues. Should the authorities pursue an activist stabilization policy or follow nonreactive rules? Should monetary or fiscal policy be the chief instrument of demand management? Should policy makers (and their advisers) worry most about the short-run unemployment problem or the long-run inflation problem?[2] It is almost a foregone conclusion that questions that begin with the word *should* can never be given a definitive answer by research results alone. At minimum, value judgments and political considerations enter. So these questions continue to be debated. That fact is no condemnation of economics as a science.

The new-classical debate was, in stark contrast, largely over positive issues. Do all markets clear (approximately) instantly? Is anticipated money neutral? Do shocks to aggregate demand principally move real output or the price level in the short run? Are economic fluctuations dominated by mainly demand or mainly supply shocks?[3] This second list of questions is not about what policy makers should do but about how the economy works. Such questions ought to be resolvable by economic research—by the process of normal science—and perhaps by now have been. The fact that such issues remained controversial for so long is a strong condemnation of our profession.

One final important point has not been brought out in the discussion but should be. So-called new-Keynesianism has come in for a great deal of criticism, but little praise, at the conference so far. One main reason is its starkly nonempirical flavor. It is difficult even to imagine taking most of these models to the data; and few (but not no) new-Keynesians seem so inclined. But I think this criticism is unfair, for it entirely ignores the historical context. New-classical counter-revolutionaries sacked the Keynesian temple not because its empirical content was found wanting, though some falsely argued that point,[4] but because its theoretical underbelly was so soft. The challengers did not offer superior empirical predictions, but rather models that were smaller, cuter, and more consistent with maximizing behavior. It was therefore rational for younger economists seeking to defend the Keynesian tradition to work on strengthening the theory, not the empirics—which is precisely what they did.

Were they misguided? Consider this metaphor. You are the commander of Fort Keynes, which guards the intellectual frontier from dangers believed to lurk principally on the empirical east side. Though your fortress is far from beautiful, it is functional—and functioning. You are aware of both homely aspects and structural weaknesses in the consumption, investment, and money-demand towers arrayed along the east side, where most of the fortifications have been built. And you are working hard to repair them. In the meantime, you have allowed yourself to live with meager defenses on the theoretical west side, believing that there is little danger of attack from that quarter. Then events prove you wrong. Enemies from the theoretical west mount an attack whose ferocity was previously unimaginable. Soon they are scaling the walls. You suffer heavy losses for a while, but then fresh troops arrive. My question is simple: Where do you send them? That, I believe, is the story behind new-Keynesian economics. It both explains and rationalizes its nonempirical flavor.

2 A Time Line of Macro Models

Let me now try to illustrate the main message of the conference by turning to the achievements, or rather lack thereof, of what is here being called the second debate. To do so, consider the following simple macro "model;" it is really no more than a schema, a way to organize thought:

$$y^d = D(P, e_1, e_2, \ldots) \tag{1}$$

$$y^s = S(P, u_1, u_2, \ldots) \tag{2}$$

$$\dot{W} = \alpha \dot{P}^e + \lambda(y^d - y^s) \tag{3}$$

In this schema, equation (1) is the aggregate demand curve relating real GNP negatively to the price level; the e's are demand shocks such as money, government purchases, tax rates, and the like. Money presumably enters the model as M/P, so the derivative D_p indicates (with sign reversed) the strength of monetary impulses. Equation (2) is the aggregate supply curve, whose positive slope derives from some sort of nominal rigidity (fixed money wages, for example) and which can be perturbed by various supply shocks, the u's. Equation (3), a Phillips curve, summarizes the evolution of the money wage, here modeled as a state variable. This schema is incomplete since, among other things, it does not specify how P evolves (it could, for example, have its own dynamic equation) nor how y is determined when y^s is not equal to y^d (Keynesians usually specify $y = y^d$). But it suffices to make my points.

Table C–1 presents a "time line" of macro models that encapsulates the two debates. History here begins in the mid- to late 1960s. Reflecting my age,[5] the left-hand column is called "early" Keynesianism. Monetary effects on aggregate demand were not denied, but they were believed to be empirically minor (D_p small). Demand shocks from other sources—such as "autonomous spending" or fiscal policy—were, on the other hand, believed to have large variances. The aggregate supply curve was thought to be quite flat, perhaps even horizontal, in the short run (S_p large), but it was not thought to shift much over the business cycle (var$(u) \approx 0$). Finally, we come to the Phillips curve. As previously noted, early Keynesians cited empirical evidence that the sum of the coefficients of lagged inflation—which they mistakenly identified as *expected* inflation, $\dot{P}^e$—was considerably less than unity.[6] These expectations were modeled as a mechanical distributed lag ("adaptive" for short). And the coefficient λ was estimated—I repeat, *estimated*, not assumed—to be quite small, indicating sluggish adjustment of wages and prices to excess demand.

The second column of table C–1 represents the monetarist challenge, and my main point—it is also Laidler's—is that the challenge was entirely empirical. Monetarists argued that the effect of money on aggregate demand (D_p) was much larger than Keynesians allowed. Some of the zealots even argued that fiscal impulses were inconsequential, so that

Table C–1. A Time Line of Macro Models

	Early Keynesian	*Monetarist*	*Early New-Classical*	*Real Business Cycle*	*New/Old Consensus*
D_p	Small	Large	Large	Zero	Sizable, but erratic
var(e)	Large, especially C, I, G	Large, mostly M	Large; M	Small	Large; G and M
S_p	Large (infinite?)	?	Zero if anticipated	Zero	Usually large
var(u)	≈ 0	≈ 0	Small	Large	Usually small, sometimes large
α	$\ll 1$	≈ 1	$= 1$	$= 1$	$= 1$
λ	Small	Small	∞	∞	Small
$\dot{p}^e$	"Adaptive"	"Adaptive"	Rational	Rational	Rational?

monetary impulses were the dominant source of macroeconomic instability. Here too their argument, though weak, was primarily empirical. Like the Keynesians, the monetarists pretty much ignored supply shocks (var(u) $\approx$ 0). Since it is not clear that there was a "monetarist position" on the slope of the aggregate supply curve, I have left a question mark in that position, inviting Laidler or Michael Parkin to fill it in. Finally, an important monetarist innovation was the insistence that α had to be 1.0. Otherwise, monetarists more or less accepted the Keynesian position on the Phillips curve—including, importantly, the small value of λ.

The resolution of the Keynesian–monetarist debate, or rather the positive aspects thereof, can be thought of as a process of normal science. Evidence accumulated that D_p was in fact sizable, that fiscal policy did matter, and that α really was approximately unity. The monetarists won some and lost some; in the process, Keynesianism became less crude and monetarism became less monotheistic. These empirical debates were essentially over when the "second debate" burst on the scene.

Those of us old enough to remember the early 1970s will recall that new-classicism was originally dubbed "Monetarism II." My time line shows why. The early models adopted the Quantity Theory of Money, thereby elevating M to pre-eminence as a determinant of aggregate demand (D_p large, fiscal shocks small). This, however, can and should be interpreted allegorically; it was not essential to the new-classical approach and I will not belabor it. The key differences all came on the supply side. Supply shocks were recognized—the Lucas supply function did, after all, have a disturbance term—but I think it fair to say that they were not emphasized. The monetary misperception models, like their Keynesian and monetarist forebears, were demand-driven.

Where new-classical economics departed radically from the macroeconomics that came before it was in its view of the Phillips curve. Expectations were modeled as "rational," meaning consistent with the model, and λ was asserted to be extremely large, if not infinite. Notice that the first of these was not an empirical statement at all; no evidence for rational expectations was offered, as if none were needed. The second innovation was worse: It was patently antiempirical, contradicted by mountains of empirical evidence. Consistent with this view, the aggregate supply curve was assumed to be vertical for anticipated changes in money. Robert Barro subsequently offered empirical evidence to support this assumption, but his evidence did not withstand the intense scrutiny it received.[7]

After about a decade, monetary misperception models passed from the scene and were replaced by real business cycle models, the fourth column of table C–1. Taken literally (which is probably not appropriate), these models deny any role for money as a determinant of real aggregate demand ($D_p = 0$) and denigrate the importance of demand shocks more generally (var(e) small). Need I point out that these assumptions are not empirically motivated?

Since misperceptions are no longer a central issue, real business cyclists simply adopt a vertical aggregate supply curve ($S_p = 0$). But this supply curve is subject to substantial shocks, even at business cycle frequencies (var(u) large). There is considerable controversy over the extent to which this last aspect of the model is empirically based. Finally, RBC models tacitly adopt the same Phillips curve specification as the early new-classical models. In particular, that means accepting the nonempirical view of expectations and the antiempirical view of price adjustment. Is it any wonder that Laidler and Fair question the extent to which real business cycle analysis is empirically based?

In the final column of table C–1, I am bold (foolish?) enough to announce a new, post-RBC consensus. The title is meant to suggest that this "new" consensus is not very different from the consensus we almost had reached in 1972. In this new and unarticulated model, large effects of monetary policy are accepted, but instability in money demand makes them erratic. Both fiscal and monetary shocks are taken to contribute significantly to the variability of aggregate demand. The aggregate supply curve is *usually* taken to be quite flat in the short run, an exception being when the economy is pressing up against capacity constraints. Supply shocks, we learned in the 1970s, can on occasion be extraordinarily large and disruptive.[8] But, for normal quarter-to-quarter economic fluctuations, the contemporary consensus is that supply shocks are quite small.

And then there is the Phillips curve, which, despite much bad-mouthing, has proven to be a remarkably sturdy empirical regularity once supply shocks are appended. The contemporary consensus is that $\alpha = 1$ and λ is small, just as in the second column, and that expectations are *probably* rational. I use the qualifying adverb because, while most economists nowadays accept the rational-expectations hypothesis, the empirical evidence in its favor is at best weak and at worst damning. In fact, my personal assessment is that the weight of the evidence is against it.[9]

3 Back to the Future

In conclusion, I invite you to compare the last column to the first two in table C–1—thereby skipping over both versions of equilibrium macroeconomics. Other than recognizing the potential importance of supply shocks—which was forced on us by events, not by the new-classical revolution—and the wholesale adoption of rational expectations, perhaps for unsound reasons, the "new" consensus is the same as the "old" consensus that had been reached in 1972. Was that progress?

Well, that's the past. What of the future? Can macroeconomists, equipped with this new/old consensus, get back to doing normal science? Five and a half years ago, when I wrote an evaluation of the "second debate," I thought the answer was *no*; we were not ready yet.[10] Now I think the answer may be *yes*. If we can break the habit of shouting "Lucas critique" or "rational expectations" or "unexploited profit opportunities" in a crowded theater, then workaday macroeconomists may be able to return to the task that was so unfortunately abandoned in 1972.

Notes

1. I pick 1972 over 1971 advisedly. By 1972 the "vertical-in-the-long-run" view of the Phillips curve had won the day.

2. It will be noted that this last question presupposes the existence of a short-run tradeoff. Keynesians and monetarists did not and do not dispute this.

3. The grammatically awkward adverbs are in deference to Benjamin Friedman's admonition that most supply shocks affect aggregate demand and conversely.

4. See, for example, Robert E. Lucas, Jr., and Thomas J. Sargent, "After Keynesian Economics."

5. Professionally speaking, I was age −2 in 1969.

6. It remained for Thomas Sargent to correct the error that identified the sum of the lag coefficients with the effect of anticipated inflation. See his "A Note on the 'Accelerationist' Controversy."

7. See Robert J. Barro (1977). Ultimately definitive criticisms were offered by Frederic Mishkin (1982) and Robert J. Gordon (1982).

8. I must correct the mistaken intellectual history offered by Blanchard. He suggests that supply shocks were not successfully incorporated into the Keynesian paradigm until "the late 1970s and early 1980s." In fact, this had been done by the first months of 1974, as I showed in "The Fall and Rise of Keynesian Economics" (1988, note 16, p. 282). Given that the first supply shock hit in October 1973, that was a very short lag.

9. See, for example, the summary of empirical results in Michael Lovell (1986).

10. Alan S. Blinder, "Keynes After Lucas," (1986).

References

Barro, Robert J. 1977. "Unanticipated Money Growth and Unemployment in the United States." *American Economic Review* 67: 101–115.

Blinder, Alan S. 1986. "Keynes After Lucas." *Eastern Economic Journal* 12: 209–216.

——. 1988. "The Fall and Rise of Keynesian Economics." *The Economic Record* 64: 278–294.

Gordon, Robert J. 1982. "Price Inertia and Policy Ineffectiveness in the United States, 1890–1980." *Journal of Political Economy* 90: 1087–1117.

Lovell, Michael. 1986. "Tests of the Rational Expectations Hypothesis." *American Economic Review* 76: 110–124.

Lucas, Robert E., Jr. and Thomas J. Sargent. 1978. "After Keynesian Macroeconomics." In *After the Phillips Curve: Persistence of High Inflation and High Unemployment*, Conference Series No. 19, Boston, MA: Federal Reserve Bank of Boston.

Mishkin, Frederic. 1982. "Does Anticipated Monetary Policy Matter? An Econometric Investigation." *Journal of Political Economy* 90: 22–51.

Sargent, Thomas J. 1971. "A Note on the 'Accelerationist' Controversy." *Journal of Money, Gredit and Banking* 24: 721–725.

Commentary: Business Cycle Developments and the Agenda for Business Cycle Research

by Herschel I. Grossman

Important changes in the agenda for research into the business cycle in modern industrial countries have occurred over the past two decades. These changes have included the end of the single-minded concern of researchers with the determination and management of aggregate demand and a new emphasis instead on the cyclical implications of shocks to available resource endowments and on cyclical aspects of regional and sectoral economic development.

Prior to the mid-1970s, conditioned by the cyclical experience of the preceding hundred years and especially by the experience of the Great Depression, we took it for granted that in modern industrial economies, cycles in the economic activity reflect fluctuations in the utilization rate of existing endowments of labor and capital and that these fluctuations in the utilization rate are proximately the consequence of fluctuations in nominal aggregate demand. It seemed obvious then that, with the exception of the damage associated with major wars, the possibility of sharp changes in existing resource endowments was not something worth worrying about, at least not in the context of modern industrialized economies, which had conquered the old problems of famine and pestilence. In addition, although we were concerned with problems of economically depressed regions and industries, we regarded these problems as involving secular issues of economic growth and stagnation and as distinct from the agenda of business cycle research. In sum, we believed that, if we were able to understand fluctuations in nominal aggregate demand, then we would have understood economic fluctuations, and that, if we were able to prescribe how to stabilize nominal aggregate demand and, thereby, to stabilize aggregate economic activity at the national level, then we would have largely solved the problem of economic fluctuations.

Accordingly, the business cycle research agenda prior to the mid-1970s focused on the determination of nominal aggregate demand, on the relation between nominal aggregate demand and real aggregate demand, and on the management of economic policy to stabilize nominal aggregate demand. This research agenda generated a variety of distinct, but related, controversies. One controversy concerned the source of fluctuations in nominal aggregate demand—specifically, the importance of disturbances to tastes and technology, as manifested in changes in the marginal efficiency of investment, in the propensity to consume, or in liquidity preference, relative to the importance of perverse shifts in monetary and fiscal policy. Another controversy concerned the problem of rationalizing the apparent failure of disturbances to nominal aggregate demand to be translated immediately into changes in the level of wages and prices and the resulting impact, at least in the short run, of disturbances to nominal aggregate demand on real aggregate demand. This controversy probably was most fundamental, because, in addition to its practical implications for business cycle research, it raised questions about the logical structure of neoclassical economics. A third major controversy concerned the potential for actively using monetary and/or fiscal policy to stabilize nominal aggregate demand.

Although these three controversies remain incompletely resolved and continue to be the subject of active theoretical and empirical research, they no longer monopolize the agenda for business cycle research. The agenda now also emphasizes issues other than the determination of aggregate demand. It seems to me that we can identify three historical developments, beginning with the oil price shock of 1973, that have been largely responsible for this evolution of the business cycle research agenda. First, the oil price shock of 1973 suggested that even modern industrialized economies could face sharp changes in available resource endowments and that it might be relevant to think about such changes as a possible source of economic fluctuations in modern industrialized economies. Second, in the United States the recessions of 1974–1975 and 1981–1982, as well as the last recession, were surprisingly uneven in their regional and sectoral impact, with the implication that the business cycle research agenda should include questions about the determination of regional and sectoral economic activity. Third, the experience of recent years has suggested—the cyclical expansion and contraction of the late 1970s and the early 1980s as well as the last recession notwithstanding—that the Federal Reserve, and probably the monetary authorities of the other major industrialized countries as well, is now both willing and able to conduct monetary policy in such a way as to preclude large fluctuations in nominal aggregate demand.

Let me elaborate on the last observation. In the mid-1960s President Johnson claimed that recessions were a thing of the past. Given the then ongoing economic expansion and the evolving belief, which probably was correct, that we had learned how to use monetary and fiscal policy to achieve effective control of nominal aggregate demand, Johnson's claim seemed plausible at the time. In fact, one of my senior colleagues at that time advised me that interest in business cycle research was dying and that as a young assistant professor I would have little chance of making a reputation by working on Keynesian problems like the determination of aggregate demand.

As we know, subsequent cyclical experience made President Johnson's claim seem overly optimistic and served to restimulate interest in business cycle research. This experience included the inflationary surge of the late 1960s—which apparently resulted mainly from the political imperative to try to finance the war on poverty and the war in Vietnam with both minimal borrowing and minimal explicit tax increases—followed by the recession of the early 1970s and the inflationary surge and recession of the mid-1970s—both of which apparently resulted from the combination of the oil price shock of 1973 and a policy response to the oil price shock that probably mitigated its impact but aggravated its cyclical effects—and the unprecedented inflation of the late 1970s, which apparently resulted mainly from an unperceived increase in the natural rate of unemployment, followed by the recession of the early 1980s. But, this experience notwithstanding, developments since the late 1970s, and two important events in particular, have now made the view expressed by Johnson again seem plausible, at least if we interpret Johnson as having in mind cycles in the national economy associated with fluctuations in nominal aggregate demand.

The first of the two events that I have in mind was the sharp reversal of monetary policy midway through the Carter administration, marked dramatically by President Carter's appointment of Paul Volcker to replace his earlier appointee, William Miller, as chairman of the Federal Reserve Board, together with similar policy reversals by the Callaghan Labor government in Britain and by the Mitterand Socialist government in France. These developments showed that by the late 1970s even the political left was willing to accept the idea that resource endowments are a relevant constraint on aggregate output and that, to paraphrase Prime Minister Callaghan, "we cannot spend our way to prosperity." Given this new consensus, it would seem reasonable to hypothesize that the sort of policy decisions that in the past have generated unsustainably rapid expansions of nominal aggregate demand and resulting cycles of inflation and recession will not be a problem in the future.

The second event that I have in mind was the apparent confirmation for this hypothesis provided by the performance of the American economy during the 1980s. The Volcker Fed, after apparently having erred in the early 1980s on the side of disinflating more rapidly and with a sharper recession than either the Reagan administration or the Fed itself wanted, was then able to manage a sustained noninflationary expansion of aggregate demand through the rest of the decade. Only the mildest of recessions as measured at the national level, probably resulting mainly from a contractionary fiscal impulse, interrupted this expansion. And the Fed seems sufficiently cautious in its reaction to this last recession that we have little reason to fear an unsustainably fast expansion of nominal aggregate demand that would lead to a major new cycle of inflation and recession at the national level.

But a single observation does not provide a powerful test of an hypothesis. Were the 1980s merely a lucky drawing from an unchanged economic and political structure? Or are we actually living in a new era in which we have no need to worry about major cyclical fluctuations in nominal aggregate demand at the national level? To try to answer this question, we can begin by trying to account for the two events that I have emphasized—the policy reversal of the late 1970s and its apparent consequence, the macroeconomic stability of the 1980s. Two explanations, which are potentially complementary, occur to me as good candidates for such an accounting.

The first explanation emphasizes the effects of the accumulation of new knowledge about the economy during the 1970s. This new knowledge included both new theories—especially the natural-rate hypothesis, and also the rational-expectations hypothesis—as well as new empirical evidence—especially, evidence that the natural rate of unemployment is not a constant and, in particular, that by the late 1970s the natural rate of unemployment was much higher than in the 1950s and 1960s. According to this explanation, policy makers, who by the 1960s were confident of their ability to manage nominal aggregate demand, learned during the 1970s the limitations on the ability of aggregate-demand management to deliver high levels of economic activity. The inflationary surges of the late 1960s, mid-1970s, and late 1970s were all plausibly part of this learning experience.

The second explanation emphasizes that since the late 1970s the major industrial countries have seen no exogenous economic or political disturbances of the type that have led to inflationary monetary policies in the past. Most obviously, there have been no adverse disturbances like the oil price shocks of the 1970s. In addition, the large increase in military spending in the 1980s, in contrast to spending for the war in Vietnam, had wide political support, support that precluded the need to risk an inflationary surge to finance it. The more recent easing of international tensions has reduced further the strain on resources that potentially would generate political pressures for inflation.

But, we have no guarantee that the future will not bring less favorable developments. Most basically, there has been no obvious change in the structure of preferences and political constraints underlying economic policy, and especially monetary policy. It is one thing for policy makers to know how to manage aggregate demand to mitigate fluctuations in aggregate economic activity. It is another thing for them to give priority to this objective. Even if policy makers have learned the dangers of underestimating the natural rate of unemployment and of trying to exploit the short-run Phillips curve to drive unemployment below its natural rate, without a change in preferences and political constraints we cannot preclude the possibility that some future economic or political development will cause policy makers knowingly to risk producing a possibly unsustainable expansion of nominal aggregate demand and a consequent cycle of inflation and recession. For example, can we be sure that the large and growing fiscal obligations implied by current budget deficits and other currently legislated spending commitments will not undermine future monetary discipline?

Returning to the current agenda for business cycle research, it seems to me that we still have to be concerned about fluctuations in nominal aggregate demand. But the present priority does not seem to be to refine further our knowledge either of the determination of nominal aggregate demand, or of the relation between nominal aggregate demand and real aggregate demand, despite the fundamental importance of this issue for economic modeling, or of how to manage economic policy to stabilize aggregate demand. Rather the experiences of the past two decades suggest that the present priority, in addition to studying the cyclical implications of shocks to available resource endowments and the cyclical aspects of regional and sectoral economic development, should be to improve our understanding of the political-economic structure underlying monetary and fiscal policy. I leave a discussion of the directions for such a research agenda for another occasion.

Acknowledgments

I am grateful to William Poole for constructive comments.

Commentary: Where Do We Stand?

by Michael Parkin

Albert Einstein is reputed to have said:

> Creating a new theory is not like destroying an old barn and erecting a skyscraper in its place. It is rather like climbing a mountain, gaining new and wider views, discovering new connections between our starting point and its rich environment. But the point from which we started still exists and can be seen, although it appears smaller and forms a tiny part of our broad view gained by the mastery of the obstacles on our adventurous way up.[1]

The mountain for macroeconomics is a particularly tough one. (Actually, it has three peaks—growth, inflation, and business cycles—and they keep getting separated from each other's views by periodic dense clouds. Here, I plan to remain on the business cycle's peak.) We stand on the side of this mountain. In this position we are doing the best we can to achieve macroeconomic stability and also making a series of attempts to climb higher—to gain wider views. A variety of routes—research programs and efforts—have brought us to the place where we now stand, and we are exploring the promise of new routes—new research programs—the ultimate utility of which we'll know only when we actually get to a higher vantage point and can see them all in perspective—when there has been another major *theoretical* advance.

The first debate was about how we got to here. Although it *was* a debate, it was a debate among the crack mountaineers who were leading the way up and their immediate followers. The rest of us watched, sometimes in awe and admiration, sometimes in dismay. But most of us made our personal climbs up well-worn paths.

My own climb (as that of many of my generation) started out along the traditional Keynesian track. Educated in England in the 1950s and early 1960s, I *knew* that the interest elasticity of investment demand was zero and that the interest elasticity of the demand for money was infinity. These "facts" had been established by solid empirical evidence, most notably survey data on investment intentions and the experience with attempting to push interest rates down to 2% in the immediate postwar years and finding it impossible to do so. The "textbook" on which I was brought up was the *Radcliffe Report* (1959), which endowed these views with an additional aura of authority.

Given this "knowledge," the *IS-LM* apparatus, while correct, was irrelevant. With a vertical *IS* curve and, lest there be any doubt about that fact, with a horizontal *LM* curve as well, the aggregate demand curve (the equilibrium locus in price-output space) was vertical, so the entire apparatus was irrelevant. All one needed to determine aggregate economic activity was the 45-degree cross model of the consumption function and autonomous expenditure.

Arnold Zellner has recalled that in the early 1960s while a member of President Kennedy's Council of Economic Advisers, James Tobin was asked whether he used large-scale econometric models to form his advice to the President.[2] Tobin responded that he did not. Instead he used an envelope on which he drew the 45-degree cross model to generate his multiplier results. Remarked Tobin, "I don't believe the results but at least I know what I am doing." The only difference between the 45-year-old Tobin and the 25-year-old Parkin was that I did believe the results and didn't know what I was doing!

Many of us left the traditional Keynesian track sometime in the 1960s. For me the departure was dramatic. It was in the fall of 1967. I had just arrived at the University of Essex, where I met David Laidler, fresh from Chicago and Berkeley. He was as fast on his feet, well read, and well equipped to do verbal battle as anyone I had ever met. After one or, at most, two sessions in which I resoundingly lost all the arguments—because I was ignorant of some crucial, by then well-known, pieces of empirical evidence, especially Laidler's own work on the demand for money function and Jorgenson's work on investment demand—I quickly recognized that the *IS* curve indeed was not vertical and that the *LM* curve was not horizontal. The *IS-LM* apparatus was not only elegant but useful.

Given this view of the *IS-LM* curves, the aggregate demand curve sloped downward and to determine equilibrium output we needed an aggregate supply curve. Thus I was ready to buy into the *IS-LM, AD-AS* Phillips curve mainstream. Actually, accepting the Phillips curve part of the story was really easy because I had already been convinced (on the basis of the same ignorance that led me to my earlier conclusions on the *IS* and *LM* curves) that the Phillips curve was the most robust of the empirical relationships available!

As the mainstream flowed and the expectations augmentation of the Phillips curve was absorbed into it, a great deal of constructive work was done. Though the mainstream flowed strongly, it did not flow up the mountain. (Karl Brunner was fond of reminding us—usually when putting down some absurd statement based on factual error—that water does not flow up hill, not even in Switzerland.) As the mainstream flows it fills in the cracks and sorts out the details. That's what was happening in the late 1960s.

But while the aggregate demand-aggregate supply-expectations augmented Phillips curve mainstream was flowing, a few macroeconomists were looking for ways of "gaining a wider view." Robert Lucas (the leading macro mountaineer of our generation) did most of this work (helped of course by some extremely able colleagues). Lucas' work had *two* distinct effects.

First, it enabled the near completion of the old way up the mountain. The incorporation of rational expectations, combined with the institutional features of overlapping wages on the supply side and the more sophisticated, dynamic *IS-LM* model on the aggregate demand side, gave the mainstream a respectable completeness on its own terms and enabled it to form the basis of Cowles' style econometrics that has given us medium-scale econometric models developed by, among others, Ray Fair and John Taylor. The completion of the framework also informed and continues to inform the selection of variables to use in time series/transfer function work of the type described by Arnold Zellner in this volume. It yet further enabled the tight formulation of the early versions of new classical macroeconomics and to the speedy rejection of those models.

And this *is* where we stand today. This is what we "know" about business cycles. We know the rich fabric of fact displayed by Victor Zarnowitz in this volume. We have a coherent rationalization of those facts in the form of mediumscale econometric models or a series of single equation (or *VAR*) time series models. And we *think* about these models with the aggregate demand-aggregate supply-expectations augmented Phillips curve framework.

But Lucas' work had a second effect. It offered some glimpses of what it might be like up a particular mountain path. That path is not classical macroeconomics made new. It is not any particular kind of economics. It is a research method and one that could take us anywhere. It was given important impetus by Kydland and Prescott (1982) in their work on real business cycles, but it is not real business cycle theory.[3] It has, however, become associated with real business cycle theory and new-classical macroeconomics, and so the two do get confused.

To clarify the distinction I want to quote (fairly extensively) from an unpublished paper by Jean Pierre Danthine and John B. Donaldson (1991). I use Danthine and Donaldson for three reasons. First, they are typical of young macroeconomists who have no political or ideological position. They are doing what they see as constructive work and the approach they are taking to their work was, in my view, badly misrepresented in Olivier Blanchard's paper on the second debate.[4] For me that was a one-sided and misleading presentation of the nature of today's debate, and in part I want to present what I believe to be a corrective to Olivier's characterization of it. Third, I quote from this paper so extensively because I agree with it.

First, Danthine and Donaldson suggest:

> The RBC [real business cycle] label is unfortunate as the major contribution of this body of research is not a denial of any substantive role for money in explaining business cycle phenomena, but rather the establishment of a new research methodology for the study of the business cycle. The first component of this proposed methodology is an "empirical reassessment" which calls for a more systematic and complete statistical characterization of the economic fluctuations to be explained. The second component is the recourse to what has been called "quantitative theory"; i.e., the building of small, intuitive, computable, general equilibrium dynamic models which can be evaluated not only qualitatively but also quantitatively in terms of their ability to replicate the basic business cycle stylized facts.

I want to emphasize the order in which the material is placed by the new macroeconomists. Macroeconomics is fundamentally an empirical enterprise. Elegance is not its objective. We have not gone back to basics so that we can build beautiful models. We've gone back to basics so that we can build models that work and explain the phenomena of interest.

Danthine and Donaldson go on to say that three important consequences for the whole of macroeconomic theory are likely to flow from this research program:

> First, . . . a move toward a more inductive approach to macroeconomic research, with the accent being placed on a more systematic qualitative and quantitative description of the facts to be explained. Second, . . . developing "quantitative theory" will spread to other applications, mitigating the importance attributed to purely qualitative results. Thirdly, added research discipline will come from the view that a successful theoretical model must be one which not only explains the stylized facts at its focus but which is also broadly consistent with other accepted aspects of reality. Models calibrated successfully to explain one fact (or set of facts) but which do so while contradicting other accepted empirical findings will not be accorded much value.

They then go on to talk about the research strategy:

> A natural strategy for the execution of such an ambitious program is first to examine well known existing dynamic models to determine how well they perform. Such logic fully justifies the attention given the stochastic growth paradigm—a Walrasian model without money—by RBC authors to date.

Next they offer some instructive comments on the reception that these efforts have received:

> These initial attempts to construct a theory have, however, generated substantial misunderstanding and dogmatic posturing while revealing how we macro-

economists have been accustomed to think. Indeed, the idea of even proposing and "testing," in the above sense, a purely Walrasian model of the cycle has generated heated objections, sometimes aggravated by the misguided claim that these initial attempts conclusively demonstrated that business cycle phenomena were nothing more than the optimal reaction of rational agents to exogenous productivity shocks.

My final quotation from the Danthine–Donaldson paper is one that shows how they view the enterprise and what they see as the possibility of progress:

> In reality, RBC methodology is by nature ideologically neutral in the sense that it prefers the model or set of models that is (are) best able to replicate the stylized facts independent of the hypotheses underlying it (them). *The best RBC model may thus ultimately be a demand-driven money model with substantial non-Walrasian features.* [My italic.] Such a convergence will ultimately occur, however, not on the basis of prior views but as the outcome of a process of building increasingly richer models and confronting them with an increasingly richer set of stylized facts.
>
> . . . It is . . . premature . . . to claim victory of one model paradigm over another given the modest set of facts which current models are able to replicate. . . . However, a clear achievement of the RBC literature has been to free us to reconsider what we know about the business cycle.

I believe the foregoing statements by Danthine and Donaldson represent the point of view of the vast majority of young macroeconomists working the field today. They certainly represent the views of my colleagues who work in this area and of all the young macroeconomists with whom I have discussed the subject in the past several years. Olivier Blanchard's (1991) characterization of the research program on which these young economists are embarked is severely at odds with the picture that I have painted and, I think, is wrong.

The approach has already led to the development of models with enormous diversity. There are papers that explore a variety of alternative types of technology shocks,[5] international aspects of the business cycle,[6] alternative interpretations of the Solow residual—seeking to understand the possible deeper sources of shocks[7]—and non-competitive market structures.[8]

This new method of *quantitative theory* joins the other research methods in macroeconomics—the Cowles method, qualitative models, and case or episode studies—the outstanding example of which is Friedman and Schwartz (1963) but a modern example of which is Romer and Romer (1990).

If the new method of macroeconomics is doctrinally neutral, what has become of the new-classical and new-Keynesian labels that are at the centerpiece of the second debate and of Olivier Blanchard's chapter? These classifications are orthogonal to the alternative research methods. The distinctions between new-classicals and new-Keynesians are distinctions based on views about which abstractions might turn out to be useful and which might not. New-classical macroeconomics downplays problems of coordination. It does not deny that they exist, and it does not deny that they are important for some purposes. But it speculates that they are not important for explaining the fluctuations in the economy. Instead, it conjectures that intertemporal substitution is at the heart of aggregate fluctuations. This may turn out to be a brilliant short-cut giving a huge ratio of payoff to machinery (to paraphrase Blanchard). Or it may turn out to be wrong. The research methods at our disposal—the traditional methods supplemented by the new quantitative theoretical method—will help us figure out whether it indeed is a brilliant simplification.

New-Keynesian macroeconomics accepts the importance of intertemporal substitution but adds coordination failures and rigidities to the list of important factors influencing the *fluctuations* in the economy.[9]

New-Keynesians and new-classicals alike use all four of the research methods that I have identified. Increasingly, new-Keynesian ideas are being explored using quantitative theory. Typically they are not being done by new-Keynesians (at the present time), but no doubt as the method begins to pay off, new-Keynesians will start to use them. As we saw in the second debate new-Keynesians, for the most part, are using qualitative theory (and partial equilibrium theory at that) and thus are not really addressing the quantitative issues that Ray Fair would have had them address. But nor are new-classicals, with their use of quantitative theory, addressing quantitative issues in the traditional way. Thus far quantitative theorists have concentrated on explaining data described in moment's space—means, variances, covariances, and autocovariances. Traditional macroeconomists have worked with time series and been concerned to make predictions about next quarter's GNP, not the variance of GNP over some long period. Concentration on moment's space is consistent with the broader view that policy is a process, not an event, and that policy discussions can only usefully assess the consequences of employing well-defined policy "rules."[10] This view of policy, embraced by new-classical economists, is compatible with the moment's characterization of data.

But it is not consistent with a view held by a large number of economists. They want to get back to time-series predictions. Will new-classical (or for that matter new-Keynesian) economists ever get around to couching their predictions in terms of the more natural time series? I believe it is too early to say. If they don't, it will be either because we all recognize that "policy is a process, not an event"[11] and there is, therefore, no need to operate in the time domain, or because other methods have superseded quantitative theory.

Finally, what about policy itself? What does the current state of knowledge imply for policy choice? First, there does not exist a feasible commitment technology that permits us to establish policy rules. All policy is inevitably discretionary. In this I agree with Ben Friedman's assessment. Second, given where we stand, policy can do no better than use the traditional econometric models rationalized through the aggregate demand-aggregate supply-expectations augmented Phillips curve view of the world, in its attempt to steer a course between recession on the one side and inflation on the other. Third, given the political and institutional constraints on policy making, it is all but certain that policy actions will be imperfect and will from time to time exacerbate the very cycles they seek to smooth.

The more interesting and important policy questions, it seems to me, are not those concerning the details about which instrument to assign to which target, with what intensities and timing, but those concerning the way in which policy makers react to the evolving economy and the ways in which alternative institutional arrangements—central bank law and operating procedures—operate to stabilize the economy. I recommend strongly to our hosts and organizers that they consider this topic as a suitable one for a future St. Louis conference.

Acknowledgments

I could not have prepared these comments without the help of my colleagues Jeremy Greenwood, Andreas Hornstein, and David Laidler. Although I do not hold them responsible for what I say, I acknowledge my debt to them.

Notes

1. Attributed to Einstein in a letter by Oliver Sacks to *The Listener* 88, No. 2279, 30 November 1972, p. 756. (I have not been able to track down the original Einstein quotation.)

2. A remark made at the Sixteenth Annual Economic Policy Conference, Federal Reserve Bank of St. Louis, October 17–18, 1991.

3. See Kydland and Prescott (1982).

4. The reader is referred to Olivier Blanchard (1991), not the revised version of his paper published in this volume.

5. Such as Greenwood, Hercowitz, and Huffman (1988).
6. Enrique Mendoza (1991).
7. Mary Finn (1991).
8. Hornstein (1991) and Danthine and Donaldson (1991).
9. I believe this to be a correct characterization of the new-Keynesian research program. When I coined the term new-Keynesian in 1980 I used it to describe a set of models then developed by Edmund S. Phelps, Stanley Fischer, and John Taylor, models with rational expectations but Keynesian implications—see Parkin (1982). I recognize that coining a term does not give ownership to the way it is used and claim no more than that the characterization I've just given does accord well with the way people align on these issues.
10. I use rules here in the sense of systematic policy reactions, not fixed rules. All policy is discretionary in just the sense that consumer choice is discretionary but can be characterized as rule-based in just the same way that consumer choice can be characterized by a set of decision rules (demand functions).
11. I attribute this phrase and the initial insight to Neil Wallace.

References

Blanchard, Olivier. 1991. "New-Classicals and New-Keynesians. The Long Pause." Boston: MIT.

Danthine, Jean Pierre, and John B. Donaldson. 1991. "Methodological and Empirical Issues in Real Business Cycle Theory." Discussion paper, Universite de Lausanne and Columbia University.

Finn, Mary. 1991. "Energy Prices, Capacity Utilization and Business Cycle Fluctuations." Unpublished Paper, Department of Economics, Michigan State University.

Friedman, Milton, and Anna J. Schwartz. 1963. *A Monetary History of the United States 1867–1960*. Princeton, N.J.: Princeton University Press.

Greenwood, J., Z. Hercowitz, and G. Huffman. 1988. "Investment, Capacity Utilization and the Real Business Cycle." *American Economic Review* 78: 402–417.

Hornstein, Andreas. 1991. "Monopolistic Competition, Increasing Returns to Scale and the Importance of Productivity Changes." University of Western Ontario.

Kydland, Finn E., and Edward C. Prescott. 1982. "Time to Build and Aggregate Fluctuations." *Econometrica* 50: 1345–1370.

Mendoza, Enrique. 1991. "Real Business Cycles in a Small Open Economy." *American Economic Review* 81: 797–818.

Parkin, Michael. 1982. *Modern Macroeconomics*. Toronto: Prentice-Hall.

Radcliffe Committee. 1959. Committee on the Working of the Monetary System (1959). *Radcliffe Report*, Cmnd. 827, HMSO, London.

Romer, Christina D., and David H. Romer, 1990. "New Evidence on the Monetary Transmission Mechanism." *Brookings Papers on Economic Activity* I: 149–213.